DAYS OF HOPE
AND PROMISE

DAYS OF HOPE

AND PROMISE

The Writings and Speeches of
Paul J. Hallinan

Archbishop of Atlanta

edited by
Vincent A. Yzermans

a memoir by
✠ Joseph L. Bernardin

a tribute by
John Tracy Ellis

THE   LITURGICAL   PRESS

Collegeville   Minnesota

Printed by Sentinel Publishing Company, St. Cloud, Minnesota.
Copyright © 1973 The Order of St. Benedict, Inc., Collegeville, Minnesota.
Library of Congress Number 73-75293.
International Standard Book Number 0-8146-0424-2.

This work is a labor of love both on the part of those who have collaborated in its production as well as, I am sure, on the part of those who will read it. The book is but a symbol of one small flame of the fire of love that enkindled the hearts of countless persons who were touched by the consuming love of Paul J. Hallinan who is the author of this volume.

Two men who, perhaps, knew and loved the former archbishop of Atlanta most of all have contributed their recollections to this volume. The first, the Most Reverend Joseph L. Bernardin, served as his chancellor in Charleston and later as his auxiliary bishop in Atlanta. Their relationship was not as religious superior to subordinate but, as all such relationships in the Church should be, as brother to brother. The second, Monsignor John Tracy Ellis, was both a colleague in the area of church history and a confidant in the realm of ecclesiastical polity.

It was this writer's good fortune and honor to be asked two years ago to edit the major addresses and writings of the late archbishop of Atlanta by our mutual friend, Bishop Joseph L. Bernardin. The task could not have been accomplished without the continual assistance and support of the present Archbishop of Cincinatti and the opportunity for leisure and study afforded by the writer's own Ordinary, the Most Reverend George H. Speltz, Bishop of St. Cloud. Bishop Bernardin not only supplied the necessary papers but also, with the assistance of the late archbishop's secretary, Miss Sally K. Grubbs, assisted in the necessary citations and documentations. The task has not only been an intellectually stimulating effort for this editor, it has been, even more, a deeply spiritual experience. It is both my hope and conviction that the reader will share the same experience.

An editor need not, and in this case dare not presume to offer a commentary on another's writings. If the Archbishop could speak today, he might make his own the scriptural phrase, "What I have written, I have written!" The reader will be able to see for himself that Hallinan's words had stood, and for years to come will stand, the test of time. If a reason be sought, it is this writer's conviction that the Archbishop, either knowingly or unknowingly, played a prophetic role in the exercise of his office. An editor—any editor—however, at times may offer, and in this case must offer, an *apologia pro vita sua*.

Between the years of 1962 and his untimely death on 27 March, 1968, Archbishop Hallinan delivered over one hundred major addresses and penned over a score of pastoral letters. This excludes the sermons and addresses that any Ordinary is expected to deliver in the exercise of his office. It also excludes the numerous statements he issued on such occasions as the National Conference on Religion and Race in 1963; his statement opposing sterilization before a committee of the Georgia General Assembly in 1965; his testimony on behalf of Dr. Martin Luther King in 1965; his tribute to Miss Flannery O'Connor upon her death in 1964; or his interventions at the Second Vatican Council. The last-mentioned have already been published in the work of the present editor, *American Participation in the Second Vatican Council.*

The critic might well question the editor's judgment in the selection and omission of some of the Archbishop's works. Such reservations will be gratefully accepted, for that is precisely the role of the critic, and every editor worth the name knows and appreciates respectful and reasonable criticism. In reply to the question, "Why did he include this address or omit that pastoral letter?" the editor can only cite the following criteria he employed in the selections that comprise this work.

A glance at the table of contents will show that the selection was drawn from eight areas of interest that seemed to have held special importance for the Archbishop in the last decade of his life. We have chosen to arrange the selections in chronological order to show the development as well as the interests of the former metropolitan of Atlanta. Secondly, the editor strove to choose those addresses and letters that were at the time, and still remain, of more than passing interest and value. Thirdly, those addresses and documents were incorporated that seemed to exhibit most strikingly the breadth of the vision and creative daring and scholarship that so singularly marked Paul J. Hallinan to all of those privileged to know him.

It is this writer's conviction that if Hallinan had not been a military chaplain, a Newman chaplain, a bishop, and an archbishop, he would have been extremely successful as a journalist. At one time during the Second Vatican Council he confided to me that as a young priest he often wished that he could have been associated with the *Catholic Universal Bulletin,* the weekly newspaper of his native diocese of Cleveland. At another time, he approached this writer concerning the possibilities of publishing his doctoral dissertation, a biography of Richard Gilmour (1824-1891), the second bishop of Cleveland. Members of both the secular and Catholic press held the Archbishop in high regard and this, perhaps, is why he consistently received a "good press." His interest in the *Georgia Bulletin,* the weekly newspaper of the arch-diocese of Atlanta, was proverbial, and editors of Catholic newspapers throughout the country deeply admired and at times envied his cordial and professional relationship with the editors of that publication. His interest undoubtedly explained the reason for its excellence.

His journalistic flair also accounted for some of the realistic titles he gave to his addresses. One was entitled, "Will the Real Crisis Please Stand Up?" and another, an article he wrote for *The Critic,* was simply titled, "I Was Wrong." For this reason it has been thought best to let all but one of the titles of his addresses and pastoral letters stand as he gave them.

Of the thirty-six selections contained in this volume there are four sermons, two articles written for the *Georgia Bulletin,* twenty-one ad-dresses, two interviews and seven pastoral letters. Each selection ˙is prefaced by a short introductory paragraph with reference to the time, place, and circumstance of each document. The reader will notice in Monsignor Ellis' introductory essay that I suggested as a title for his contribution, "Days of Hope and Promise." I am now happy that he chose his own title for his essay, thus leaving me with a title for the work. Surely, few titles could be better chosen for such a volume, not only because Archbishop Hallinan lived through an era of high hopes and great promises, but also because in his own life and work he ex-hibited the hopes and promises that were the motivating forces of his life.

If this writer be permitted, at least in this brief introduction, to introduce his own personal conviction it would be that Paul Hallinan by his life, even perhaps more than by his words, instilled an abiding sense of Christian hope and optimism among all who knew him and admired him. In an era that seems to be so lacking in leadership in both church and state, Paul Hallinan seems to come through as a man and a Christian who practiced these virtues to an heroic degree. Well might both young and old learn from his suffering, and sometimes heroic, example.

A future historian of the Catholic Church in the United States will, from the perspective of time, assess and evaluate the stature of Paul J. Hallinan at a critical period of religious development in this country. This volume is offered with the conviction that the words of the first

Archbishop of Atlanta will be of immeasurable value in assisting clergy and laity today in surmounting the confounded confusion and desperate despair that today afflicts so many noble spirits in our nation.

Vincent A. Yzermans

Feast of St. Francis de Sales, 1972
St. Rosa, Minnesota

A MEMOIR: PROPHET AND PRIEST

by ✠ *Joseph L. Bernardin*

One of the most refreshing things about Paul Hallinan was that he never thought of himself as a suitable candidate for the office of bishop. One of his favorite stories — and he told it frequently precisely because he could not understand why he, of all the priests of Cleveland, was chosen — was a conversation which took place outside the Charleston Cathedral shortly after it was announced that he had been named Bishop of Charleston. An elderly lady whose recently deceased brother had been a distinguished priest of the diocese for nearly forty years expressed astonishment at the appointment.

"What has *he* done to deserve this?" she asked. The only thing her friend could offer was the fact that he had been a Newman chaplain for a long time. "Why," she said, "that's no accomplishment!" and she walked away indignantly.

It was not long, however, before everyone knew why he had been chosen. In Paul Hallinan they saw a true leader. They saw a person who had not only talent but also a great vision. They saw, too, a person who had courage. He had a deep faith which seldom permitted him to falter or to become discouraged when he was convinced of the rightness of a decision or a course of action. He was a humble yet secure man who never held back because he was afraid of the personal repercussions his stand might have. And the people who came to know Paul Hallinan as a bishop soon discovered what his friends had known all along: he was the most human of persons; he was extraordinarily sensitive to the feelings and needs of those around him; status and fame never affected his relationship with people. Whether he was enjoying himself at a party for dependent children or dealing with a pastor who had not paid his diocesan assessment, the Archbishop was always kind. He always knew just what to say to bring out the best in a person. And he literally died with that infectious smile which, over the years, brought so much warmth and happiness to those who knew him.

At the beginning of the Year of Faith in 1967, the Archbishop wrote a remarkable pastoral letter entitled "Faith and the Human Condition." (He flattered me by signing my name to it too, but he was really the author.) In this pastoral, one paragraph sums up well, I think, the motivating force behind his constant effort to make the gospel message relevant to the people of today: "Faith can be weakened, and it can be lost. Our present society does little to help. Materialism, relativism and secularism are poor soil if we expect a good harvest from our faith. But it is more likely that the torpor starts within us. If a man fails to relate his faith to the everyday facts of life, the bond intended by God becomes weakened. If he is harsh and critical to other persons and institutions, without love and compassion for them, his vision of the Church grows bitter . . ."

He felt that as a bishop one of his main responsibilities was to help those around him see how their Christian faith *was* related to their daily life. He was convinced, as he said at the University of West Virginia in January, 1968, that we must be "realistic enough to accept the world as it is — its culture and its changing knowledge — and then permeate it by the Word, Christ, and His enduring wisdom."

To accomplish this he constantly addressed himself to the real issues of the day regardless of how controversial they might be. He was one of the first bishops, for example, to speak out on the moral implications of the war in Vietnam. He disagreed completely with those who considered the war a matter which should be left exclusively to the generals, the diplomats and the politicians.

He once said: "We must speak out; we cannot remain silent. In his novel, *War and Peace*, Tolstoy asks how men can ignore the continued disasters in which 'Christians, professing the law of love, murder one another.' Christian consciences and voices must be raised against the savagery and terror of war. We must speak out — for justice, for truth, for freedom and for peace."

When he called for a halt in the bombing in North Vietnam, he was severely criticized in many quarters. His file was soon full of angry letters he received from all parts of the country, some accusing him of being a Communist and others simply saying that he was a misguided idealist. You can well understand, then, the impact of President Johnson's dramatic announcement that there would be a partial halt in the bombing of North Vietnam in an effort to create a climate favorable to negotiations. For that announcement was made on March 31, 1968, the evening before the Archbishop's funeral. And it came precisely at a moment when a number of us who had gathered in the Atlanta Cathedral rectory were recalling the many things he had said and done, including those relating to the war.

The Archbishop's record in the field of race relations is known to all. His voice was constantly raised on behalf of those who were suffering because of prejudice or injustice. He insisted that the heart of the race question is essentially religious and moral and he never ceased to appeal to the conscience of the Catholics of the archdiocese and the community to accept all men as brothers.

He was a personal friend of the late Dr. Martin Luther King. After Dr. King had won the Nobel Peace Prize, he was one of three Atlantans responsible for a testimonial dinner in his honor. Shortly before the event, however, he was hospitalized because of a recurrence of hepatitis. On the day itself, at the last moment, he persuaded his physician to let him attend at least for a little while. The audience, including Dr. King, was completely surprised and, of course, delighted when he made his appearance, even though they could tell that he could hardly walk.

"Non-violence, the answer to the Negroes' need," he said in his brief tribute to Dr. King, "may become the answer to the most desperate need of humanity. This, we believe, it was that the committee of the Nobel Peace Prize found in you and your work. This is really the reason for Atlanta's pride tonight. It is no small feat to make non-violence a dynamic of peace. It is no mean achievement to make America aware of the great formula of man's dignity: 'I will walk in liberty because I seek thy precepts.' Dr. King, you have done both. We are indebted to you. God bless you."

The Archbishop was perhaps best known for his vital interest in the liturgy. He was convinced that the liturgy was one of the chief ingredients of renewal of the Church. He understood that to have this effect it must be a living liturgy, intimately related to the realities of daily life. It is within this context that his constant plea for liturgical adaptation must be understood.

"This is the hour, this is the day," he said, "when we must find our identity as a people whose worship flows from their very life." And then he was quick to point out that life is not static, that it is subject to growth and development. So, too, must the worship of God's people grow and adapt, pruning off what is outdated and grafting on what is needed.

He was well aware that there were many forces at work in the current liturgical renewal — forces which, because they are sometimes contradictory, cause unrest. He was firmly convinced that much of this unrest could be dealt with effectively through creative experimentation carried on in properly authorized and supervised ways. He was also realistic enough to know, however, that experimentation would not completely end the unrest. Indeed he thought that some unrest was needed for authentic liturgical growth.

"If Catholic leaders," he said, "listen to this unrest, no matter how untrained the voices are, they will catch some authentic sounds. Under the twanging of the guitars are sounds of hope and hate, of bitterness, joy and even despair. The rhythms of the new beat are part of our society. But it is not enough just to listen. Those who guide the new liturgy should live with those caught up in today's grossness. They must talk with them, share with them, and even suffer with them . . . and because the pastor and bishop are leaders for the Lord, each should take the lead in opening up new channels for the Lord's children . . . . He should stand, not in a shady corner, but in the midst of his people. There he serves by love and compassion, but also by pointing the way."

Another great interest of the Archbishop's was ecumenism. He found it very easy and satisfying to work with those of other churches and faiths. This was because he loved people. He always saw the good in them and believed that this goodness was a bond which already united them. Beyond this, he was convinced that unity was Christ's desire and that all men of good will, under the inspiration of the Holy Spirit, must sincerely strive to prepare the way for it. He was realistic enough not to expect more than the human situation would allow. He always insisted on personal integrity because he believed that the watering-down of religious convictions would impede true ecumenism rather than foster it. Because of his tremendous confidence in God's grace, however, his hopes were always high. He watched these hopes materialize into the spirit of brotherhood that has become characteristic of our era.

In his optimism he frequently alluded to Newman's vision of the Church entering into a second spring. A short time before he died, in a talk entitled "Ecumenism in the New South," he said that he believed that we could look forward to a second springtime because God "has spurred on our instinct for religious unity and corked the bottles of venom and violence distilled from our peculiar grapes of wrath . . . ." Later in the same talk, after speaking of a new South emerging from all the crosscurrents of the past — all the ugliness and glory, all the boasts and humble prayers — he returned to the theme of a second spring. "We are haunted with spring," he said. "If we stay apart in sectarian isolation, it will be a cruel, deceptive spring. But if we climb unity's ladder, step by step, with courage and patience, it will be a spring of Christian hope."

There was one other sphere in which the Archbishop felt completely at home — academe. His natural talents — his inquisitive mind, his ability to write in an imaginative way — equipped him to be a scholar. His work on the university campus for many years prior to his appointment as bishop gave him an opportunity to put those talents to work, for he was not only pastor but also student. His determination to continue working on his dissertation after he had exchanged his student's cap for a miter finally earned him a doctor of philosophy degree in history and the reputation of a first-class Church historian.

In an article in *Thought*, Monsignor John Tracy Ellis, a close friend and advisor of the late Archbishop, paints a vivid portrait of him as an able historian. In the article he refers to a foreword that the Archbishop had written for one of his books, *Perspectives in American Catholicism*. "Those four and a half pages," Monsignor Ellis stated, "contained much of Archbishop Hallinan's philosophy of history, which, he said, is often called a craft, 'and such it may be, but history-writing is more than that. The term *vocation* is not too lofty to designate the life-work of the real historian.' The latter, he continued, must seek and strive for objective truth. 'The perspective he maintains,' the Archbishop declared, 'will be the measure of his success,' and then he stated: 'If it is pure and true and balanced, the past event will come alive. But exhaustive research and profound study are needed. So is honesty, and often, so is courage'."

During his many years as a chaplain to university students, he acquired a great insight into their thinking and their attitudes. In August, 1967, in an address given to the chaplains at the National Newman Congress at Northern Illinois University, he drew a very revealing profile of today's university student. He spoke of a new kind of Church, a new kind of world and university — and a new Pandora's box of tensions and concerns in every student's ID kit. He described many of those tensions and concerns that stem from their disgust, their frustration, their revolt against many of the ugly realities of today's computerized life. And with that understanding and compassion which were also so characteristic of him, he challenged the chaplains:

"What I am pleading for, in an audience well tuned in by your own experience, is that we take their side, espouse it and defend it.

Reach them by every new and honest approach. Share with them, not their hatred, but their agony when they find teamed up in American life: righteousness and racial hate, affluence and starvation, national honor in war but little national honesty in peace, the *status quo* and the *aggiornamento*."

One of the reasons for Archbishop Hallinan's success as a Church leader was his ability to interpret correctly the signs of the times. He never buried his head in the sand; he never retired from the world and its problems because of fear. On the contrary, he was always out front, ready to meet the challenge no matter what it might be. A proof of this is that in his writings one can see a steady development in his ideas. He was able to detect the radical changes which began to take place during the last few years of his life. More importantly, he understood the implications of those changes for the Church. While the substance of our faith, as Pope John told us, can never change, relating that faith to the contemporary world is a process which necessarily changes. Archbishop Hallinan was prepared, both intellectually and temperamentally, for this change.

At the time of his funeral I stated that there might be some who thought the Archbishop was ahead of his time. I said then, and I am even more convinced now, that his genius was that he saw that time was running out. This is why he was usually a step ahead. Thank God he had the courage to take that step — that necessary, decisive step needed to bring the Church into the mainstream of contemporary life. It was for this reason that he was such a prophetic figure. It was for this reason he gave us all so much hope. It was for this reason that his influence will long be felt.

Some time ago I came across these words: "The news of his death leaves the world saddened, and the Church bereaved. For this beloved father spoke not only to us — his children — but to all men because he loved the whole human family. His thoughts were never narrow and doctrinaire; they stretched out to all the confusing issues of a weary world. His heart beat not only for the anxieties of Catholics, but for the longings of all men of good will . . ."

As I read these words I assumed that they were a tribute which had been paid to Archbishop Hallinan at the time of his death. But then, having read to the end, I realized that these were the Archbishop's own words, spoken in tribute to Pope John XXIII. In my opinion they vividly and accurately reflect the mind and the heart of Paul Hallinan, that extraordinary man, that prophetic priest and bishop whose memory is honored in this volume.

TABLE OF CONTENTS

A TRIBUTE: ". . . WITH PRUDENCE, WITH COURAGE, WITH DETERMINATION."

by John Tracy Ellis

"May I take the liberty of asking your help in a matter relating to American history?"[1] With this question the late Archbishop of Atlanta and I inaugurated a correspondence that ranged over a wide spectrum of topics during the following twelve years. That first letter was postmarked March 23, 1955, and the last in the series bore the date of July 19, 1967, at a moment when the archbishop was on the eve of departure for Land O'Lakes, Wisconsin, to attend a conference of about twenty-five or thirty experts called by Theodore M. Hesburgh, C.S.C., President of the University of Notre Dame, to discuss the future of Catholic higher education. Something of the spirit and the infectious enthusiasm of this extraordinary man were conveyed in a paragraph of his final letter. He had just concluded, he said, an interview with a lady reporter from the *Atlanta Constitution* in preparation for an article the paper was to carry on the churches' involvement in civil rights, war protests, inner city, housing and related areas of social concern. He mentioned that several of the *Constitution's* reporters had previously spoken with some of the young priests of the Archdiocese of Atlanta who were then active in various civic affairs. The archbishop wondered if the reporters had not doubted the priests when the latter told them that "they not only had the freedom but that the two bishops were shoulder-deep in the work too." My friend then stated what he had summed up for the lady reporter in this way:

> Bp B [Joseph L. Bernardin] and I returned from the Council deeply convinced that the Church & the Modern World could not live apart. By serving on welfare, civic and social boards of all kinds and getting into the neighborhoods themselves, we think of ourselves as simply opening the doors. And we are blessed that about 42 of our 56 priests are under 35, are vital, restless, imaginative, creative, full of faith and hope, and with a band of brave sisters and an increasing number of laity, they are working where the action was . . . .[2]

i

I first met Archbishop Hallinan, if I recall rightly, at one of the annual meetings of the American Catholic Historical Association after he had accepted my invitation to become a member in March, 1955; it was, I think, at either the Washington meeting of Christmas week, 1955, or the following year in Saint Louis. At any rate, an acquaintance at first restricted in the main to mutual professional interests gradually evolved into a warm personal friendship. Once he began work for the doctorate in American history at Western Reserve University in 1955, an institution he had served since 1947 as Catholic chaplain, our correspondence quickened as he proceeded with his research and writing of the dissertation, a biography of Richard Gilmour, second Bishop of Cleveland. But since I have treated that aspect of our relationship in an article published some months after the archbishop's death,[3] I shall say no more about it here.

I should prefer to dwell on a number of traits and characteristics of this remarkable man's personality that left a deep impression on my mind, as they did on the minds of numerous men and women who had the good fortune to know Paul Hallinan. Some months ago a distinguished priest scholar wrote me of the concern he felt about a distorted news story — accompanied, needless to say, by the inevitable sensational headline — of a statement he had made on a delicate theological issue. "You circulate among the hierarchy," he said, and should I encounter any bishops disturbed over the account, he asked that I suggest they withhold judgment until the complete text was published. I assured my friend that I would, indeed, be glad to be as helpful as possible in the circumstances, but in honesty I felt compelled to disabuse him of the notion that I 'circulated among the hierarchy.' Actually, in my thirty-four years as a priest I have been on terms of intimate friendship with very few bishops. True, I have known several in the way one comes to know one's contemporaries in the seminary. I was on friendly terms with several others before they were made bishops, for example, Archbishop Humberto Medeiros of Boston, Archbishop Philip Hannan of New Orleans and Bishop Cletus O'Donnell of Madison, with all of whom a cordial relationship has been maintained over the years. There were still several more with whom I became well acquainted after meeting them as bishops, for example, Archbishop Michael Curley of Baltimore and Bishop Peter Ireton of Richmond who always received me with warm hospitality when I came periodically to work in their respective diocesan archives.

With the exception of Archbishop Hallinan, however, in only a single instance could my relationship to members of the hierarchy be accurately described as approximating close and enduring friendship. That exception was John M. McNamara, Auxiliary Bishop of Washington, who died in November, 1960, at the age of eighty-two, a man who, I believe, had a deep affection for me as I had for him. In the case of one or two other bishops, as they made their ascent toward the ecclesiastical Mount Olympus, an earlier first-name relationship was left behind in the valley below. In this category I think of the eminent prelate who, perhaps to his surprise, caught sight of me one morning in September, 1965, on the floor of Saint Peter's during the final session of Vatican Council II, and who rapidly found a more congenial object for his gaze. Nothing of that kind was ever experienced in the years that I knew Archbishop Hallinan or Bishop McNamara.

Since the editor of this volume has left me free to write whatever I like, and since Bishop Bernardin and Monsignor Yzermans will have given their own versions of Paul Hallinan's claim to an honored place in the memory of future generations, I shall confine what follows to a few observations on two or three aspects of the man's character that, I believe, may be studied with profit by anyone concerned about the American Catholic community in this troubled era of the late twentieth century.

If there is a single personal trait which beleaguered humanity stands in desperate need of finding in the leaders of both Church and State today, it is, in my judgment, a rebirth of what was once called by the old fashioned term 'honor.' By honor in this context I mean the code of honesty and truthfulness that must, regardless of one's racial origin, nationality strain, religious affiliation, or social classification, inspire and inform the relations of men and women in every one of the varied walks of life with their equals and with those above them and below them, as well as the dealings that heads of state and the ruling element of nations have with one another. It is the kind of thing that within the last year an editorial writer for *The Tablet* had in mind. He commented on the gravity of international tensions at that moment and he then remarked:

> There is one fundamental qualification to be made: good faith, credibility, trust in the pledged word must be restored. The currency of international political speech has become debased to such a degree that scepticism and cynicism are universal.[4]

The currency of speech, whether in an ecclesiastical or secular framework, was never debased by Paul Hallinan, even when he could maintain its integrity only at a personal price that cost him dearly. To one who came to know him well and who followed his career, as

iii

I did, through his final twelve years as university chaplain, graduate student, bishop, and archbishop, the memory is not taxed to recall a variety of circumstances in which this rare and priceless quality shone through what this forthright churchman said and what he did. In his later years one of the archbishop's most absorbing preoccupations and principal objectives, both for the universal Church and for the Church of his own country, was centered in a reform of the liturgy. In this respect to no member of the American episcopate of the 1960's would the judgment of the hierarchy's founder, John Carroll, have made more immediate sense and point than to Archbishop Hallinan when as far back as 1787 Carroll had himself treated the subject of liturgical reform. In a letter to an English priest he asked if there could be anything more preposterous than the Catholics of the relatively small territory in and about Mount Libanus having a liturgy "in their proper idiom," while the vast English-speaking lands were obliged to perform divine services in an unknown tongue. A language which, as Carroll remarked, meant that the great part of the American congregations "must be utterly ignorant of the meaning and sense of the publick offices of the Church."[5]

Months before the opening of Vatican Council II on October 11, 1962, the Archbishop of Atlanta had been carefully preparing for the event, and the council was not three weeks old before he mounted the podium in Saint Peter's and opened his vigorous intervention with these words, "I speak for many bishops (although not for all) of the United States of America who hope for the more vital, conscious and fruitful participation of our people in the Mass."[6] From that day until his fatal illness forced him to bed in the early weeks of 1968 he continued to hammer away at this theme. In the meetings of the American bishops at Rome while the council was in session he insisted repeatedly on the importance of the vernacular, on the need for liturgical experimentation in designated centers, and on the freedom that the bishops should encourage among qualified scholars in the liturgy so that all might benefit from their research. On one of my visits to him in Atlanta he showed me — with the merry twinkle so characteristic of this fun-loving man's eyes — a colored snapshot of Cardinal Spellman and himself taken at the close of one of these Roman meetings. The archbishop's arm was thrust forward in an emphatic gesture before the cardinal whose grave countenance reflected a mixture of puzzlement and annoyance. It was no secret that the late Archbishop of New York had at first viewed the liturgical changes with a jaundiced eye, although once the council had voted them in, he quickly fell in line.

It would not have occurred to Paul Hallinan that by arguing with the powerful cardinal in the presence of their episcopal colleagues he was taking his ecclesiastical life in his hands. The careerists, of whom the American episcopate has its fair share, would have thought of that, and they would have paused, regardless of how eagerly they may have desired liturgical reform. Had someone at the time called the archbishop's attention to the jeopardy to which he had exposed his ecclesiastical future, the puzzlement — if such be the proper description of Cardinal Spellman's expression as caught by the camera — would then have been transferred to the broad and beaming face of Atlanta's new metropolitan. And if the idea that he should give thought to his personal advancement over his dedication to the new liturgy had not brought puzzlement, the suggestion might well have been met with his customary grin as he suddenly thought to remind his interlocutor that so dire a fate need not necessarily follow the displeasure of the Archbishop of New York. For had it not been reliably reported that the cardinal's chagrin over criticism of New York's Saint Patrick's Cathedral by a certain Bishop of Reno,[7] had prompted His Eminence to comment, "He must like Reno," only to have the same bishop promoted eight years later to an archiepiscopal see while the cardinal was still alive? In any case, it would have been the kind of sally that the Archbishop of Atlanta would have thoroughly enjoyed.

The fidelity of Archbishop Hallinan to his high personal standard of honor, to his pledged word, and to deep convictions that on occasion he believed should merit a public ideological position or a specific course of action in controversial questions, could be illustrated from numerous episodes in his life. Always a staunch defender of the accepted principles of academic freedom, in his role as a trustee of the Catholic University of America he clearly felt that there had been a violation of these principles by the Board of Trustees at their Chicago meeting in April, 1967, in regard to renewing the contract of Father Charles E. Curran, assistant professor of theology. At that memorable session the archbishop was the sole trustee who cast his vote against the board's proceeding without first giving the priest an opportunity to be heard. When news of the trustees' action reached Washington it set off the most significant demonstration to date in American Catholic higher education in behalf of academic freedom. An overwhelming vote of both faculty and students for a boycott of classes brought the institution's life to a standstill. The controlling element among the trustees sensed the gravity of the situation, hurriedly conferred, and ended by completely reversing their Chicago action. Amid all the

v

national publicity that attended this historic incident the Archbishop of Atlanta was the only trustee who emerged from the fray with his honor entirely intact.[8]

Mention has been made of the high price that Paul Hallinan had at times to pay for his promotion of liturgical reform and for other causes in which he believed profoundly. Probably no episode illustrated that fact more dramatically than his prolonged defense before the Washington meeting of the National Conference of Catholic Bishops in November, 1967, of further advances in matters liturgical such as the establishment with the hierarchy's approval of centers for experimentation. On that occasion he was grilled and harassed for five or six hours by certain episcopal opponents to the point that when this already mortally ill man had finished the ordeal he returned to his hotel room in a state of complete exhaustion, threw himself on his bed, and wept. By this time he was only about four months removed from death, yet he bravely battled on to the end for what he believed to be the best interests of the Church.

Some time later the American request for centers of liturgical experimentation was denied by the Roman Curia, and the archbishop was naturally disappointed. But even then he would not give up. Three weeks before he died he telephoned me early one morning and we talked for almost an hour. I later learned that he had similarly called a number of friends to say 'good-by,' for he was fully aware that the end was near. During our converation I alluded to Rome's refusal and the fact that I had found slight consolation in the concession that had accompanied the negative response, namely, that permission had been granted to the Americans to substitute another hymn at Benediction for the *Tantum ergo!* The voice in far-off Atlanta — by this time so weakened that, in fact, I lost a considerable amount of what he said that morning — was ever so faintly heard to say, "We'll go back again, John, we'll go back again." In the sequel, his associates of the bishops' liturgy committee did go back again, and this time they succeeded in winning what had originally been denied. One would like to think that the courageous spirit of Paul Hallinan had assisted those concerned ultimately to win the day.

When the editor of this volume sent me the texts of Archbishop Hallinan's addresses for the purpose of the present essay, he suggested a tentative title for the latter in "Days of Hope and Promise." As one reviews the life of the archbishop one is prompted to think that his had, indeed, been 'days of hope and promise.' I decided, however, to substitute another title for reasons that bear on what I have been saying here, a substitution which I wish to explain. On March 29, 1962, the erstwhile Bishop of Charleston preached at his own installation in the Cathedral of Christ the King as Atlanta's first archbishop. The sermon was relatively brief, but like all the public statements of this remarkable person, it said something that was worth his audience's remembrance.

It could truthfully be said, I think, that Paul Hallinan's nature and temperament would not allow him to indulge in the type of vacuous pronouncements — not infrequently a tissue in good part of quotations from papal and curial documents — that certain high prelates seem called upon to make on such occasions. In the sermon of March, 1962, the most arresting remark, I suppose, was the archbishop's forceful pronouncement on the most delicate public issue of the hour, and that not only in Georgia but throughout the United States, namely, racial equality and justice. Enlightened mind that he was, he had long been painfully conscious of the traditional prejudice against the blacks harbored for generations by countless white Americans, and he knew, too, that certain priests and laity of his new jurisdiction had not remained immune from this national disease. There must not be the slightest doubt, therefore, about where their new archbishop stood on this burning question. He lost no time in affirming that it was the manifest duty of the Catholic Church to champion racial justice. "Neither in the North nor in the South," he declared, "can she bear the ugly blemish of prejudice and fear." With that he proceeded to set the course for the clergy and laity of the new Archdiocese of Atlanta in what he would probably have conceded privately were to some degree wishful words when he added:

> Small in numbers but great in loyalty, our Catholic people are trying to reflect the unity of Christ's Mystical Body as they move toward the reality of full racial justice, — with prudence, with courage, with determination.[9]

Upon reading those final words I was immediately struck by their appositeness as a description of both the manner and spirit of Archbishop Hallinan, a spirit that accustomed him to move forward on every issue of his public and private life, no matter how controversial it might be. For informed persons will, I believe, agree that in his handling of sensitive subjects the archbishop never lacked fundamental prudence in his approach, this his expression embodied a courage that was evident for all to see, and that his pursuance of a goal, once he had become convinced that he was on the right road, was fortified by a determination that no contrary interest, personal or otherwise, could dislodge or turn aside. In this respect he resembled another archbishop for whom he entertained a deep admiration and esteem, namely, Cardinal Leo Joseph Suenens, Primate of Belgium. Those of less creative and adventuresome mind than these two men have at times been highly critical of both as dangerous radicals who deepened the Church's anguish during Vatican Council II and the years that followed. As is true of the careers of all men, the final verdict on the role played by a Hallinan and a Suenens will be pronounced by history. But at this writing I find it difficult to dissociate their contribution from the ecclesiastical lineage that numbers Saint Paul, Saint Athanasius, Hildebrand, and Newman. Should this judgment prove to have been an accurate one, the ultimate assessment of their lives as Catholic churchmen cannot be in doubt.

As I read through Archbishop Hallinan's addresses I jotted down numerous notes with the thought of employing them for the present task. But were I to attempt to use them all, this introductory essay would assume a length quite out of proportion to the editor's original intention. By way of drawing this effort to a close, then, let me choose a few items from these notes that will serve to illustrate other notable traits of my lamented friend. He was plainly delighted when he was chosen for the hierarchy in 1958, but never was the new rank permitted to make the slightest difference in his relations with friends of a former time. I am certain that others would say of him what I say here with the utmost sincerity, that though he never for an instant was unmindful of the dignity that should ever be the hallmark of a bishop's bearing, Paul Hallinan remained completely open to the easy and casual approach of his friends. In this he could have made his own every word of a letter written by Prospero Lambertini, the future Pope Benedict XIV, when in 1728 at the age of fifty-three he was made a cardinal. "What you can be sure of," he told this friend

> is that in this new transformation I am changing nothing but the colour of my clothes, and that I am still the same Lambertini in my character, my lightheartedness and my lasting friendship for you.[10]

I have never known, nor have I ever heard of a friend of Paul Hallinan's who could not witness to precisely that kind of treatment from him after he became a bishop in 1958 and an archbishop four years later. To some it may seem to belabor the commonplace to dwell on the point; but the trait in those of high station in either Church or State is not that universal, and when one observes its unvarying presence in a prelate it says more about the latter's integrity than lengthy discourses on that virtue could convey.

An interview of the archbishop's in October, 1964, intended for *Continuum* and entitled "Our Own American Trademark," exemplified characteristics of another kind. It was no surprise that journalists, and especially Gerard Sherry, who became editor of Atlanta's Catholic weekly, the *Georgia Bulletin,* early in 1963, should have found the archbishop so congenial a 'boss,' if that is not too incongruous a word to apply to Paul Hallinan. The latter had his own very real journalistic flair, and if at an early date he had not been taken captive by Clio he might well have made his mark with the Catholic press. Elated at the prospect of Mr. Sherry's advent to Atlanta, he confided the news to me some months in advance, ending the paragraph with the terse comment, "Mum's the word."[11] In the interview mentioned above, one meets a number of flash phrases that succeeded with a minimum of words in encompassing a wide spectrum of truth; for example, in noting the press' constantly changing moods he remarked, "One decade's Pulitzer may become the next decade's pot-boiler."[12]

In the same piece the archbishop's kinship with the thought and style of John Ireland, Archbishop of Saint Paul, was apparent. Ireland, said Hallinan, was the kind of man "who posed further direct challenges that called for an even more dynamic response," a stance that he very much admired, and he then wove together several quotations from Ireland's addresses, of which the following sample showed unmistakeably why Saint Paul's first archbishop held so strong an appeal for him. In this instance Ireland had said:

> Go down in sympathy to the suffering multitude, bringing to them charity, and, what is more rarely given, justice. Seek out social evils, and lead in movements that tend to rectify them .... Laymen need not wait for priest, nor priest for bishop, nor bishop for pope.

The Archbishop of Atlanta hailed what he described as Ireland's call "for engagement, commitment, involvement," and he then proceeded to quote his hero once again where he had declared:

> To sing lovely anthems in cathedral stalls, and wear copes of broidered gold while no multitudes throng nave or aisle, and while the world outside is dying of spiritual and moral starvation — this is not the religion we need today![13]

Words of this kind never failed to stir Atlanta's archbishop and to touch off within him an immediate sympathetic reaction.

Speaking of involvement, an almost dramatic passage from one of my friend's last letters gave a striking example of how his personal involvement was implemented in the case of anyone who crossed his path and was in need of help. At the time he was on the eve of departure from Atlanta for what he called "an hon. degree spree" with engagements at the College of the Holy Cross in Worcester and Western Reserve University in Cleveland which, he said, were to be "sandwiched in between" his thirty-fifth anniversary of graduation from the University of Notre Dame. He then continued:

> Just returned from an exciting evening — mayor's Human Rel. Commission at the Tabernacle Baptist Church, crossed swords with an angry Negro preacher-cum-politician, & caused a slight riot when a number of the community still wanted to speak, so when I was asked to close with prayer, I made a motion to continue the mtg. instead! [This is Boulevard Ave. where the riots were last summer] — a 6-year old Negro boy had been hit by a truck driver (white) & knocked to the street. About 70 had gathered in a foul mood — we got an ambulance & I drove the mother, the grandmother, & 3 other little kids to the Hospital. It looked bad when I left after about an hour — hope he makes it. Of such stuff are riots made. (This is detailed not as a 'success story,' but to indicate why my correspondence is so badly neglected!).[14]

The incident was entirely in character. It documented what I had in mind when some months after his death in an obituary notice for an historical journal I wrote, "He was a warmhearted man, quick to sympathize with the problems of others . . . ."[15] Moreover, the episode of that early June night of 1967 demonstrated that Archbishop Hallinan had meant what he said in his installation sermon five years before. Alluding on that occasion in warm and gracious words to the presence in the cathedral of representatives of Atlanta's Protestant and Jewish communities, he affirmed that his own people, "speaking their deepest Catholic convictions," would work side by side with their fellow citizens of other religious faiths. He then added:

> Our first task is to save our souls, but we cannot save them in heaven, nor in the sanctuary. We can save them only in Atlanta, in Georgia, in America, in the world in which we live.[16]

A year later he returned to this favorite theme in addressing an audience of men and women engaged in higher education when he reminded the educators, "Men will save their souls on Main Street, on Wall Street, on Madison Avenue, and every other thoroughfare in the world, or they will not save them at all."[17] To use another of the fatigued expressions of our day, here, indeed, was a truly 'out-going' churchman, and his 'going out' was a kind that citizens of every religious persuasion, and of none, and of every social class in Cleveland, in Charleston, in Atlanta, and in other places where he was a resident were aware that in their midst was a genuine man of God whose concern for each of them left an indelible impression of Christ-like love that lingered in their hearts and memories.

Paul Hallinan was a person who believed profoundly in the saving grace of humor in the relationships of humankind, even when he was himself the object of other people's laughter. When, for example, he caused a general inquiry to be made as to what people felt the archdiocesan weekly newspaper should contain, one man wrote in to say that it should cover "first communions, confirmations, and the funerals of priests." Quoting the man's preferences, the archbishop commented:

> It can be presumed that all Catholics are in favor of the first two, but those who enjoy reading about the clergy being buried might well be suspected of a rather morbid anti-clericalism![18]

On another occasion he extolled the openness of the new Church, of the priest and bishop moving among the people after the model of the Master, and of the incongruity in the old days of priests offering Mass with their backs to the people. "I recall no artist," he said, "who ever painted a Last Supper that had Our Lord facing the wall."[19] His humor never left a sting, although frequently he strengthened a point with a twist of irony. As Monsignor Yzermans has said, the archbishop's championing of women's role in the Church anticipated the Women's Liberation Movement, his views having been formalized at Vatican Council II by an intervention that he called, "Equality of Women in the Church." A year later he followed this up in an address to a group of Catholic women in Omaha in Stepember, 1966, in which he enlarged upon his concept of the new role that he thought they should fill in the post-conciliar Church. He told them that he was still receiving reactions to his conciliar intervention of October, 1965, whereas a second intervention of the same date entitled "Racial Injustice" was, insofar as he knew, never again referred to by anyone. At Omaha he made special mention of the women religious, supported the demands of some of their spokeswomen for a really significant participation in decisions relating to their future, and, in alluding to what was then a lively topic of discussion, he wryly remarked, "After all, it is rather absurd to have celibate prelates, some of them 70 years old, judging the styles of sisters' habits." [20]

It was in his final article published after his death that Archbishop Hallinan gave the most conspicuous example of his ability to laugh at himself. The point revolved around the answers he had given to a newspaper reporter's questions concerning Pope John XXIII who had been elected on the day that Paul Hallinan was made a member of the College of Bishops. He and the new pontiff, he said, had gotten off to a bad start in that Cardinal Roncalli's election coming as it did while the episcopal ordination ceremonies were in progress in Saint John's Cathedral in Cleveland, there was a sudden switch in the headlines. The archbishop described it this way:

> RONCALLI ELECTED POPE was spread-eagled across eight columns. HALLINAN A BISHOP was relegated to page 4 somewhere between 'Dear Abby' and the Dow-Jones averages. Somehow, John XXIII took the first round.

Reviewing the interview, the archbishop stated, "I marvel at the accuracy of my observations. History will surely be reluctant to alter any detail." As the questioning continued the new bishop sank deeper and deeper into a quagmire of faulty predictions. No, John XXIII was seventy-seven and would, therefore, be only an interim pope, he would introduce no alteration in the liturgy, he would foster no fresh approach to the other Christian churches, he would hold fast to his predecessors' anti-Communist policies, nor could he be expected to change the Church's attitude toward the world. "I summed it all up," he bravely wrote, in this fashion: "No, Pope John is a good, simple man. He will do little that history will note. He will keep the Barque of Peter high on a mountain top while the tillers sow the seed." In closing this brief but revealing piece the archbishop listed John's summoning of Vatican Council II, the memorable encyclicals, *Mater et Magistra* and *Pacem in Terris*, noted the pontiff's inauguration of a new policy toward the Communist world, called attention to the presence of the Protestant observers at the council, and remarked the replacement of Latin by the vernacular in the liturgy. In a final great rhetorical guffaw at himself he then concluded, "I have recently been asked to assess the 1968 Presidential race. It's Harold Stassen all the way!"[21] Was ever more convincing proof than this offered by any man, to say nothing of an archbishop, of magnanimity of character and basic humility of soul? There may, indeed, have been such, but personally I have never known or heard of an example in our time exactly to parallel or to excel it.

Were it not that as I now write I am several weeks late in meeting the editor's deadline for this essay, I should be tempted to say more about my friend's many attractive qualities of mind and heart as reflected in our personal correspondence, in his public addresses, and in the memories that I cherish of a relationship through over a decade that became a deep and enduring friendship. Archbishop Hallinan had many helpful things to say on a variety of subjects that are still very much in the public mind, a judgment that will be sustained, I believe, by a careful reading of the thirty-six items included in this book. It is well to remember, too, that all these date from his installation as Archbishop of Atlanta in March, 1962, for there had been significant statements as well during the previous three years and four months that he served as Bishop of Charleston. If here and there one comes upon a treatment that may now seem somewhat dated — Catholic women may feel that during the past six years they have moved beyond what he had to say to them at Omaha in September, 1966 — in most of what he wrote and spoke in the years between 1962 and 1968 there lingers a surprising air of contemporaneity.

The quality of relevance (it is difficult to avoid entirely that exhausted word) probably shows to advantage as much in the archbishop's views on higher education and on war and peace as in any other topic. For that reason administrators and faculties of colleges, universities, and seminaries of the American Church can still read with profit counsel offered to their kind at Saint Louis in April, 1963, when with his customary clarity and tact he urged more collaboration between Catholic schools of all levels, while he deplored the folly of proliferation of more feeble institutions in a wasteful competition and heedless individualism.[22] On the second topic, war and peace, the archbishop, in fact, anticipated the joint statements of the American bishops on more than one occasion. That appears in the pastoral letter that he signed in October, 1966, along with his beloved auxiliary, Bishop Bernardin, when an open and constructively questioning and critical attitude toward American involvement in Vietnam was advocated, thus adumbrating in a way the hierarchy's remarkable pronouncement of November, 1971, on that burning question. Just as the public lectures and published essays of Wilhelm Emmanuel von Ketteler, Bishop of Mainz, and of Henry Edward Manning, Archbishop of Westminster, had clearly foreshadowed in the 1870's the encyclical, *Rerum novarum*, of Pope Leo XIII of May, 1891, on the problems of the new industrial order, so in a lesser way it may be said Archbishop Hallinan's arresting public stance and forceful pronouncements on the tragedy of the war in Vietnam, prepared the way and hastened the collective action of his fellow bishops in 1971. No special perception was needed, therefore, in placing a high evauation on his pastoral letter of 1966 and in choosing it as the final entry in a revised and enlarged edition of my readings in American Catholic history some months after it had appeared.[23]

At the time there were those, even among his own, who were prone to wonder about the appropriateness of Archbishop Hallinan's public stand on this very controversial subject and to question his patriotism and loyalty to the Republic, so unaccustomed were they to hear a Catholic bishop openly criticize American foreign policy. Such people forgot this man's notable contribution to his country during World War II when he served for several years as a chaplain in the south Pacific with the Army Corps of Engineers and distinguished himself sufficiently to win the award of the Purple Heart at New Guinea. While Paul Hallinan lacked nothing of what constitutes true patriotism, he was adamantly opposed to any late twentieth-century version of Stephen Decatur's unfortunate response to the Norfolk dinner toast of 1815: "Our country! In her intercourse with foreign nations may she always be in the right; but our country, right or wrong." Nor did the archbishop hesitate to affirm his position on this point in the presence of powerful figures who strongly differed with him. For example, at a dinner at Miami in September, 1962, in Cardinal Spellman's honor following the latter's ordination of Father Daniel Sanchez, a native Cuban, the Archbishop of Atlanta spoke in a vein that could scarcely have been acceptable to the guest of honor. Recounting the reasons that people had for their fears, as well as the reasons that should inspire their confidence, he said:

> What must we fear? Communism, of course, but our own noisy nationalism and our own private apathy are just as dangerous. Communism is evil, and it is our public enemy. Nationalism and apathy are just as evil, but it is easy to forget them . . . . Communism is monolithic, and quite easy to spot. But nationalism wears many coats, and speaks many tongues. It may be raucous like fascism, vicious like Naziism, or polite and smug and condescending. When it is winning, it cries: 'My country, right or wrong.' When it has won, it speaks self-righteously of 'white supremacy' or the 'white man's burden.' But when it is less sure of itself, it looks about for a scapegoat, and the nearest one at hand is the 'foreigner.' . . . . Nationalism is you and I closing our eyes to the beauty and warmth and truth of another culture, and squinting only at what is ugly and mean and degrading. It is the refusal to share, to learn, to sympathize. These were the sins of the levite and the priest on the road to Jericho. It was a foreigner, let us never forget, who gave our world the beautiful term, 'the Good Samaritan.' [24]

In everything that he said and that he did, Archbishop Hallinan always put the highest premium on truthfulness and honesty. It was for that reason, I suppose, that he never seemed to lose a chance to promote this spirit in those whom he believed he might influence. When he spoke before the annual national Newman meeting at the University of Southwestern Louisiana on August 26, 1963, he was in the presence of those whose apostolate he had served for over a decade with conspicuous success. It was these qualities that he urged on his Newman friends, and in doing so the man's magnanimity showed once again when he told them:

> We must honor the scholar who honestly seeks the truth in his field, whether he is on our side or not, whether we like him or not, whether he likes us or not. Anything else is intellectual dishonesty.[25]

It would be difficult to conceive a more helpful mandate than this for an archbishop to give to young Catholics from secular college and university campuses. Two years later I made that the general theme of the annual Wimmer Lecture at Saint Vincent College in November, 1965, with variations on the grave injury that I felt had at times been done to the Church by Catholics' infractions against truthfulness and honesty. When the lecture was published I sent the archbishop a copy, and in the last letter I received from him he told me that he had that summer completed the updating of his personal files. He then remarked:

> I think I have about all the major pieces you have done; either you were kind enough to send me a copy, or I have got one from the news-services. Of everything you have done, I like *Commitment to Truth* the most.

He then wished me length of years and a 'heavy output,' as he expressed it. There followed a sentence that, I trust, I may be pardoned for quoting since the opinion of this good friend, biased as it was in my favor, yet meant then and still means much to me. "Every line you have written," he said, "has been in the service of the Church."[26] I would ask for no higher tribute from any source than those words from Paul Hallinan.

The imagination is not taxed nor is the memory burdened when one seeks to evoke the striking characteristics of the first Archbishop of Atlanta. Actually, the task is an easy one. He was an engaging speaker, an historian of genuine promise, a Catholic churchman to whom ecumenism meant more than a superficial compliment or a passing smile, a man born to lead, a first class mind, a dynamo of tremendous industry, and a keenly responsible person whether that responsibility related to parishioners, to soldiers, to students, to the clergy and laity of the dioceses he ruled, or to the general community of which he was a resident. He was, indeed, all these things, and he was more. Yet it would, I believe, be a serious omission were one to conclude a brief essay of this kind without a final word about that which was the informing principle of Paul Hallinan's entire life, the source, as it were, from which he derived his inner strength and that lighted every day of his nearly fifty-seven years in this world.

That most fundamental and enlightening of the archbishop's many notable qualities and characteristics was his supernatural faith which, in turn, accounted for this man's passionate love for the Church, for the priesthood, and for every man and woman who crossed his path and in whom he saw mirrored the image and likeness of the Master. In a word, Paul Hallinan was a deeply pious man whose piety was as devoid of any suggestion of pretense or display as was that of Cardinal Newman, one of the prime inspirations of his life. One sensed this inner light in a hundred different ways in all that he said and wrote and did, whether he was engaged in formal address before a large public gathering or in a quiet conversation with a friend in the intimacy of his study. Moreover, his quick sensitivity to the needs of others told him that relatively few were blessed with the same degree of enlightened and secure faith that he was. And he realized this in a special way as his life drew to a close amid the most distressful and frightening turmoil that his beloved Church had known in more than 400 years.

Knowledge of that fact prompted the archbishop in June, 1967, to address a final pastoral letter to his people, a message that revealed how much he was at pains to make known his sympathy with those who were plagued with doubts. As in previous pastorals, this one was also signed at his request by Bishop Bernardin, and it was obvious that they sought to lead their spiritual charges out of what was for many a lifelong habit of dependence on the Church to furnish an answer for every problem they encountered. In other words, these two wise churchmen attempted to guide their people gently over the void that had been left in their lives when the whirlwind of the revolutionary situation that descended on the entire Catholic world in the 1960's had seemingly swept away the prop of the Church's reputed omniscience. Far from wishing to weaken further the Church's authority in their minds, the Atlanta bishops sought rather to render it more secure in the minds of their people by reminding them of the price that is often asked of those who have the gift of faith. In a word, the pastoral letter led the Atlanta Catholics toward a mature and sophisticated attitude vis-à-vis life's inevitable mysteries, sorrows, and sufferings. "Our vigilance must be constant. We must meet difficulties with wisdom," said Archbishop Hallinan and his auxiliary, and they thereupon explained what they meant:

Even doubts can have two effects: although they can enervate and weaken faith, they can also try and test it. Catholics must not rest comfortably on their belief. They are called to suffer many a struggle of doubt. Under pain of decline, the habit of faith must keep stretching toward a perpetual renewal and growth. It is not an insurance policy or a guarantee of a serene mind. Its exercise, amid difficulties and even with the resolution of doubts, is a necessary part of God's discipline.[27]

This final formal message of Archbishop Hallinan was eminently fitting for a time of widespread doubt and disbelief. Not only did it constitute a strong affirmation of his own lifelong faith, but it afforded his people a solid theological signpost. In this it was, as it were, the archbishop's spiritual bequest before he departed, a guideline for souls who had looked to him for direction and who were given herewith a lifeline to the mature approach that Catholics should cultivate in all that pertained to their supernatural destiny.

As one reviews in retrospect the life of Atlanta's first archbishop it is not difficult to think of his relatively brief time in this world as having fulfilled what his beloved Newman had in mind in the latter's prayer on life's ultimate purpose. Those who knew Paul Hallinan well would, I think, say that at the end he could, if his modesty did not forbid him, fittingly make his own Newman's words in the serene assurance that he had endeavored through all his years to implement them in his daily life. In a measure known only to the ultimate Judge of humankind he had realized what Newman intended when he said:

Let us ever make it our prayer and our endeavour, that we may know the whole counsel of God, and grow unto the measure of the stature of the fulness of Christ; that all prejudice, and self-confidence, and hollowness, and unreality, and positiveness, and partisanship, may be put away from us under the light of Wisdom, and the fire of Faith and Love; till we see things as God sees them, with the judgment of His Spirit, and according to the mind of Christ.[28]

[1] Paul J. Hallinan to John Tracy Ellis, Cleveland, February 5, 1955; although the letter was dated February 5 it was postmarked March 23, 1955.

[2] Same to same, Atlanta, July 19, 1967.

[3] "Archbishop Hallinan: In Memoriam," *Thought,* XLIII (Winter, 1968), 539-572.

[4] "The Search for Security," *The Tablet* [London], CCXXV (October 23, 1971), 1018.

[5] Carroll to Joseph Berington, Baltimore [1787], copy, Archives of the Archdiocese of Baltimore, Special C, C-1, quoted in John Tracy Ellis,

"Archbishop Carroll and the Liturgy in the Vernacular," *Worship*, XXVI (November, 1952), 547-548.

[6] Intervention of Archbishop Hallinan, October 31, 1962, Vincent A. Yzermans (Ed.), *American Participation in the Second Vatican Council*. New York: Sheed and Ward. 1967. p. 157.

[7] "Death to the Cathedral," *Time*, LXXII (September 1, 1958), 46.

[8] For an historical survey of academic freedom among American Catholics, see the writer's chapter, "A Tradition of Autonomy?" Neil G. McCluskey, S.J. (Ed.), *The Catholic University. A Modern Appraisal*. Notre Dame: University of Notre Dame Press. 1970, pp. 206-270, especially pp. 260-262 for the Curran case.

[9] "A New Archbishop," p. 37, Xerox copy.

[10] Renée Haynes, *Philosopher King. The Humanist Pope. Benedict XIV*. London: Weidenfeld and Nicholson. 1970. p. 41.

[11] Hallinan to Ellis, Atlanta, August 20, 1962.

[12] "Our Own American Trademark," p. 30. Xerox copy.

[13] *Ibid.*, p. 25.

[14] Hallinan to Ellis, Atlanta [June 5, 1967].

[15] *Catholic Historical Review*, LI (July, 1968), 408-409.

[16] "A New Archbishop," pp. 3-4, Xerox copy.

[17] "Catholic Higher Education — A New Chapter," p. 12, Xerox copy.

[18] "Dialogue Within the Church," pastoral letter for Lent, 1966, p. 4. Xerox copy.

[19] "The Church — The Open Circle," p. 3, Xerox copy.

[20] "Wanted: Valiant Women," p. 2, Xerox copy.

[21] "An Archbishop, Of All People, Admits I WAS WRONG," *The Critic*, XXVI (April-May, 1968), 30-31.

[22] "Catholic Higher Education — A New Chapter," pp. 3-5, Xerox copy.

[23] "War and Peace. A Pastoral Letter to the Archdiocese of Atlanta, October, 1966," John Tracy Ellis (Ed.), *Documents of American Catholic History*. Revised and enlarged edition. Chicago: Henry Regnery Company. 1967. II, 696-702.

[24] "The Same Reasons for Confidence or for Fear," pp. 4-5, Xerox copy.

[25] "Forming Catholic Leaders," p. 3, Xerox copy. These sentences were spoken in the context of the Archbishop bidding farewell to the Index of Forbidden Books that had recently been disbanded by the Congregation for the Doctrine of the Faith.

[26] Hallinan to Ellis, Atlanta, July 19, 1967. At this point he added in a parenthesis: "(By the way, do you have an extra copy of the OBEDIENCE talk to the Paulists at Washington) with the citations from de Chardin and Congar? If you could spare it, I would appreciate it." The reference was to the diamond jubilee address at Saint Paul's College, Washington, D.C., January 25, 1965, which was published as "A Seminary Jubilee," *Chicago Studies*, IV (Summer, 1965), 115-136.

[27] "Faith and the Human Condition," pastoral letter of June 29, 1967, p. 7, Xerox copy.

[28] "Wisdom, As Contrasted with Faith and with Bigotry," a sermon preached on June 1, 1841. *Fifteen Sermons Preached before the University of Oxford*. New York: Longmans, Green & Company. 1906. p. 311.

DAYS OF HOPE
AND PROMISE

A NEW ARCHBISHOP

*This is the text of the sermon Archbishop Hallinan
delivered upon his installation as the first metropolitan
of the Province of Atlanta, 29 March, 1962. The Scriptural text he chose was from 1 Thessalonians 1:2-7: "We
give thanks to God for you always ... being mindful of
your work of faith, and labor, and charity, and your
enduring hope in Our Lord, Jesus Christ ... so that you
became a pattern to all the believers in Macedonia and
in Achaia."*

One hundred and fourteen years ago, the sacrifice of the Mass
was first offered in Atlanta. There was no church; in fact, there was
hardly a city. The priest was Father Thomas Shannahan; the place,
a clean table in a simple Irish home. But the faith was here. As the
historian of the Church in Georgia and the Carolinas described it, "If
there had been ample notice, every Catholic from Rabun Gap to
Dahlonega . . . would be gathered round, waiting their turn for confession, and fasting." The faith was here indeed, among the Georgians
as among St. Paul's Thessalonians. And it grew and became a pattern
to all the believers, a pattern of growth against tremendous odds, of
struggle against thorns and thistles, against poverty, and distance, and
the epidemics that cut down priests and sisters, and reduced the tiny,
scattered flock. No great waves of Catholic immigration came, as in
the north, to build the churches and to fill them. War destroyed the
homes and harvests and left behind it incredible misgovernment and
bitter frustration. Every decade brought its own peculiar tragedy to
the South and to the Church. When war and reconstruction had done
their worst, there were probably less than 40,000 Catholics in the four
states which today comprise the new metropolitan province just established by the Holy See.

But what Catholics these people were! The old man in Marietta
who knew the Scriptures by heart, and won the respect of many fine
Protestants when he outquoted an anti-Catholic Bible salesman in
public debate. The veteran priest of forty years on the Georgia missions,
Father Peter Whealan who lived most of his life on quinine, emaciated

1

and worn out, at the end almost hanging on to the altar in Savannah as he offered Mass. The pioneer Catholic families of Milledgeville who offered their homes for Mass before the church was even built. Bishop John Barry who, as a priest in Augusta during the cholera, turned his rectory into a hospital while he nursed, consoled and then buried the victims, anointing the Catholics among them. Martyrs, confessors and apostles they were, and a litany of the saints could well be sung of the men and women who lived and died for their faith on the Georgia missions.

The origin of the Church of Savannah and Atlanta is essentially the same as the growth of the Church in the dioceses of Raleigh and Charleston to the north, and St. Augustine and Miami to the south. It is a heroic account of staunch faith and daily struggle. It was a long winter, and the world grows old, but the Church is ever young. The rhythm of the seasons moves along. We are privileged to live in the springtime of the Christian year, not as Cardinal Newman predicted for England a century ago, a "second spring," but for the southland of America a "first spring." We can still expect, in Newman's words, "keen blasts, and cold showers, and sudden storms," but the bright promise and budding hopes cannot be denied.

The first soil of Catholic planting for the South was in the mother province of Baltimore. Within her boundaries the seeds of faith were planted, in North Carolina by Gibbons and the Benedictines, in South Carolina by England and Lynch, in Georgia by Gartland and Becker, in Florida by Verot and Kenny. Under the steady care of good priests, the seeds have sprouted; the strong young shoots have flourished. The breath of the Holy Spirit has warmed the land; Catholic souls have trebled in the past decade, and the Holy See has taken formal notice. Because the faith is deep, and the charity of our people is open-hearted, the bishops of this youngest American province face the future with strong, confident, Christian hope. We are few in priests and sisters, small in physical plant, short of mission funds. But out of the sacrificial record of a century there remain faith, hope and charity; these three, and the power and the promise of God who said, "My grace is sufficient for thee."

The Catholic Church in the South faces her own special challenge. Large cities have grown out of industry and commerce. Urban and suburban parishes have their own problems: crowded schools, capacity congregations, changing neighborhoods. But the basic challenge in our states lies between and beyond these cities, the rural area, the small town, the crossroads. This dilemma is confronted in every diocese in the province. How to care for Catholic thousands in the cities. How to reach the villages and counties where the Church is not known. Then, cutting across almost every problem, there are the difficulties of a nation in transit: thousands of military personnel, shifting populations, and (in one notable instance) refugees from the island of Communism. Finally, as St. Paul had his daily pressing anxiety in the care of the churches, so does the Church today face the daily task of putting into practical effect her clear-cut teaching on racial justice. Neither in the North nor in the South can she bear the ugly blemish of prejudice and fear. Small in numbers but great in loyalty, our Catholic people are trying to reflect the unity of Christ's Mystical Body as they move toward the reality of full racial justice, with prudence, with courage, with determination.

These are the elements of the challenge within the Church itself. But the Church does not live only to itself. It lives *in* society and *for* society. In any nation that calls itself religious, the Church must provide the vision of what society should be. It is society's yeast, society's sentinel, society's ideal. Our Catholic, Protestant, and Jewish people are the citizens of the community. That community will be what all of them, working together, decide that it will be. Our Catholic people, speaking their deepest Catholic convictions, will work side by side with citizens of other faiths toward a community approved by God. Our first task is to save our souls, but we cannot save them in heaven, nor in the sanctuary. We can save them only in Atlanta, in Georgia, in America, in the world in which we live.

Our Holy Father, Pope John XXIII, has marked this springtime of the South with an event of profound significance, the creation of a new ecclesiastical province. I know you join me in this expression of our gratitude to him. We warmly welcome to Atlanta his personal representative, the revered Apostolic Delegate, Archbishop Vagnozzi. We greet the distinguished bishops of the new province, men of zeal and vision: Archbishop Hurley of St. Augustine, Bishop Waters of Raleigh, Bishop McDonough of Savannah, Bishop Carroll of Miami, and a hearty welcome to my as yet unknown, but fortunate successor, the next Bishop of Charleston. We are proud to greet the honored metropolitan of our mother province of Baltimore, Archbishop Shehan. To this joyful event have come archbishops, bishops and abbots, priests and religious, family and friends from every part of the United States, and the nearby islands, to witness this latest sign of Rome's paternal care. They rejoice in this blessing for the South, as the South rejoices in their coming.

At the heart of this event are the devoted priests, religious and laity of the new archdiocese of Atlanta. Their faith, their leadership, their cooperation have merited this new honor and its corresponding new responsibility. Side by side with our own splendid diocesan priests, the members of nine religious orders have blessed our soil. In the extension of Christ's Kingdom, all priests have worked together. They wear different cassocks, they bear different names, but there is really only one kind of priest: God's priest. Priests, sisters and laity recall with me today the blessed labors of their beloved Archbishop O'Hara when all Georgia formed one diocese. They are profoundly grateful — as am I — for the firm foundation laid in five short years by that gentle and zealous man of God, the first bishop of Atlanta, my predecessor, Bishop Francis Hyland. To all who love Atlanta, and Georgia, and the South — to all who love the Church — this is a day of thankful prayer and joyous hope.

We are especially honored by the presence of distinguished officials and representatives of the civic community, and by friends and guests who profess a different faith, but join with us in mutual respect and charity. In the meaningful words of Pope John, we greet them all as brothers, and this fraternal greeting could cease only if the Lord's prayer, the Our Father, would cease to be said.

Because we are Catholics, we cannot be blind to the worldwide Church beyond our boundaries. For, in a world of distress and fear, the Catholic Church is experiencing her own splendid springtime of hope and promise. When he convoked the ecumenical council, our Holy Father called the Christian community today "vibrant with vitality." It has been, he added, "transformed in great part, and renewed . . . strengthened socially in unity . . . intellectually reinvigorated . . . internally purified, and is thus ready for trial." This fragrant hope, this holy anxiety is in the air we breathe today. We are not living in ordinary times. A great pope and a historic council stamp the year of 1962 with momentous distinction. No prelate, no priest, no Catholic can ever look upon it again as "just another year."

In this spirit of mutual hope and charity, I pledge to you, my beloved priests and religious, Catholic men and women of the new archdiocese of Atlanta, my best efforts, humble as they are, in the sacred vocation of your spiritual father. When a bishop is consecrated, the Church speaks but four words: "Receive the Holy Spirit." When a bishop is installed, nothing is said at all. He is simply seated and handed the crozier of his authority. The Catholic conscience needs no further mandate; the Catholic heart instinctively recalls the promise of Our Lord: "As the Father has sent Me, I also send you." St. Paul in his letter to the young bishop, Timothy, gave him a series of vigorous directives: "Fight the good fight . . . guard the trust . . . stir up in you the grace of God . . . preach the word, be urgent in season, out of season." These are not maxims for serenity and repose. They are rules of action that bind the men who are called to be faithful stewards in the house of God.

And yet no bishop governs in solitude, just as no human act can occur in a vacuum. The bishop works through his priests, his religious, his faithful people. Thus St. Ignatius of Antioch urged the Christians of Smyrna and their bishop, Polycarp, to "toil together, run together, wrestle together, suffer together, rest together, rise together." As you promise to me today your obedience and your loyalty, I promise to you, as best I can with God's help, the practice of those particular virtues which St. Paul required of a bishop: "Justice, charity, mildness, patience."

Our cathedral is dedicated to Christ the King. Our patron is His Blessed Mother. United with our King, joined in prayer with Our Lady, we take today a new turn on the old road that leads to God. In that unity of purpose that was the subject of Our Lord's last formal prayer in the garden, we will reach together our eternal destiny with Him. It was already said today, in the ceremony of installation, in the prayer for the new archbishop. May God "enable him to further, by his teaching and example, the salvation of those over whom he is placed, so that he may — with the flock entrusted to his care — attain everlasting life."

CATHOLIC ADULT EDUCATION:
Necessity and Challenge

The Archbishop's knowledge of Newman's writings and his own deep admiration of Newman the man is evident in all his addresses and writings. Perhaps more in this particular address he revealed that knowledge and admiration. He delivered this address on 26 April, 1962, in Detroit, invited as the principal speaker by the Catholic Adult Education Commission.

Everyone who has struggled through high school Senior English is aware of Cardinal Newman's famous definition of a gentleman: "One who never inflicts pain." But most of those who quote it are not aware that it is not a definition at all. It is a satire, almost a joke. As part of his little joke, Newman warns us that it is "almost a definition." To bring it to the full measure of satire, he carries it out for two full pages — his mirror of the Oxford type of man who concurs with others rather than take the initiative himself; avoids what would jar or jolt their minds; looks upon all forms of faith with an impartial eye; in short, says Newman, he might even pass for a disciple of Christianity itself. This mild and bland creature is what happens when the cultivated intellect operates without religious principle.

I introduce Newman's little joke right at the beginning not because I intend to inflict any more pain than is ordinarily connected with listening to convention addresses, nor because I have a low regard for gentlemen. But it is refreshing to learn that complacency is not just our contemporary problem. Newman's times knew it well, and so do we. We still like to take our liturgy as we take our athletics — from the comfort of a grandstand seat. Our educational process has developed with that same occupational disease. We want philosophy without tears, theology without dogma, poems in anthologies, and novels in digests. Are we willing today to struggle with ideas, sacrifice for ideals, suffer for consequences? Certainly when put to the test many of us are quite willing, but the tide of complacency is strong, and full, and persuasive.

This involvement in struggle is part and parcel of the whole process of adult education. To learn is to expend energy, to engage in that work, both pleasant and painful, by which pieces of the unknown are chipped off, digested, made part of our own self. The soul groans while it grazes, whether it be the ten-year old who would rather watch television, the teen-ager who would rather watch another teen-ager, or the college student who has more joy in one class that is cut than in ninety-nine others dutifully attended.

But at no point on the academic spectrum is there more struggle than at the point of adult education. This is not because adults do not want to learn; they would not otherwise have enrolled. Nor have their minds hardened against the thrill of new ideas. It is simply that we live in a busy, distracting world, and it is no mean accomplishment for the workingman, the housewife, the young executive, or the nurse to complete an evening course in anything. Against this round of duties and distractions, we must, of course, set the determination to learn and the fascinating prospect of opening up new roads of mental adventure. That this is going on all over the United States and that Catholic adults are taking their fair share of the benefits is a decided plus in our educational scales. That we have advanced to a point where a national Catholic organization meets annually to find out how it can be better planned and more widely carried out is good news of the very first order.

May we simply state the necessity of adult education and then go on to what is called the challenge? May we not take for granted that most mature Catholics capable of adult education are well aware that it is necessary? Must we stress that Catholics should be well informed in this Joannine year of 1962, when John Glenn went 'round the world, John Kennedy went 'round Big Steel, and the ghost of John Birch still goes 'round the anxious precincts of the fearful and the insecure? As the year goes on, it will become Joannine in an even more profound sense (indeed, a papal sense) as contemporary historians record for later times the general council called for October by our valiant and vigorous Holy Father, Pope John XXIII. These are not ordinary times. They call for all mature Catholics to seek fresh insights into their own mental inventory, and fresh approaches to the agenda of disorders that history is always setting before us.

The challenge, the great opportunities, the situations full of hope and promise, these strike me as more compelling than the need. Men marry not only because of need, but because of the hope of happiness in marriage. Medical students study not only because there is disease

to be treated, but because they hope to cure it by their skill. So
Catholic men and women enroll in evening courses not primarily because there is need of an informed Catholic laity, and not just because
of their own need to pass the time profitably, but because the challenge
of the unknown is one of the most compelling in the experience of man.
There is a joy in truth, a *gaudium de veritate,* as St. Augustine said.
There is a purpose in education beyond the immediate practical use to
which it can be put, as John Henry Newman said. There is a link,
a cause and effect bond between truth and man's cherished freedom,
as Our Lord Himself said. And although He was speaking primarily
of that truth which only faith can reveal when He said that it would
make us free, it is proportionately true of all knowledge. Man's freedom
grows as he learns the truth from any source.

The challenge, then, of adult education has certain dimensions.
It is not our task in this field to reform the world, nor to hunt out
communists, nor to aid and abet, nor to say, "Cease and desist!" to
the United Nations. It is a task much more modest, but for all that,
much more demanding. Newman called it "the reconsecration of the
intellect." If that term seems pretentious today, it is because we have
grown accustomed to the mediocre mind. We have sneered too long
at the "brain-trust," and "quiz-kid," and "egg-head." We cannot expect
excellence in life unless we have excellence in education. We pay little
honor to journalists who think, critics who criticize, churchmen who
judge. We want journalists, critics and churchmen who soothe and
console; we pay high royalties for their positive thinking and their
adjusted complacency. Ideas have become cheap, and in our college
and university world we are far more concerned about a free market
for all kinds of thoughts than about the value of the thoughts themselves. Newman's phrase, the reconsecration of the intellect, strikes
us as embarrassing. Too many intellects have been bought and sold.
We are aware that there is a sin of simony, when sacred things are
put into commerce. But the practice had dulled our conscience. We
have forgotten that the intellect too is sacred, and falls under the same
prohibition.

Adult education has taken up the formidable job of reconsecrating
the mind. And the range of human problems stakes out the dimensions
of the task. How deep shall we probe? How far out shall we range?
How high shall we reach? An exploration of our boundaries should
prove worthwbile for the men and women responsbile for the national
growth of the post-academic, post-formal pursuit of wisdom known
today as Adult Education.

How deep? Deep enough to get to the strata of ideas, far below the surface of opinions, feelings, prejudices, old mental habits and odd personal views. In his essay on "The Idea of a University," Newman explored the thing he called viewiness, the preoccupation of a man who has a view about everything, a grasp of nothing. Yet those who found Newman hard going a century ago have descendants today who are just as superficial. Much of our modern conversation today is merely an exchange of assorted prejudices. What passes for thought is only a search for the newspaper or magazine which agrees with one's likes and dislikes. There is a certain pleasantness in all this; it reminds us of the definition of a gentleman: polished, inoffensive, no edges, all surface. But this surface knowledge can be found in partisans as well as in gentlemen, the stalwarts of the extreme right and the extreme left. There is a curious affinity in their thinking, an extreme simplicity on both sides. On the right, there are the Matt Dillons of the status quo, grim and determined, with only one enemy — the Communist — and only one heresy — that which is new. On the left, there are the Chesters of the far, sophisticated left, confused and whining, with only one answer to every charge — McCarthyism. One need not sympathize with either Khrushchev nor the late senator from Wisconsin to disdain both approaches. They are just too simple, just too superficial. The educated Catholic adult distrusts "viewiness" wherever it is found. In the new world that Father Weigel says has replaced the old world of 1914, a great deal of wisdom must be put to work. Wisdom is a gift of the Holy Spirit that gives point to facts, gives meaning to ideas. Opinions are important because they are the stuff from which ideas come. But opinions untried by facts, untested by experience, undisciplined by courses of logical study can suffocate us all. The first dimension of adult education must be to deepen our learning, to dig for wisdom, to sift out the dross of today's headlines in the search for things that are true because they have been touched by eternity.

How far shall we range? Keep in mind that we are speaking here not of the professional intellectual, the scholar. We are talking about the average man, that human specimen subjected in our times to the sociological probing of popular scientists like Dr. Reismann and Dr. Packard. A dozen years ago, each of us were ciphers in Reismann's *Lonely Crowd.* Now we have been assigned our proper ladder and bar in the jungle gym of Packard's *Status Seekers.* There is something of the comic in all this. What about the lonely fellow who has never been examined by these scholars? How anonymous he must feel. He gets written up in nothing more exciting than the decennial census.

While thousands of Ph.D. candidates are plotting the profile of the average American, he waits at home in obscurity for the doorbell that never rings, for the knock that never comes, with the gnawing fear that no one will ever ask him about his politics, his religion, his income after taxes, or even his preference in comic strips. But if the anonymous cipher is comic, there is tragedy in the life of the man for whom the sociology bell has tolled. Once he has been assigned to his proper bulge on the graph, or his status rung on the ladder, what happens to him then? Certainly, he is "upper-middle-class" or "substandard low." But is he content, hugging his status symbol? Is he happy? Is he virtuous? Is he even alive? In the quiet murmur of his conditioned reflexes, isn't there room for one unconditioned yelp of pain? Doesn't he sometimes want to cry out, "I know all that. But I am tired of all this wall-to-wall monotony. My question is simple: how do I get out?"

How far should adult education range? Far enough to draw the average American out of his statistical niche, to call him down from his precarious rung of status. Knowledge is inexhaustible, and the range of courses possible is almost without limit. Some will like the direct approach: philosophy, history, psychology, the languages, the classics, theology, Scripture, liturgy, social action. Others will start with "gimmick" courses, but they can be led by package deals to the spiritual wellsprings of honest learning. The point is to offer a curriculum that will make a man want to break out of his tight circle of boredom, a syllabus that will lead to the mastery of a subject, or even more than a subject. Here the Catholic school has a tremendous advantage because nothing should be considered foreign to the Church. There is something immediately odd about a Christian Scientist studying medicine or a Jehovah Witness studying government. But to be a full Catholic means to be universal. The courses may have to be departmentalized for convenience, but in the Catholic institution there is no reason for them to be cut up into narrow, airtight compartments. If our depth must touch wisdom, our range should reach out to the whole horizon of man's concerns.

Finally, how high shall we reach? The human intellect itself points to the answer: "The calm, clear, accurate vision and comprehension of all things, as far as the finite mind can embrace them, each in its own place and with its own characteristics upon it." Knowledge is a pyramid that leads to God. The senses and the intellect dig down and stretch out far. In man's more enlightened moments, they also reach up. But the infinite can be exasperating, and for some tragic souls it can be full of despair. We must have God's assistance. It comes through faith. And once God has spoken, not only does the fact of God become more clear, everything else does too. Faith unlocks the tower of the Trinity, the Incarnation and the Redemption. But it is not only a tower; it is also a lighthouse. These mysteries, revealed by God, cast a fine light over human affairs, and over biological facts and psychological theories, and over everything else.

> Admit a God [said a man who did], and you have introduced among the subjects of your knowledge a fact encompassing, closing in upon, absorbing every other fact conceivable.

The speaker was Newman. Although he is usually associated with the university mind, he had the concern of both a priest and a layman for the non-university mind, the education of all those who really want to learn. He would have grasped and applauded the objective of your association, the point that brings you here.

That point is to restore a beautiful, old Christian word, the term "witness," as the role of the adult Catholic. To be informed, responsible, loyal, and apostolic, these are the hallmarks of the Christian witness. It is not necessary for him to be a scholar, only that he love to learn. It is not necessary that he preach on streetcorners, or be active in a cell. There is a place for that in the contemporary Catholic scene, but there is a more pressing need for the witness. Simply put, the Christian witness knows his faith and lives his faith. He is an ordinary citizen, an ordinary workman, an ordinary parishioner, but he is extra-ordinarily concerned about the present and the future of his Church and his world. He studies the liturgy, learning how to live out the worship of his God. He studies *Mater et Magistra,* and the other papal directives, that he might measure his own community by the social teaching of his Church. He follows the coming Vatican Council and sees Christian unity in a new light, not only as a problem for the Fathers of the Council, but as his own personal and social problem, too.

In apostolic terms, he is a witness to the faith. He is aware that he is a witness to his Church at one of the most critical moments of her history. Perhaps the main step that he took was his enrollment in Catholic adult education. As a Catholic, he learned the secret of knowledge. That to be fully educated, he must have grown to adult-hood; that to be fully adult, he must continue his education.

THE CHRISTIAN WITNESS IN THE WORLD

Every close observer of the Archbishop knew that he was most at home in the halls of academia and to this experience he brought the practicality of a mid-twentieth-century bishop. The addresses and writings before university audiences attest to that fact. The first, presented as a baccalaureate sermon at his alma mater, the University of Notre Dame, and given on 3 June, 1962, was but one among many baccalaureate sermons he would be called upon to give. The editor has taken the liberty with the text in those cases where the Archbishop used the word "student" to replace it with the word "Christian."

The year 1962 is not likely to be lost in the limbo of "just another year." Whether history will be kind or cruel to it is not ours to know, at least right now. The Second Vatican Council has already stamped it with greatness. The scientific break-through reminds us of 1492. The steady crumbling of racial barriers in our country may make effective in 1962 what became merely legal in 1863. The recent events in the stock market have recalled uncomfortably the year of 1929. It is too early to place this year in the focus of world events. But it is never too early to examine the task of the educated man in terms of his times. It is always urgent for the Church to appraise her leaders in the context of their decade, in the longer view of the century in which we live and move and have our being.

A Catholic bishop's view will always be chiefly pastoral; only by exception will it be academic or professional. But to call a bishop's concern pastoral is not to limit it to the diocese or the parish. It will always be apostolic in its origin, and universal in its horizons. Every Catholic bishop in the world is a successor to the apostles, and the coming Council is only the historic occasion, not the fundamental cause, of our universality, our Catholic world-mindedness, our deep and lasting concern that our leaders are ready for the task.

Only a man who is devoid of Christian hope can look at the world today and throw up his hands. Only a philosophy that is drained of all meaning can find expression today in a shudder, or worse, a tired yawn. The world into which Our Lord sends us is still the same world in which He makes His constant presence felt. It is a world inhabited by that human society which He himself did not disdain, from which He refuses to take us, in which His prayer keeps us not from contact, but only from evil. The flesh is still weak, and it must be trained away from sin. The devil is still energetic, and he must be exorcised from human hearts. But the world, that third source of moral trouble, is our world, our homes and our cities, our industry and our labor, our government and our responsibility. Our salvation is from Christ, His death, His Mass and His sacraments. But we will save our souls not in the sanctuary nor in the confessional. We will save them on Main Street and Wall Street and Madison Avenue, and every other thoroughfare in the world, or we will not save them at all.

That is the objective of our baptism: grace enough to expel sin and to toughen the moral fiber of our being. That is the objective of our confirmation: strength and wisdom enough to grow to maturity as full-time Christians. That is the whole process of our liturgy: to offer God our human efforts, through the headship of His Son, Our Lord, and to draw from the experience of worship that totality of communion with God's presence and cooperation with His saving power that we may return to our duties, consecrated and sanctified, to continue our lives and to help the world.

The layman's responsibility in this division of churchly labor is well summed up in the term "Christian witness." That is what Christ called us to be; "You shall be witnesses for me in Jerusalem and in all Judea and Samaria and even to the very ends of the earth." The word "witness" is almost a definition of the Catholic layman.

In the third century, in the midst of a Christian community which was poor, uneducated, and without great influence, the great African bishop, St. Cyprian, proudly explained what the rudimentary Catholic society must be: "As for us, we are philosophers not in word, but in act; we do not say great things, but we do live them." Much more recently, a French missionary described the "pre-mission" stage of the Church in some areas: "We must be and do, before we talk." The hazards of much speaking and little Christian living were contained in Our Lord's warning to those who often said, "Lord, Lord," but failed to obey Him. The Christian witness must live his faith. There is an urgency about this today that comes only in a time of true crisis.

But if the Catholic layman is being repeatedly called to this role with such urgency by popes and bishops today, does not the university man, the Catholic scholar, the partner in the Catholic intellectual elite, have a special duty? We are entering, in the United States, the long-desired era of the Catholic university graduate. Two centuries of sacrifice and toil for Catholic education are drawing to a close, leaving a glorious record of courage, vision and generosity. The heritage of that record is bearing fruit today in Catholic scholarship, cultural efforts, and some intellectual leadership in our society. Our challenge is to continue to penetrate the world of science, and letters, and art, the world of government and trade and communication with Christian principles and with lives of authentic Christian charity. "The true scholar," said Etienne Gilson in 1927, "is essentially a man whose intellectual life is part and parcel of his moral life."

This imposes on the Catholic lay leader a certain relationship to truth, and to his Church. The pursuit of truth, especially in a society accustomed to rather shabby handling of it, is a difficult occupation. It means much more than honesty in expense accounts and tax payments. It goes farther than basic honesty in our pronouncements on radicals and reactionaries, communists and fascists, and other people we do not like. The search for truth must go on at every humble level; in the laboratory, in books and newspapers, in political speeches, in our own secret thoughts. The mind is a power of the human soul, and because it is intended by God for a holy purpose, truth, it partakes of a sacred character itself. We know that simony is a grave crime because it is the buying and selling of sacred things. Are we as aware that the use of the intellect for any sordid purpose — the writing of a dishonest advertisement, the twisting of a sociological survey, the reading of an evil book — is a certain form of simony? The mind was not created to be bought and sold for unworthy gain; it was created by God to find out for men the truth about its Creator, and the truths about His creatures.

St. Augustine spoke of a *gaudium de veritate* — the joy of the truth. This joy will warm your lives, and it will warm our world if we do what Augustine urges: "Love the intelligence very much."

I have mentioned the term Christian witness. That is our common role. To bring Christ into your office, your recreation, your home, is not to make a preacher of you. Rather, a witness. It means that the great burden which Pope Pius XII placed upon the Catholic laity, the reconsecration of the world, rests proportionately upon your shoulders. Already the Catholic world is aware of the work of lay readers at Mass, lay teachers in our schools, lay catechists in our missions, lay editors and publishers, lay leaders in the St. Vincent de Paul societies and the Legion of Mary, laymen of influence in parish and diocesan administration, marriage counseling, interracial and economic conferences, and a score of other areas.

We are living, in this respect, as in any other great and exciting historical moment, in both optimism and tension. The optimism springs from the spirit of Pope John and his recent predecessors, from the Church's opportunities, but fundamentally from the providential breath of the Holy Spirit over our distracted and discouraged world. But there is a tension too. It rises from areas of uncertainty and lack of clear instruction, as well as from the inertia of old ways and a shortage of tact. If your entrance as a layman into the vital activities of the Church is made with deep faith and due competence, and above all, good humility and good humor, you will be welcomed and ultimately honored. But if it is made with arrogance and impatience, you will slow down the process that is surely taking place. The increase of the proper role of the laity today, explained and urged by our modern popes, is the result of the mutual efforts of what Cardinal Suhard called "the inseparable pair, priests and laity, a kind of organic composite, the complete evangelist." We are grateful that today none of us can say, in violation of St. Paul's counsel, "I have no need of thee." In the mansion of the Church, the laity can be thought of as the door, the clergy as the knob. If a door is useless without the knob, what shall we say of a knob without the door? As Pius XII warned us five years ago, "The tasks before the Church today are too vast to leave room for petty disputes." It is a time for mutual effort, each in his proper role, each with his proper grace. It is a time for the collaboration in the Church of that inseparable pair, the Catholic priest and the Catholic layman.

Economic and political individualism should have died long ago. Intellectual individualism is almost a contradiction in terms. But individualism in the Mystical Body of Our Lord slows the growth and weakens the full vitality. A gifted English prelate, Bishop Andrew Beck of Salford, said four years ago, in a splendid address on Catholic higher education, "We need to be lifted out of our individualism to catch a glimpse of the grandeur of our work in the Church."

To find the truth is a social task beyond the scope of any single human mind. To reconsecrate the world, in the full sense of the phrase, is a mutual work of all concerned, men and women, scholars and workmen, bishops, priests and laity. The Church calls lay leaders in a very special way to this double task of finding truth and making holy the society in which we live. You are not invited out of the world; you are invited into it. You are not shielded from the struggle; you are armed and prepared for it. In His last formal prayer, Our Lord prayed for those whom He was sending into the world, to change it and to save it. He was praying for you and me.

THE SAME REASONS FOR CONFIDENCE
OR FOR FEAR

Archbishop Hallinan knew how to make the most of any situation. On 2 September, 1962, he was invited to be the principal speaker at a banquet honoring Francis Cardinal Spellman in Miami, Florida, on the occasion of the priestly ordination of the Reverend Daniel Sanchez. He took the occasion to speak on inter-American cooperation as a means of securing understanding and development for a lasting foundation of peace.

This afternoon when His Eminence, Cardinal Spellman, began the solemn task of ordaining young Father Sanchez, he spoke these ancient words of the Church to the vast congregation:

> Dearly beloved brethren, just as all those on a ship, both the captain and the passengers, have the same reasons for confidence or for fear, they should act together with one mind, seeing that their interests are the same.

This concept, the passengers and captain on a ship, facing an uncertain voyage over unpredictable waters, is surely not new to Christian people. Jonas' experience in the Old Testament, and St. Paul's many journeys in the New immediately come to mind. So too does the drama in Simon's fishing boat when there was a great squall, and Our Lord had to say "Why are you fearful? Are you still without faith?"

A ship speaks to us of discovery and travel, of danger and adventure. At the great Eucharistic Congress in Rio de Janeiro in 1955, the high altar was designed by the talented Brazilian architect, Luis Costa. To Father John Considine, that gifted Maryknoll priest who may truly be called "a man of the Americas," the most impressive sight was the canopy — a ship in full sail. High above the sacred table, this ancient caravel was a reminder of the precious cargo of faith and grace and wisdom, of justice and charity that the Spanish and Portuguese priests brought to the new world.

17

Now as we look ahead thirty years to the 500th anniversary of
the discovery of this world, another "man of the Americas" sees a
ship — or rather, three ships — as symbols of the future. Mr. Jaime
Fonseca, the skillful Catholic journalist from Costa Rica, has called
for Catholic initiative in this historic commemoration. Speaking two
weeks ago in Buenos Aires, he asked that this anniversary in 1992
point up the Christian sense of discovery and give a Christian content to the new culture that is flowing from the best of the New
World and the best of the Old.

Columbus' ships are true symbols of the Christian past, but as
Fonseca points out, they point to the Christian future too. Ships trans-
port people; they communicate ideas. Ships load goods to be ex-
ported and imported. They make war too, but this is only one more
proof that the finest products of God and man can be twisted into
tools of destruction. Today, for good and for evil, mankind has gone
far beyond the water-bound limits of sailing ships. Planes, capsules
and satellites fill the heavens and must confuse even the angels. But
the memory of civilized man is not likely to forget the sailing vessel
as the first step toward the knowledge and peoples of other lands.
When Columbus and his three ships left Palos, there was no radio by
which he could speak with Ferdinand and Isabella, no camera to catch
that first flicker of light on Watling's Island, no second missile waiting
back on the launching pad at Palos. He and his men were alone in
a more profound sense than any cosmonaut has ever been.

Ships — space ships as well as sailing ships — have made our world
much smaller. But it only adds to that old cliché to say that the
human mind has been much slower in transporting truth, and the
human heart has lagged in the export of love and sympathy and
understanding from nation to nation, from continent to continent.
The power of the gospel to speak to all men has been diminished
by man's refusal to live by the gospel he has heard. The great driving
force of Christian grace has been hobbled by the way Christians themselves neglect and abuse it. History records how man's science leaps,
and how man's religion drags behind. In our nation, we are only
starting to rid ourselves of the bitterness engendered by the fact of
racial color, and indeed by the fact of religious creed. We have much
to learn and much to repent.

There seems to be no area of human relationships in which there
is more room for really Christian effort than in the great hemisphere
in which we Americans live — on both sides of the Rio Grande. Nearly
five centuries after Columbus, we still live like strangers in our two

continents, forgetting that Columbus came first to the islands, then to South America, then to North America. He was truly the first "man of the Americas." In Europe today, a wise Frenchman, a perceptive German, a thinking Italian is proud to be called a "European man". It is regarded as a step toward universality, away from a narrow provincialism. But we are still hesitant, slow to learn the lessons of the Western Hemisphere. The North American and the South American differ widely in history, but we do share an authentic heritage of good, solid, revolutionary principles. We differ in language, but most of us share the same roots in Greek philosophy and Roman law. We differ in religion, but the majority still cry "Abba" to the common Father, and millions pray to our Brother, Christ Our Lord.

It is high time to explore and discover ourselves. We need not lose one whit of proper pride, loyalty and obedience to our particular nation. Nor need we abandon a common concern for all humanity of every color in every land. In one sense, it is a simple matter of geography. Since we all live on a long slice of land, it is imperative that we try to live like brothers. But while geography is fairly static, history moves ahead. It took nearly two hundred years for the people of what is now the United States to stop calling each other "Virginians," "New Englanders" or "Pennsylvanians." Now we have painfully learned that a man may keep all that is great and fruitful of his citizenship in the city of Miami, the state of Florida, and the nation of the United States. If we avoid fuzzy schemes and idle dreams, can we not walk forward to a fuller title — "a Citizen of the Americas?" Only the little mind and the faint heart will see this as a denial of national identity and national rights. It is rather an affirmation of national responsibilities and national duties. It is true of the human family, as it is true of the human body. St. Paul reminds us, "The eye cannot say to the hand, 'I do not need thy help'; nor again the head to the feet, 'I have not need of thee.'"

This afternoon we witnessed a stirring event, filled with symbolism and with practical lessons for us all. A priestly young man from Cuba was ordained by the Cardinal Archbishop of New York. At the beginning of the ceremony, we were reminded that all of us who live in the Americas have the same reasons for fear and for confidence. What are these reasons? What must we fear? Communism, of course, but our own noisy nationalism and our own private apathy are just as dangerous. Communism is evil, and it is our public enemy. Nationalism and apathy are just as evil, but it is easy to forget them.

Communist leaders have fastened a gross materialism upon millions who once worshipped God. Why have they been so successful in lands which once were Christian? Because Communism thrives where Christian justice is forgotten, where Christian love has died. When Christian men of influence live public lives that are a travesty of Our Savior's teaching, we have good reason to fear. We are not doing enough, states Bishop Pinera of Chile. Unless the Church moves, says Bishop Tonna of Uruguay, it will be too late. The exiled bishop of Havana, Bishop Eduardo Boza, has put his finger on the exact cause of Christendom's shame and Communism's gain: "The selfish class differences must disappear whereby some have too much, and others die in poverty . . . our peoples, our countries, and our nations must find help in the social Christian doctrine." There is reason to fear Communism, but there is no reason to fear it blindly. This warning was put bluntly by Bishop Tonna: "The blind fear of Communism, the custom of seeing it where it does not exist, and an inclination to combat it more with words than with deeds, have made us belittle every serious proposal of social and economic reform as being suspect of Marxism, leaving to the Marxists a monopoly of all that the working people desire." When the social order of lands that are heavily Catholic is sickly with injustice, we have good reason to fear the cancer of Communism. But let us fear it with purpose and direction, not with blindness and panic.

Of the second threat, nationalism, we are hardly aware. When the chest swells with proper national pride, that is one thing. But when the head swells with national ego, that is something else — something far worse. Communism is monolithic and quite easy to spot. But nationalism wears many coats and speaks many tongues. It may be raucous like fascism, vicious like Nazism, or polite and smug and condescending. When it is winning, it cries, "My country, right or wrong." When it has won, it speaks self-righteously of "white supremacy" or the "white man's burden." But when it is less sure of itself, it looks about for a scapegoat, and the nearest one at hand is the "foreigner." Nationalism is a business man absorbing another country's oil, or a ruler absorbing another nation's territory. Nationalism is a Yankee preacher in South America sneering at the people's devotion to Our Blessed Mother, or a foreign visitor to the United States sneering at the pragmatism, the "practicality," of our Catholicism. Nationalism is you and I closing our eyes to the beauty and warmth and truth of another culture and squinting only at what is ugly and mean and degrading. It is the refusal to share, to learn, to sympathize. These were the sins of the Levite and the priest on the road to Jericho. It was a foreigner, let us never forget, who gave our world the beautiful term, the Good Samaritan.

But deeper and more personal is a third cause for fear — our own apathy, our complacency. Do millions in Latin America fail to get the minimum food requirement of 2200 calories a day? We have our own problems. Do 400,000 people live in the slums of Rio? How unfortunate! Does Latin America have only one priest for nearly 5,000 Catholics? How blessed the United States is to have one priest for every 700! Are we our brothers' keepers? Pope John can hardly be more serious when he repeats an earlier warning in *Mater et Magistra*: "We all share responsibility for the fact that populations are under-nourished." What a surprise we will get on judgment day when we find the verdict based on those divine requirements: "I was hungry, and you did not give me to eat . . . ."

In these three causes there is room for rational fear: Communism, because it is on the move; nationalism, because it arrived long ago; apathy and indifference, because we do not even realize how they have sapped the Christian vitality. The pessimist totals up the fears and cries out in despair, "Enough!" But the man who is cast in a different mold, the mold of the apostles and their smiling, hopeful successor in the chair of Peter, Pope John XXIII, cries, "Enough," for a different reason. Whether he be North or South American, he counts his resources, and he is confident. Whether he cries out in Spanish or Portuguese or English, his cry is trusting and clear. He understands the reasons for fear, but he sees beyond them the reasons for Christian hope and confidence.

First, the vigor of the Church on both sides of the Rio Grande. In 1955, the bishops of Latin America formed a Council, unique in the history of the Church, to confront these fears with a plan of united action. In 1959, a group of them met with prelates from the United States and Canada to review common problems and work out a common agenda. Meanwhile, the program was blessed by the formation of a Pontifical Commission for Latin America. The vast program calls for bold action and constant improvement in five vital fields: more personnel, more schools, more religious education, more social justice and charity, and more communication. With blunt questions and honest answers, the priests and religious and lay apostles of Latin America are meeting the fears that disturb their beloved nations. From the United States and Canada, and from Europe too, allies are coming to march side by side with their Latin colleagues in a remarkable demon-

stration of Catholic cooperation. We have only to read of the radio
schools in Columbia, the credit unions in Chile, the rural life conferences and the Papal Volunteers, to realize that today the consecration, not the repudiation, of the world is the full-time task of Church
leaders, both priest and lay.

In happy parallel to such Catholic cooperation in the Americas are
the secular efforts of the nations to work together in the new Alliance
for Progress. This forward-looking program is only one year old, and
it is already being criticized for many things. But it is a giant step in
the right direction. It faces challenges of almost superhuman difficulty.
It must do a great deal in a hurry. It must blend an insistence on reform
with assistance to the desperately needy. It must harmonize Latin
dignity with North American organization and system. But any program that can plan and execute in two short years projects benefitting
about 35,000,000 people is a program to be applauded, pushed and
helped. Teodoro Moscoso, administrator of the Alliance for Progress,
sees the plan and its blessings in terms of the "voiceless ones." He tells
of walking through an ugly slum while on the one side Leftists denounced the United States and the Alliance and on the other Rightists
sneered at the need for reform. Out of the slum crowd that watched
in silence and curiosity ran an old man. In one phrase, he linked the
Catholic spirit of the Latin Americans and the hope they have for the
Alliance for Progress. He simply cried out, "May God bless you!"

At this point in history, in the Americas, we have the framework
for cooperation, both religious and secular. We do not need more
apparatus; we need more understanding and love. We, in the United
States, are indebted to the Spanish for a fine word that has no exact
English equivalent, the word *simpatico.* Somewhere in the semantic
jungle, our word sympathetic got mixed up with grief and commisera-
tion. The Spaniard takes it straight, feeling with, responding to, sharing
with another. But we are indebted for much more than a word. We
can learn from the Latin American's sense of dignity. It comes naturally,
as well as supernaturally, to the Latin to identify himself as a child
of God. We can learn from his example of deep faith. With few priests
and little instruction, this has grown into a mighty tree, and not the
least of its blossoms is the tender charity that exists, particularly among
the very poor. There is much more to be learned in the cultures of
the vast and varying lands that lie to the south.

And we can give to Latin America our own good gifts as Catholics
in the United States: our love of the sacraments; our sacrifices for
Christian education and for Christian works of compassion; perhaps

most significantly, the working example of how we live without loss and without compromise in a society of many religions. These are not small gifts. They are a deeply important part of the Catholic history of our times. We are proud of them, just as Latin Americans are proud of their distinctive gifts. Every good gift is from God, and His grace can energize the Christian of every continent.

What we need is not more apparatus and more organizations. We have a superb framework already. Ours is the task of perfecting each his own spirit — the Latin spirit, and the North American spirit. Will the priests and sisters and lay apostles now on loan from the north return home inspired and motivated by the genius of the Latin American faith, that deep sense of human dignity, the inclination and the will to be *simpatico?* Will the 12,000 Latin American students now studying in the United States return to their homes with a new appreciation of the proud buoyancy, the straight-forwardness, the blessed practicality of our Catholicism? If this comes true, we will be closer to the dream of every true man of the Americas. Diverse cultures should feed, not starve each other.

Archbishop Paul J. Hallinan, first Archbishop of Atlanta, Georgia.

Archbishop Hallinan enters the sanctuary of the Cathedral of Christ the King for his installation March 29, 1962. He is preceded by Fr. John O'Shea, cross bearer, and Monsignor Michael J. Regan, J.C.D., master of ceremonies. At the right is Rev. Lawrence Murphy, C.SS.R.

Archbishop Hallinan greets those attending the reception held in the Sacred Heart Auditorium following his installation.

Monsignor William J. Gallena, the priest who gave Archbishop Hallinan his First Communion, congratulates the new Archbishop at the reception following the installation.

Pope Paul extends an audience to Archbishop Hallinan, Archbishop John J. Krol, of Philadelphia, and Andrew P. Maloney, vice president of the Bankers Trust Company of New York and president of the Newman Foundation.

An ardent supporter of the vernacular in the liturgy, Archbishop Hallinan celebrates the first English language Mass in the archdiocese.

THE TWO LAWS AND THE CHRISTIAN LAWYER

On 19 September, 1962, a few brief weeks before the opening of the Second Vatican Council, the Archbishop was invited to address the Catholic Lawyers Guild in Baltimore at its annual Red Mass. The Archbishop returned to a theme he had frequently used — the example of the Good Samaritan. The address reveals his own deep personal commitment to the needs of humanity.

> But the Advocate, the Holy Spirit, Whom the Father will send in My Name, He will teach you all things, and bring to your mind whatever I have said to you. *John 14:26*

An incident that happened on the road from Jerusalem to Jericho, told to us in parable form by our blessed Lord, throws into sharp and terrifying relief the tensions of our own society. A man was beaten, robbed and left to die. A priest and a levite passed by, unmoved. A stranger gave the victim help and kindness. In the parlance of today's police report, the incident might have been recorded thus:

> Robbery and brutal attack on the Jericho Road this afternoon. Assailants escaped. Victim in critical condition, multiple lacerations and bruises, found at nearby motel. Owner of motel said he was brought there by some foreigner, whom he suspected was a Samaritan. Owner stated that victim had been given first aid. The Samaritan promised to pay for motel room on his return, but owner doubted he would ever see him again. Two witnesses, a priest and a levite, apparently saw the victim by the road after the beating took place but said they were on their way to a meeting and could not stop. They acted surprised when questioned. They said they didn't even know the man.

It was a lawyer who had occasioned Our Lord's parable by asking the simple question, "Who is my neighbor?" After Christ laid down the two fundamental principles of the new law, Love the Lord thy God, and Love thy neighbor as thyself, the lawyer sought some clarification. "And who is my neighbor?" To answer him, Christ told the little story. It gave the definition of the term "neighbor." But it did more. It put our human actions into the light of the new law of Christ, more compassionate than human law, more far-reaching than the divine law already revealed through Moses. In the police account and in popular thought, there had been a double crime, the robbery and the beating. But in the light of the parable it is clear there was another crime, that of omission. The priest and the levite, passing by, were guilty of gross indifference in the presence of urgent need, a brutal apathy where human compassion should have prevailed.

The tensions that try men's souls in today's society are deep, complex and frustrating. Some of them are rooted in the home and family, husband against wife, children against parents. From these tensions issue a host of human dislocations: incompatibility, infidelity, desertion, separation and divorce. At another level, children are abandoned or ignored. Their surface needs are pampered, their basic needs neglected. The sickness spreads through the community, in juvenile misdemeanor and crime, neighborhood bitterness, racial strife and the deterioration of a community spirit. National and world tensions are too numerous to list, too well known to require comment. True, thousands of families live God-fearing, loving lives; hundreds of communities are healthy examples of faith and hope and charity. But the tensions are here, and they affect us all. It is not really important whether the world is any worse than at some other historic point. It is *our* world and *our* responsibility right now, because as Christians we are not called out of the world; we are sent into the world. Its sickness is our sickness, its wounds are our wounds.

In the midst of this disarray of human aspirations stand the lawyer and the judge, the one to plead the law, the other to apply it. Out of its Judeo-Christian tradition, our western world has drawn a great respect for the law and a great trust in it. In Europe, the settlement of rough tribal disputes came gradually under Roman law. Just as slowly but surely, the feudal kingdoms, the city-states and then the modern Western nations accepted the rule of law. Because no human statute can be perfect, the keepers of the law are charged with a grave burden: to conserve the principles, but apply them with equity; to teach all men, the ruler as well as the ruled; to deal with all manner of malefactors without jeopardizing their own integrity. For the far greater part, the men of law in our modern society bear this awesome role with honor and courage. Together with healing and teaching, the pursuit of law is acknowledged as an honorable profession. As the doctor extends the health of the body that is God's creation, and the teacher extends the mind's knowledge that is God's truth, so the lawyer and the judge defend the proper human equation that reflects God's justice. The sacred character of the courtroom oath, usually taken in God's name, is our recognition of the sacred nature of the work of the men who conserve, interpret, plead and apply the positive statutes of the public body. Even in the steady push toward the secularization of our public institutions so evident in the United States today, it is likely that the courtroom will be the last place to expel those words and symbols which remind man that he is God's creature.

The Catholic lawyer — in fact the Christian lawyer, indeed the godly lawyer of whatever faith — faces the contest of tensions today with a very special concern. Aware that human law is both necessary and salutary for human beings, he is equally aware of its limitations. Just as the whim of a king made St. Thomas More's decision an agonizing choice, so may the whim of an electorate today. There are useless laws, such as federal prohibition was yesterday. There are unjust laws, such as state segregation is today. The new industrial revolution is loaded with a thousand agonizing questions. Automation is only one of the more obvious. And yet whatever its caprice, whatever its short-comings, human law must be enacted and obeyed. You are its practitioners; you are its apostles.

In the first centuries of Christianity, Catholic apologists were not sure of the precise role of human law, except that in the words of St. Peter, "We must obey God rather than men" (Acts 5:29). It was St. Augustine who taught, in his magnificent *City of God,* what might be called the long view of human law:

> It is incredible that God would leave the kingdoms of men and their bondages and freedoms loose and uncomprised in the laws of His eternal providence.

A modern theologian, Father Bernard Haring, repeats that same teaching today in his recent book of moral theology entitled *The Law of Christ*:

> In the last analysis, in a rapidly changing society, necessary guides given by competent authority are an expression of divine wisdom and providence.

In yesterday's world, a majority of civilized men accepted human law in the greater light of the divine law. But today's tensions have darkened society's understanding of God's law. Civilized man's respect for human life called abortion a crime. Today's sentimentality pronounces it a blessing. Christian people traditionally called divorce a violation of a sacred bond. Today's conventions welcome it as an easy way out. In Hitler's day, the world called human sterilization a totalitarian trick. There are hospitals today where it is standard practice, especially on the defenseless and confused. Have the statutory laws failed? Not as long as they reflect the immutability of the divine commands. What has failed, once again, is human nature. Men and women have failed.

Now the man of law views this deterioration of our society with even greater gravity than the clients who come to him. Because the fabric of statutory law is so laboriously prepared and so delicately sewn, it is often mocked. Yet it is our chief social covering. If it can be easily torn, it can also be destroyed. The good lawyer, aware of this, is deeply concerned not just with society's law, but with society's members. At all times, he seeks beyond the text of the statute the context of reality, both human and divine. The Catholic lawyer sees the solution not in more stringent laws, still less in a forsaking of his chosen profession. For he is a lawyer by choice, and he is a Christian by grace. He knows there is a law above all municipal and state law, above federal law, above even the law of nature. It was foreshadowed when the prophet Jeremias reported the Lord's words, "I will give my law in their inmost being, and will write it into their heart." It was promulgated when Jesus spoke the beatitudes, beginning with that stirring decree, "Blessed are the poor in spirit, for theirs is the Kingdom of heaven." And it was codified when He commanded, "Love the Lord thy God . . . love thy neighbor as thyself." This is the law explained by St. Paul, the law of grace. It is the foundation of the whole Christian community, the central objective of the Catholic Church itself and the continuing reason for that "revival of the spirit of the gospel" which Pope John gives as the cause of the coming Vatican Council.

This is not just a pious concept, either for human society or the men of law who are its guardians. It is a part of that reality that must be understood. The lawyer's realization of the law of Christ, the law of grace, will not solve his dilemma about a particular divorce suit nor his quandary about an alleged violation of the law on income tax. This concept of the law of Christ does not mean that the Christian lawyer is called upon to fashion the Beatitudes or the Decalogue into some statutory law of the state. Christ's law and Ceasar's law are quite distinct. No union of church and state, in the Byzantine or medieval sense, nor in the Anglican or Calvinist sense either, is going to heal the sickness of modern man.

The Christian lawyer is both lawyer and Christian. In his deeper grasp of the reality that is his Christian faith, he is a better lawyer. He works at his Christianity no less than he works at the law. Incompetence in the latter may disbar him from its practice. Incompetence

— or ignorance or neglect, or worse, violation — in his Christian person incurs a far graver penalty. He approaches his task with humility because so much is at stake. But he comes with confident Christian hope because so much is in store — the redemptive resources of grace, sorely won on the cross by the Son of God. He opens each day's dossier with dedication. His own morning prayer has already centered that dedication. He deals with the weak and the oppressed, the vicious and the foolish, the regretful and the unrepentant, and remembers that Christ did too. In this, he finds fraternal encouragement because Christ is his Brother. But more important than encouragement is grace, because Christ is his Redeemer.

We are not runners on a meaningless treadmill. We are not figures in a mechanistic puppet show. Our human efforts count in the scale of justice. All God asks is men of good will. Against the thousand dislocations of our changing society, the million frustrations of this period of transition, God arms the man of good will with wisdom and courage. The larger realities become clearer — man's soul, man's destiny, man's Creator, man's Redeemer. Our Lord promised to send us an Advocate, One who pleads the cause of another. This Holy Spirit of God, the third Person of the Blessed Trinity, has never left the Christian community. In times of distress, this Advocate is ready to enlighten our darkness with His wisdom, to warm cold hearts with His love.

To the lawyer in the United States of today, God offers this supreme opportunity: to stand professionally for the principles of human law; to stand, Christ-like, for the principles of the law of grace. Assured of the presence of the Divine Advocate, he takes his dual role, as lawyer and as man, with confidence. He honors his profession, and more, he honors the American community of which he is at once a part, a measure, and a guide.

WHO WILL ROLL BACK THE STONE?

The necessity of hope in a Christian's life is being emphasized more and more in recent years as a theological re-discovery of Resurrection theology. The Archbishop's realization of this fact had already appeared in his Easter pastoral letter of 1963. It appeared in the 11 April, 1963, issue of the Georgia Bulletin.

In a book of meditations soon to be published, Paul Claudel, the French poet, asks us to "Lie still with our eyes closed a moment before dawn breaks on the day of the Resurrection." It is a novel suggestion, one that is apt to surprise people in our times. Why do it on Easter morning? Why at dawn? And, most of all, what would one think about?

Claudel was a man with his head in the skies of the poets, but with feet planted firmly in the reality of our world. He suggests we think about the question that the three holy women asked, "Who will roll the stone back from the entrance?" They had brought ointment to prepare the body of the Lord. We, too, as the Christians of the twentieth century, are bringing our gifts today: prayers, good wishes, a kind word, a collection envelope. But there is a stone between us and the Body of the Lord.

The stone is our tendency to give up, to grow cold, to forget and to put off. We get busy with the things of the world, and the things of God become unappealing. The whole talk of Christian renewal, heard today in every pulpit and talked about in every mention of the Vatican Council, hinges on this. Why do our worship and our meditation need renewal? Because we offer God a routine mind. Why do we close our eyes to injustice and need and starvation around us? Because we offer God a routine heart.

The Church stood by on that first Easter morning, the Church in the person of the three women who were awake and ready, in the person of the apostles who were fitfully sleeping and frightfully scared. There was a sense of Christian urgency that day, and the Church knew it. There were people to wake up, people to stir up, people to help, and people to do the helping. It was urgent then to be a Christian. It was a day of hope, the peculiar Easter virtue.

Today our faith is strong, especially in regions where there are few Christians, in areas where there are few Catholics. We are known, thank God, as a nation of frequent communicants. Now our faith is being nourished on the words of the Scripture, much more than in past centuries. And our charity is wide and generous. Again, we are known as a nation of unselfish givers. Now our charity is affecting our hearts as well as our wallets. We are learning how all-embracing Christian love must be.

It is that third virtue, the Easter virtue of hope, that needs enkindling in our times. In the climate of fear and hate that surrounds too much of our world, too many of our communities, we must practice justice with a full confident hope. In a society that is still more concerned with material gain than the growth of the intellect, we must hope that the scholar will find elbow room, whether he be a young scientist, an old philosopher, or perhaps a little child looking for his first gem of truth. In a nation of many religions, we must hope for the best in each of them, neither compromising our own nor downgrading others.

This is hope at work in the world. It is a natural virtue for every man, but for the Christian it is a theological virtue, linked to faith and charity, produced by the grace of God. It is our special responsibility as Catholics to nurture it, to treasure it, and especially to use it. It may be symbolized by a hand, not clenched for gain or for gunfire, but reaching out to help, to comfort, to lead.

That hand, guided by Christ, can roll back the stone of our weakness.

May God renew us all and give to our beloved nation and state, our families and our homes, this Easter gift of hope.

CATHOLIC HIGHER EDUCATION—A NEW CHAPTER

*The vision that Archbishop Hallinan possessed is mani-
fested here when he invited his listeners to "turn the
page to the new chapter that is waiting for us." He
delivered this address on 19 April, 1963, at the annual
convention of the National Catholic Educational Association in St. Louis.*

If we meet this year in the dark shadow of certain world events
— increasing armaments, degrading poverty, a sunken submarine, and
a tendency to build barricades instead of bridges — it must also be
stated that there is a growing circle of light still uncomprehended by
the shadows of darkness. There is visible in this circle not only the
spires of churches, but also the upreaching towers of our legislatures
and courts, the vertical thrust of our United Nations, the uplifted arms
of the Peace Corps, and the stretching fingers of Telestar and a hundred
other instruments of communication. Very prominent within the circle
of light is the dynamism of our colleges and universities, the on-going
process of the discovery and the preservation of truth. One need not
be an incurable optimist (a curious realist is enough) to find in all this
a stubborn, persistent buoyancy rising in the work of our churches,
courts, legislatures, world bodies, volunteer associations, and media of
information, above all, in the classrooms and lecture halls, the libraries
and laboratories of the academic world. This buoyancy must not be
confused with the worship of automatic progress to which our fore-
fathers of the nineteenth century were so attached. We know better
than that now. This hope of ours will be buffeted by failure and dogged
by cynical sneers, but man's natural history demonstrates that even
in a climate of ignorance he can learn; and his supernatural history
proves that since the Incarnation he can live by grace, even in a climate
poisoned by sin and choked by indifference.

So we meet not to view with alarm, nor to point with pride, but
with a more direct burden: to sign and seal the previous chapter that
has closed; to turn the page to the new chapter that is waiting for us;

to reflect for a moment on our resources and limitations, our challenges
and our hopes, as this new chapter stands waiting to be written.

There is nothing provincial about the challenge. It is universal
rather than particularly American. A gifted English educator, Bishop
Andrew Beck of Salford, addressed a conference similar to ours in 1958
in this way:

> We need to be lifted out of our individualism to catch a glimpse
> of the grandeur of our work in the Church .... The university Catho-
> lic, perhaps because of a certain isolation of life, needs to be re-
> minded of his high responsibility in the Church.

It is a question of the world, and our relevance to it. Bishop Beck
saw this relevance in terms of truth. "The Catholic has a vested interest
in truth, and it is his allegiance to truth which should be the distin-
guishing mark of the educated Catholic." This passion for truth,
wherever it is to be discovered, has been weakened by the clean break
made several centuries ago between theology and other knowledge.
Newman made this warning the chief burden of his discourses on
university education. In our times, Gilson has pointed up the continued
tragedy of the divorce: "Those who know theology are not those who
make science, and those who make science, even when they do not
despise theology, do not see the least inconvenience in not knowing it."
We accept it so, and the dichotomy persists. We have much work to
do; we are only beginning to realize the abnormality of a Catholic
education which, in Bishop Beck's words, "would substitute deportment
for intelligence and piety for technique, and would be prepared to
disguise an intellectual inferiority under the trappings of the faith."
Beck admits to an English Catholic "reluctance to take our proper
place in the university field." But this is not only English. It is widespread, and the outnumbering of English institutions by our own should
not permit us the luxury of assuming that our Catholic students are
fully aware of the relevance of faith to the facts and figures of a career
education, and even less to the plans and programs of the agonized
human society of which they will soon be a part.

If this challenge to a narrow individualism is not restricted to the
American scene, neither is it a unique phenomenon of the present
moment. A century ago, Orestes Brownson, that outspoken curmudgeon
of Catholic criticism, was issuing the same challenge in bold and clear
language. Brownson thought of it, not so much as a challenge to be
flung, as a complaint to be lodged:

> The most approved Catholic education of our days ... tends to repress
> rather than to quicken the life of the pupil. Those who are educated

in our schools seem misplaced and mistimed in the world, as if born and educated for a world that has ceased to exist.

Hence, Catholic education, or rather the education adopted and generally approved by Catholics in our age, especially in our country, fails to produce living men, active, thinking men, great men, men of commanding genius, of generous aims, and high and noble aspirations; and hence it also fails to enable the Church to take possession of humanity and to inspire and direct its movements.

It would be a blind and foolish critic who would claim that Brownson's charge is still true today. Our Catholic colleges and universities, with meager staff and still more meager budgets, have done a heroic task. Standards have been steadily and painfully raised. Research has been encouraged and supported, and scholarship has been honored. Lay scholars and professors have come to our campuses in growing numbers to work beside priests and brothers and sisters, and in many institutions an honest effort has been made to provide the salaries and benefits proper to the academic life. Our generally healthy Catholic citizenry is evidence of a growing will on the part of our graduates to live Christian lives. If the political, economic and social life of the United States does not sufficiently reflect the ideals of a society under God, there is hopefully some ferment of Christian humanism in which our graduates have had a part. But these are hardly ordinary times; these are urgent times. In the light of the formal challenge issued last week by our Holy Father in his new encyclical, *Pacem in Terris,* we can well meditate on Orestes Brownson's bill of complaints and especially that which read:

> It is very widely and, we fear, very generally believed, that true Catholic duty requires us to take our stand for a past civilization, a past order of ideas, and to resist with all our might the undeniable tendencies and instincts of the human race in our day.

The challenge to Catholics to be a part of contemporary society speaks out on every page of the latest papal encyclical. For those who have survived the welter of charges and counter-charges in recent years about the state of Catholic higher education, it has a ringing relevance. The colleges and universities we call our own must produce Catholic witnesses, not nominal Catholics, nor safe Catholics, nor comfortable Catholics, nor well-to-do Catholics, nor famous Catholics. The urgent need is the Christian witness, and in numbers large enough to make their presence felt. This witness has been given a timely description by Pope John:

> Every believer in this world of ours must be a spark of light, a center of love, a vivifying leaven amidst his fellowmen; and he will

be this all the more perfectly, the more closely he lives in communion with God in the intimacy of his own soul.

That college and university students were very much on the Pope's
mind is surely clear in the list of rights and duties with which the
encyclical begins:

- the right to freedom in searching for truth, and in expressing and
  communicating his opinion, and in pursuit of art — within the
  limits laid down by the moral order and the common good.
- the duty of seeking it and possessing it ever more completely and
  profoundly.
- the right to share in the benefits of culture . . . to a basic education
  . . . to technical and professional training . . . to go on to higher
  studies.
- the duty to occupy posts and take on responsibilities in human
  society in accordance with their natural gifts and the skills
  they have acquired.

The new chapter of Catholic higher education opens with the
urgent need to put away individualism and take up responsibility, to
make faith relevant in the community in which we live, to produce
Christian witnesses rather than Christian bystanders. A quick survey
of our resources will convince us that the work is well begun. Aside
from our physical plant and our invested funds, these resources rest
in three depositories: the Catholic tradition of education; the gift of
dedicated lives, both religious and lay; and the peculiarly appropriate
times in which we live.

First, our historic record of teaching and learning is evidence that
the educational role is native to the Catholic Church. An intellectual
history began with the truth that would set men free, found ripe expression in the *gaudium de veritate,* the joy in truth that St. Augustine
praised, and has survived in the tireless struggle of an Aquinas in the
thirteenth century and a Newman in the nineteenth. The "holy liberty"
that Pope John praised at the close of the first session of the Second
Vatican Council is another link to Newman's statement a century ago:
"Truth is wrought by many minds working together freely." Although
strained at times and clouded, sometimes badly forgotten, this is still
our tradition, the joy in truth, the holy liberty, the freedom that flows
from truth.

Second, the gift of dedicated lives. It is our treasured resource.
It is here today in your presence, in person or by proxy, the thousands
of human lives that have caught a glimpse of the divine in what a
wise Benedictine nun once gaily called "the foolish art of teaching."
Priests, brothers, sisters, laymen — in numbers, legion; in dedication,

beyond all human computation; in potential, limited only by nature and by grace.

And finally, a strange new kind of resource, the times in which we live. These years and their events are playing an appropriate counterpoint to the heroic efforts of Catholic education. Boisterous, grim, cynical by turn, our times are best characterized as troubled times. Out of such years and moments come questions. Out of questions comes the search for truth.

In opening the Second Vatican Council, Pope John reserved the use of severity in favor of the use of mercy in the treatment of errors. In so doing, he remarked that our contemporaries are themselves inclined to doubt the omnipotence of technical progress and exclusively material prosperity, to realize that violence, might and political power will not solve the problems of the world. In such a climate as we breathe today, the lucid and charitable exposition of the Church's doctrine will better serve the present needs than the condemnation of errors that often "vanish as quickly as they come, like mist before the sun." This sound and optimistic view has been reinforced in our own experience. In our nation, whose history has been spattered by the Know-Nothings, the APA's, the Ku Klux Klan and other ugly obtrusions of bigotry, we Catholics have in recent years been asked courteously just what we teach — in the midst of a presidential campaign, in a conflict over racial tensions, in the absorbing interest in encyclicals like *Mater et Magistra* and now *Pacem in Terris,* and of course in the many questions prompted by the present Council. To our historic and our human resources, then, must be added the times in which we live. Contemporary man is asking questions of the Church, and we can be sure that he will ask many more.

The concern of a bishop in Catholic higher education is not ordinarily academic or administrative but pastoral. My principal interest is that the young people of the Archdiocese of Atlanta reach a level of intellectual excellence that will enable them to live as Catholic witnesses in our society. But the issues linked with learning do not suddenly stop at ecclesiastical or civil boundaries. Therefore, the fact that there is no Catholic college or university within our state, and very few in the entire southland, would widen my interests. Some of our collegians are enrolled in Catholic institutions all over the country; many more are students in the fine state and private schools in Georgia. But the truth is, a bishop has proportioned concern, because he is a bishop of the Catholic Church, with every development in this field — regional, national, universal. After studying some of the strengths and flaws in Catholic higher education today, I take the liberty of suggesting for your consideration three approaches. They are meant to bolster the strengths and to mend the flaws.

(1) That Catholic educators give considerably more study to the possibility of pooling their resources, especially their faculties, libraries, research facilities, efforts to maintain the highest possible accreditation, and even pooling their students. There will be in this the danger of possible loss: less "school spirit," less demonstrated love for alma mater, less response from alumni, both affective and financial. A serious loss could be a lessening of the student's identification with a preserved and historically valuable tradition. Over against all this is the prospect of greater gain: a broader scope to campus interests, less duplication of facilities and presumably better use of them, more attractive provisions for good teachers and researchers, and a weeding out of the mediocre. There will be risks, and it will take courage, and it will open up a Pandora's box of technical details that I in my non-academic innocence will never know. But in 1963, risks must be taken. If the breaching of the ivory tower renders it more vulnerable to rain, storm, hail and other acts of God, it must also be noted that it will be more vulnerable to another welcome act of providence, the entrance of fresh air.

(2) This is a corollary of the first suggestion. I would hardly dare to recommend a moratorium on building new Catholic colleges and universities, but I join with many observers of our educational panorama in urging more study, across the board, before such new establishments are undertaken. Schools are started for many reasons, but surely the principal one is to provide a good Cathoic education for young men and women who would not otherwise get one. So far, so good. But today the sheer cost of the physical plant is so staggeringly expensive that it may be costing the new institution and its founders just too much. Can a first-rate Catholic education be hereinafter provided: administration, faculty, counseling, library, research, elbow-room for the expansion of the mind, not to mention the expansion of the parking lot? Should we not beneficially look into other possibilities? A large-scale arrangement for scholarships to already-established Catholic institutions; a greater development of the affiliated college; the extension university; or as is now being done in western Canada, the inclusion of Catholic theology, and perhaps some other subjects, in an existing secular university. There is a real danger in the "Catholic roof" theory of education, that everyone is better off under a Catholic roof no matter how many leaks are in it. Unless we are ready to subscribe to that theory,

we might well practice a neglected Christian virtue which is sometimes as meritorious as zeal, the virtue of forbearance.

(3) There is at most gatherings at least a hint of Banquo's ghost, an uncomfortable remnant of the past, a piece of unfinished business. Macbeth, the realist, will see him and be disturbed. Lady Macbeth, the dreamer, will dismiss the whole thing as "... proper stuff .... the very painting of your fear." Yet Banquo is an indispensable guest. He is present because invited, but also because our conscience needs him. He is not just a remembrance of things past, but a reminder of things present, the unfinished, vital business. Banquo's ghost is here with us today as we meet in the name of Catholic higher education. This is not a reference to our obligations to the university world at large, although surely if we are to hold up a lantern of Catholic culture it must be held high enough for those in this academic world to see it. No, the specific ghost is the image of some 500,000 Catholic young men attending secular institutions, less than 50,000 of whom (according to the figures of the National Newman Apostolate) are enrolled in any kind of effective contact with Catholic doctrine or Catholic thought. These students are Catholics; they are engaged in the process of learning at the level of higher education. By what curious logic have we omitted them for so many decades as the legitimate concern of Catholic education? Two years ago Banquo's ghost was finally seated. Old fears and prejudices and misunderstandings were overcome, and now the Newman Apostolate is a duly incorporated section within the National Catholic Educational Association. The whole movement is slowly but surely coming into its own. More dioceses now have named a diocesan director of the Newman Apostolate; a Newman Foundation is seeking funds; bishops are building new Catholic centers and staffing them; Newman chaplains and (just as important) competent teachers are being assigned in greater numbers; student leaders are taking a responsible initiative. But we are only beginning. Banquo's ghost has been seated at the feast of Catholic higher education, but he is hanging on to his chair and a little nervous lest someone pick up his place card. He just isn't sure that he is wearing the proper wedding garment.

This uneasy guest and ghost is introduced as this new chapter begins, because in our new phase of Catholic higher education a great deal is going to be heard about him, quantitatively and qualitatively. By 1970, it is estimated as many as a million Catholics will be on our secular campuses. There are many reasons for this, many of them good. One practical cause is the rising cost of private education. According to the United States Office of Education, by 1970 it will cost about

$37,000 for a Catholic family to send two children to a private school for four years. But the concern is more profoundly rooted in a different question. If the historic Catholic culture is needed in our times to lift the sights of our contemporaries above the walls of the City of Man, as Michael Novak has put it, must we not provide these hundreds of thousands of young Catholics with the rudiments of that culture? If today's disease is caused by the lack of awareness of God's presence in and His meaning to the world, then we can hardly maintain a stoic indifference to the secularism which is its formula. And in training research specialists and general practitioners for its cure, must we not pay equal attention to those without, as well as those within, the halls of Catholic institutions?

It is in the ghostly light of Banquo's presence that I offer a final suggestion that we broaden the whole definition of Catholic higher education to this assembly; that we seriously consider it in terms of every Catholic student, whether he be in our Catholic institutions with which we are singularly blessed or in those secular institutions, public or private, in which we have not yet admitted our full responsibility. In 1937, Archbishop McNicholas insisted that since we had 100,000 Catholic students on the secular campus, the Church had that many reasons for being there too. Now that the figure is closer to half a million, the responsibility is obviously greater in numbers, but even graver in fact.

No one has seriously advocated a levy on the clerical and religious faculties of our Catholic schools, a sort of "share-the-cloth" prosposal. That would hurt our Catholic institutions, and these schools must continue to present to our society the unique demonstration of full Catholic education. But a number of things could be done to implement our concern. Some Catholic scholars could be shared with nearby secular schools. Young Catholic scholars could be encouraged to seek a place on their campuses. The nearby Newman chaplain could be helped in many ways: sharing lectures with him, offering campus facilities for his students, seeking means of getting courses in theology accredited in these secular institutions. Many of these things are being done, and the gratitude of bishops and Newman chaplains to certain Catholic colleges and universities is very real. Other ways and means must be forthcoming. Both the Catholic and the secular institutions will gain by this interaction. The fetish of departmentalized truth, always a problem on any campus, is being broken down within schools by cutting across the academic lines of the several disciplines. Would not this good be intensified by our efforts to cut across institutional lines as well?

Like much counsel that comes to professional groups from outside, these suggestions may seem frivolous, or even irrelevant. I have touched on none of the technical administrative or teaching tasks that plague your day. Yet when we open a new chapter is not the broader outlook called for? Footnotes, bibliographical references, and other minor directional signals are not as vital as the text that is being written. The *magisterium* of the Church is wide and diversified; you and I are a part of it, each in our proper role. What we write and what we achieve will, it is true, be conditioned by the minutiae and paraphernelia of the academic mode. But real accomplishment will be caused rather by the longer view, the wider vision, the forthrightness and courage with which we face the goals.

In asking that our facilities be pooled more effectively, and that our tendency to duplicate these facilities be curbed, I intended these two proposals to be directed to the third: that we in the United States widen our collegiate horizons, that we settle not only for what is here, but that we opt also for what is there as well as here. If this were to mean a sacrifice of standards it would be suicidal. But with our resources, and the right reasons, and relying on divine grace to transform our human efforts, this need not be. There will always be students who care little for anything but a degree. But there also will always be students who want an education. Many of the best of these are not in our schools today. Our times need Christian witnesses wherever their place of origin may be. But right now we must share our resources in order to reach them.

The new chapter we are busy opening calls upon us to find and spread the truth, to reconsecrate the world. In many ways, the Vatican Council is the turning-point in our historic road; in nothing was this clearer than in the expression of the traditional concern of the Church for scholarship. This responsibility was seen by many Council Fathers as one of helping and directing the search for truth, not repressing or condemning those engaged in it. No one expressed it with more courtesy or concern than the cardinal-archbishop of this great educational center of St. Louis, His Eminence, Joseph Cardinal Ritter. He asked for the encouragement of scholars and leadership from churchmen. On the part of the teaching Church, he made these distinctions: where possible, direct and clear answers; where not possible, then restraint. When necessary, clear and distinct, but kindly, warnings. Thus will Catholic scholars play their role in the hoped-for *aggiornamento*. Only thus will the reconsecration of the world be accomplished. The Church is calling us to this triple task, the preservation, discovery and the spread of truth, and equipping us with modern tools by which to achieve it. We are not invited out of the world; we are invited into it. We will save our souls and the souls of our students not in the sanctuary nor in the confessional. These are the well-springs of grace. Men will save their souls on Main Street, on Wall Street, on Madison Avenue, and every other thoroughfare in the world, or they will not save them at all. In His last formal prayer, Our Lord prayed for those whom He was sending into the world to change it, and to save it. He was praying for you and me, and the thousands of young men and women who will either take up their diploma and follow Mammon, or take up their Cross and follow Him.

INTERVIEW WITH AUGUSTIN CARDINAL BEA

Most of the contents of this book reveal the Archbishop as a pastor, a public speaker, an author and ecumenist. This interview reveals not only his deep ecumenical concern but also his ability as a journalist. His own introduction to the interview provides the background. It was carried in the 13 June, 1963, issue of the Georgia Bulletin *and, significantly, was one of the few copyrighted documents that the Archbishop penned.*

The brief visit of Augustin Cardinal Bea to the United States in April, 1963, gave many Americans a quick glimpse at this remarkable young/old prelate whose name has become a synonym for the hopes of Christians everywhere. On his return to Rome to continue the vital work of the Secretariate for Christian Unity, he carried with him interesting views on the progress and particular problems of unity faced in the United States. While attending the spring session of the Conciliar Commission on the Sacred Liturgy in Rome, I had the opportunity of discussing these views with him.

Their cogency in this interim period of the Second Vatican Council prompted me to request the Cardinal to approve their publication in question-and-answer form in our archdiocesan newspaper, the *Georgia Bulletin.* This he graciously did, believing that every encouragement should be given to the "benevolent explosion" in our country of ideas and energies concerned with the ecumenical movement. Since the questions also included several on religious liberty and Church-State relations, Cardinal Bea's observations following his American visit will be of interest to our wide audience of readers, both Catholics and those of other faiths.

Father Stephen Schmidt, S.J., secretary to His Eminence, in transmitting the answers wrote me that the Cardinal's many occupations render this "as a quite exceptional case," and asked that this be noted because similar requests would have to be denied. He added that Cardinal Bea composed the answers and approved their publication

41

because of the importance of the questions involved and the area concerned.

FIRST QUESTION

On your recent visit to the United States, did you find the ecumenical climate favorable? In what particular ways? In comparison with European countries?

REPLY

I find that it has improved in an absolutely surprising manner. Evidently my recent trip by itself would not authorize me to make a judgment of this type, since I hardly even touched the eastern part of the United States, and even then for only a short stay of ten days during which I was principally occupied with the conferences and lectures which I had to give. Nonetheless, the contacts I had indicated a great change. These indications also received ample confirmation from the unbelievable number of invitations which I received on the occasion of this trip. Even though it was already clear by the end of December that I would not be able to prolong my absence from Rome because of work for the Vatican Council, still the invitations continued to be sent me.

The number of invitations I had to decline, regretfully, rose to over seventy. While from among these there were about twenty which came from non-Catholic sources, the remaining fifty, among which there were twenty from universities and colleges, give eloquent testimony to the enormous interest Catholics have for the union of Christians. Since the invitations came from just about every section of the United States, they truly give evidence of the existence of this interest for the cause of union just about everywhere.

If one wishes to make a comparison with European countries — although even here there are great differences from country to country — perhaps one could say that in these countries the interest for union has been growing slowly over a period of a number of decades. In the United States, on the other hand, one feels that there has been something of an explosion, which was unforeseen, though not for that reason less useful or promising, as a result of the events of the Council and in connection with it; especially as a result of more personal and direct contacts and the exchange of ideas with other parts of the Church. This type of benevolent explosion is certainly clear evidence of the fruitful energies, ready for every type of good, which lie hidden in American Catholicism and only wait to be aroused, as if freed from their bonds, and directed along the ways of a dynamic activity. And granted the excellent quality of this Catholicism — I am thinking, for example, of the exceptional fidelity to the practice of religion, of the unbelievable achievements in the field of education and of charitable work — I would say that things could not really be otherwise.

SECOND QUESTION

Do you think that the extensive religious pluralism in the U. S. (some 300 sects) is favorable or unfavorable to the development of religious unity (e. g. by comparison with the European situation where usually one or two large Protestant confessions dominate the non-Catholic scene)?

REPLY

For the present this situation renders ecumenical activity much more difficult. Consider merely the great practical difficulties which arise in organizing meetings between members of different confessions. The enormous differences which exist among the various denominations, extending even to the point where some of them no longer recognize baptism, make the situation extraordinarily grave. In fact, what common bonds still remain if such fundamental elements are lacking? How can there be any meeting of minds on a religious level which is specifically Christian if there is a lack of some common elements? It is obvious that given this doctrinal situation, mutual esteem and charity also become more difficult. The many tensions and animosities, which unfortunately not only exist at present but even make their weight felt in private life, and above all in public life, are clear proofs of that.

Nevertheless, I would also like to draw attention to the positive aspects of your situation. There is no doubt that the widespread dispersal of forces among Christians engenders and makes more intense the nostalgia of unity. The extreme intensity of the division makes more clearly apparent all the absurdity of the division itself and spurs on the search for a remedy. It is not by chance that among the pioneers of the first rank in the ecumenical movement of the past fifty years there have been Americans such as Charles H. Brent and John R. Mott. Furthermore, the many efforts at reunification which have taken place and are continually being carried on among various groups of non-Catholics constitute a precious ecumenical experience. Finally, looking at things from the point of view of Divine Providence, it is clear that a serious situation always constitutes an appeal addressed by God Himself to each of His sons to direct their attention to all the members of the great family of God, not seeking their own proper interests, but only those of Christ. And we know that God does not appeal nor command in vain but, according to the well-known phrase of St. Augustine, commands us to do what we can and to ask for what we cannot do by ourselves.

THIRD QUESTION

Do the European countries which are progressing most effectively in the ecumenical sense have strong diocesan commissions for Christian Unity? National commissions? What do you advise in other regions, e. g. the U. S.?

REPLY

In Europe, the initiatives vary from country to country. For example, in England the Episcopal Conference has a subcommission for ecumenical questions which studies, refers and proposes measures in the national Episcopal Conference. In France, there is a National Secretariate provided by the Archbishop of Rouen, and at least a half-dozen diocesan secretariates. In Germany, there does not exist a commission in the proper sense of the term but, as part of the activities of the national Episcopal Conference, His Excellency the Archbishop of Paderborn has charge of studying the questions connected with ecumenical work and referring them to the Conference. Alongside of the commission and enterprises already mentioned, in these same countries there are sometimes also commissions or at times simple secretariates on the diocesan level, as for example in Paris and in some of the other dioceses of France. These organs are under the supervision of the Ordinary and have the task of furnishing information to the pastors and other associations and of aiding and stimulating ecumenical enterprises.

This variety in procedure is very instructive. Actually, it is not arbitrary, but reveals the great diversity in conditions which must be taken into account. Now, it is clear that such a prudent manner of acting is even more imperative for the United States since it is a country which is almost as large as a continent, with populations which are also quite different. Consider the differences of origin in countries — even in continents — as well as the traditions which each one of the groups brought over with it and preserve partly out of jealous interest, partly out of unconscious reaction. Consider also the differences in climate, in economic and cultural conditions, the differences of the religious confessions and their geographical distribution. Therefore, before establishing an organization on the national level, care should be taken to create concrete bases and stimulate initiatives on the diocesan and parochial level corresponding to immediate exigencies, to their urgency and to the possibilities and prospects offered.

In conclusion, I would say this in general about these commissions — in the present case, diocesan ones: they should properly be an organ through which the hierarchy follows, aids and stimulates ecumenical enterprises. In ecumenical work we are actually engaged, to a large extent, in a field which is new and unexplored and where it is possible to make mistakes, to take false steps. It is therefore necessary to remain in the closest contact with the hierarchy, with those whom the Holy Spirit has established to rule the Church of God. This does not mean that centralization or uniformity are necessary or desirable. Always allowing for proper initiative, these commissions can give advice, give information about the experiences of others, stimulate action, be enlightened, circumspect and prudent.

FOURTH QUESTION

In the United States, Catholics (and many who are not Catholics) are anxious that a more accurate and modern definition of religious liberty be given by the Catholic Church. Would you think that the statement in Pacem in Terris *will be a guide to more theological discussion on this and that it would lead to such a definition? Will the Vatican Council discuss and define this question?*

REPLY

I am glad Your Excellency confirms this great desire of the Catholics of the United States. As you know, it is shared by Catholics and non-Catholics of many other countries. For this the Sacretariate for Promoting Christian Unity, aware of the urgency of the matter through its own ecumenical experience, has made itself the interpreter of this desire before the Vatican Council. After long study and ample and searching discussion, a schema was presented to the Central Preparatory Commission which, as we were informed by the official statements on the work of the Central Commission, was discussed by this Commission in June, 1962. From the same statements we are informed that the schema upheld the necessity of recognizing a man's right to follow the dictates of his own conscience in matters of religion. It consists also in a recognition of the duties of civil society in all its forms, including the state, to respect in practice the citizen's inalienable right to religious liberty. This right of man, as you appositely noted in your question, was very clearly affirmed in the recent encyclical, *Pacem in Terris,* which said: "Every human being has the right to honor God according to the dictates of an upright conscience, and therefore the right to worship God privately and publicly." (Vatican English Edition, p. 4)

You ask me if the Council will discuss and define this question. Without being or wishing to be a prophet, it seems to me that there already exists the well-known declaration of Pius XII in his discourse to the Catholic jurists in 1953. We have the even more solemn declaration of Pope John XXIII in his encyclical, as we have already mentioned. Anyone who understands the actual religious situation of the world today is aware that in name, and even more in fact, there is an ever-increasing differentiation among men in the field of religion. This is most explained by the frequent migration and expulsions even from the so-called Catholic countries. It thus becomes even more urgent that the affirmation of the dignity of the human person, from every aspect, with all his rights, of which the Church through her social doctrine becomes more a champion every day, be applied also with respect to religious liberty; and although this is already well-known, I might add the great importance of this question for ecumenical work. For all these reasons, I do not doubt that those whose eyes are opened to the reality of the situation of mankind today, and who keep before their eyes the intense doctrinal activity of the Church over the past few decades in the social field, will realize the great responsibility they have of being, each one in his own position and in the field of his proper activity, a light to the world with respect to this particular question which is of such fundamental importance.

FIFTH QUESTION

The Catholic Church in the United States has flourished under our particular relationship with the State, according to her pastoral experience and the public statements of her hierarchical leaders from Archbishop John Carroll down to the present time. Can the American experience not be considered as enriching the historic teaching of the Church on this subject of Church and State?

REPLY

Permit me to be brief and not to enter into discussing the requirements of the problem itself, since this is not my particular field. Of course, I realize that this question is intimately connected with the preceding one concerning religious liberty; I believe, then, that I can briefly say the truly flourishing state of the Church in the United States, even if due to a whole series of factors, undoubtedly constitutes an irrefutable proof that your particular experience in this area has been truly fruitful and that it can make a strong contribution to the solution of this perennial and thorny problem. I can add that this experience is particularly useful today and will become more so, since it involves an experience which developed in a particular form of society, that is, a pluralistic society. Now, since religious differentiation is becoming more and more widespread today, as we say above, the importance of your experience is clear. Consequently, without wishing to give suggestion which does not fall within my competence, it is my desire and hope that out of love for the Church the leaders of the Church in your country, together with other Fathers of the Council, will, at the appropriate time and place, give to this question their strong and fruitful witness based on a rich practical experience.

SIXTH QUESTION

Will the work of the Secretariate for Unity be as important after the Vatican Council as during it?

REPLY

Undoubtedly the Secretariate will be much more important after the Council. What the Lord has accomplished in the field of unity from the beginning up to the present has truly surpassed our fondest hopes and has something miraculous about it, if one considers how great were the obstacles and the age-old barriers which have been torn down, broken or at least moved. But we shouldn't forget that even if this is a great and promising beginning, all of it still remains only a beginning. The true work of extending and deepening it, about which we have said something in our previous answers, still remains ahead of us. Now, for this work there is urgent need, not of uniformity, but of prudent coordination, assistance, support and direction. There is need to receive and furnish information, to promote the exchange of experience, to enlarge contacts. And perhaps the most urgent task of all is the spreading of the ecumenical apostolate among Catholics by carrying it into every diocese, every parish, to every social group or profession, into the life, no matter how humble it is, of each one of the faithful.

The Secretariate, for its part, is already making preparations for this task. Already at the end of the first session of the Vatican Council there was announced the establishment, under a single president and a single secretary, of two distinct sections: one for the non-Catholic oriental Christians of various rites, the other for the communities arising out of the Reform in the sixteenth century. The two sections are now already being organized. These are all reasons for making a proper comparison between the institution of the Secretariate and the decision taken by the Holy See in the seventeenth century to establish the Congregation of Propaganda, that is, for the missions. The basis for this comparison naturally does not lie in the fact that non-Catholic Christians are considered in the same way as non-Christians — for certainly they are not — but only by the fact that the institution of the Secretariate shows how the Church is more vividly aware of its permanent responsibility towards Christians separated from the Apostolic See, and how she has felt the need to establish a permanent organ to take care of them and to which our brethren have been able to turn to up to now with the security that they would find not only a ready welcome but also assistance and understanding, charity and fraternal treatment, advice and aid.

Let us conclude our conversation, then, by underlining in a special way the great obligation every Catholic has of becoming interested fraternally and practically in non-Catholic Christians and in the unity of all baptized. Let me also underline our lively hope that just as the Catholics of America have taken to themselves with energy and vigor so many other interests and preoccupations of the Church, they will do likewise in the field of Christian unity. It is certainly a very wide and difficult field. Every Catholic is called to this sublime work; every force and energy, in its proper place, is precious and indispensable. Each contribution is a stone through which the raising of the entire edifice of the Church goes on in a well-determined order toward the formation in the Lord of the Holy Temple, in which all the baptized are themselves incorporated into the fabric to form, through the Spirit, the dwelling place of God (cf. Eph. 2:21ff) so that there may be brought to realization the final prayer of Jesus, our High Priest, "That all may be one, even as Thou, Father, in me and I in Thee; that they also may be one in us, that the world may believe that Thou hast sent me" (John 17:21).

THE POWER OF THE MASS

*The editor chose to include this address because it repre-
sents the kindred spirit between Archbishop Hallinan
and Pope John XXIII. It was delivered at Duquesne
University, Pittsburgh, on 2 June, 1963. Significantly, in
his own hand-writing the Archbishop wrote on the top
of the manuscript, "On day before Pope John's death."
That explains a great deal about the contents of this
baccalaureate sermon.*

All of us stand at this moment with an uneasiness that is linked to
the greatest challenge that the Church, and indeed mankind, has faced
in centuries. This challenge can be simply stated. Can men rise to a
higher respect for each other because they are all the children of God?
Can Christians love one another with less accent on the word "separated"
than on the word "brethren"? Can Catholics live, now not themselves
alone, but with Christ living in them? Can we in our generation take
a great step forward to a second Pentecost? Have young men and
women on the threshold of life sufficient vision, enough humility,
adequate courage to be in the vanguard of this movement into the
future? Pope John during the brief four and a half years of his reign
put these questions many times. In life, he asked them clearly; in death,
the memory of this humble man of God is a goad to a greater sensitivity on our part toward the needy, the lost, the least of men with whom
Christ so pointedly identified Himself.

In the Catholic framework, the sacrifice of the Mass is the most
heavily weighted of all man's actions, a bridge weighted down with
God's infinity, and man's faith in that Infinite Personal Existence, a
bridge heavy with man's vain longings, and curious ideas, and earnest
hopes, and frightful failures — and God's great will into which this
clutter of broken, human dreams must be fitted and refined and transformed. But the Mass is not just an exercise of prayer, graced with
gestures and pageantry. It is an act, not of man alone, because man
cannot compete with God; nor it is an act precisely of God alone,

because like Moses on Mount Sinai we would faint in the presence of His face, blinded by His glory, silenced by His wisdom and His power.

No, the Mass is Christ's, Christ our Brother, Jesus the Son of God, related to us on His mother's side, offering again for us the supreme sacrifice, standing as the Head of that body comprised of all who are baptized, speaking and acting on our behalf, making the Mass the same perfect offering that it was when He first performed it on the night before His death. Only in the Mass can man grasp his own full nobility, united with the Son, in the presence of the Father. But it is also true that only in the Mass can he also sense his own broken, fallen state. The haunting question steals into our mind as we intone the awesome name of God in the Sanctus — Holy, Holy, Holy — the question: What if God had not intervened in human history? What if Christ Our Lord had not walked with us? What if the Holy Spirit of God had not filled the world, kindled in our hearts the fire of love, renewed with fresh life the face of the earth? What if man were speared on the lonely lance of his own self-interest, hoist with the petard of his precious autonomy?

In every Mass we are aware of a brief moment of truth, a divine reality without which all our other snatches of truth seem incomplete. We are joined to a power that works in us the renewal of the face of the earth. We are linked in Christ by a bond of love with God, a bond that transforms the best and clears out the worst of all human affections.

But the Mass does not cease with the last Gospel; it is not closed off when we walk out the door. It is of the very essence of the liturgy that from prayer comes action, from worship flows the sense of community. The adoration of God raises man to his full and unique human stature. The Mass is not a drama; it is life. It is not a detached part of our day; it is like man's heart, linked by a thousand vessels to every finger-tip, to every muscle and nerve of existence. If the Catholic young men and women of our generation are to break the bondage that rests so heavily on our age, the Mass must flow into their lives. This will occur only if they humbly extend their minds and wills and hearts and hands to Christ Our Lord, and put their lives at the persuasion of the Spirit of God.

The bondage of our times takes many forms. The bondage of shallow judgment is ours, what Cardinal Newman called "viewiness," having an opinion about everything but convictions about nothing. This bond can be broken only by a mind that is seeking roots, deep enough to tap revealed truth as well as discovered truth. Discouragement is a form of bondage, helplessness that withers man's will to act, hope-lessness that dogs his failures. This can be snapped only by the Christian act of hope, hope founded on God's mercy and our need. And ours, too, is the bondage of self, of personal gain, and comfort and security. In our times, this bond can be broken only by an act of love, the love of God and the love of man.

I make no pretense of highlighting the social and political, or even the theological, crises that darken our daily headlines. After World War II, colleges began to offer a bewildering array of scientific courses to match the bursting discoveries of modern industry. After a year or two, the leaders of industry begged the schools to stop, to teach, instead, the fundamentals (mathematics, physics, chemistry, the basics). Industry itself, and the future, could teach the graduates how to apply these root skills.

There is a parallel in the life of a Catholic. If the basics are grasped and lived, the future years will make the proper applications. There is nothing more basic to the Christian spirit than the Mass and its meaning. The Church can offer you nothing more real, nothing more pregnant with the acts of faith and hope and charity than the Mass. All the human sciences and skills are brought into the amplitude of its grace. All the problems and crises of the future can be touched by the reaches of its power.

At this crucial hour in our lives, which happens to coincide with a critical hour in the world's history, it is not advice we need nor moral exhortation. The need of our times is love, human love shot through with the splendor of divine love, love of God demonstrated and proved in daily contact with our fellowmen. Of this Christian love, Pentecost is the birthday, the Holy Spirit is its source, and the sacrifice of the Mass is its daily insertion into lives which without it would be dry and dull, but with it can be fresh and rich and full of the wonder that is man's measure and man's ultimate goal.

FORMING CATHOLIC LEADERS

For many years Archbishop Hallinan was the spokesman for the Newman Apostolate in the United States. As a Newman chaplain, as a graduate student at a large university, he understood better than most prelates and priests and laity the problems of the academic world. Even though he had retired from the realm of academe, he was frequently called upon to return and address students, faculties and chaplains. This address was delivered on 26 August, 1963, at the National Newman Convention held at the University of Southwestern Louisiana, LaFayette, at the annual chaplain's dinner.

This talk will be brief and circumspect. Brief, because every bishop has learned the lesson of Vatican Council II: if you can't say it in ten minutes, Xavier Rhynne will say it for you. And circumspect, because it is the Council about which I want to talk. The seal of secrecy is one reason for prudence, but the dangers of prophecy make an even greater reason for walking carefully. These are exciting and historic and uncertain times.

Who would have dared to predict a year ago that Pope John would tell us that the Church nowadays "prefers to make use of the medicine of mercy rather than that of severity"; that more than 2,000 bishops would vote in favor of liturgical reform; that the basilica of St. Peter's would resound to the beat of tribal drums? Prophecy is always a hazardous occupation even in the events of nature, and when the Holy Spirit, breathing where He will, makes His presence felt in the midst of the apostles' successors, only the handy phrase can sum it up: "Only Heaven knows."

I would like to propose to you, my colleagues, three conditional theses, and add to each the question, "Are we ready?"

1. If the Index of Forbidden Books were to be changed or abolished, would the present Newman program for the intellect be able to do by permeation what the Index was supposed to do by prohibition — preserve and increase faith?

2. If the restrictions on interreligious actions are softened by the ecumenical impulse, will our campus efforts along that line move

us a step or two toward Christian unity, or a mile or two toward confusion, misunderstanding and futility?

3. If the place of the Catholic layman in the Mystical Body is clarified and codified, is our present program of student formation mature enough to raise the annual output of such lay Catholics?

The Index of Forbidden Books was designed to preserve faith. In our day, it does not touch the university library on an intellectual plane. In fact, it does not touch anything at all on that level. It appears to most Catholics and everyone else as a moral issue far removed from the content of any volume; had any institution the right to prohibit the reading of a book? The list of named authors and named books is largely unknown to today's students; only the French novelists and certain English philosophers and a few other authors ever appearing on any college reading list. Even proscription by categories does not seem to concern the student as he looks over the highly pornographic content of the average paperback bookrack. Whatever its relevance to the past, the Index has little relation to the student mind today. It may be changed, updated, modified or abolished altogether. If it is, it is to be earnestly hoped that the prevailing reason will be the magnificent paragraph of Pope John's opening address to the Council:

> The truth of the Lord will remain forever. We see, in fact, as one age succeeds another, that the opinions of men follow one another and exclude one another. And often errors vanish as quickly as they arise, like fog before the sun.
>
> The Church has always opposed these errors. Frequently, she has condemned them with the greatest severity. Nowadays, however, the spouse of Christ perfers to make use of the medicine of mercy rather than that of severity. She considers that she meets the needs of the present day by demonstrating the validity of her teaching rather than by condemnations . . . .

Whether the Index is changed or not, the errors will continue to appear in doctrine and moral conduct. Whether it was effective or not, the Index was entirely negative. It did not increase the faith of any Christian, nor attract others to the treasures of the faith, nor penetrate the shadows of the world with the light of truth. If it should disappear tomorrow our proper positive task remains: to teach, in season and out of season; to teach the truth that is our competence — religious truth; and to foster and encourage the teaching of those truths in other regions beyond our competence — the bursting regions of the natural sciences, history, literature, the arts, and so on.

We must honor the scholar who honestly seeks truth in his field, whether he is on our side or not, whether we like him or not, whether he likes us or not. Anything else is intellectual dishonesty. Our students must imbibe this respect for scholarship from us. The Church did not suffer when St. Paul walked among the intellectuals of Athens; when Augustine urged his pupils to love intelligence, and love it very much; when Aquinas investigated the philosophy of the Arabians. This is the vast burden that is ours, the task of consecrating the intellect to God. It is difficult today because although there are more educated minds than a century ago, they are not educated in the things that pertain to God. The good news of salvation has not had a good press. It would be a mistake to assume that all Catholic students have Catholic minds. In Frank Sheed's phrase, many have secular minds with Catholic patches. Yet it is our job to awaken in all these minds the *gaudium de veritate,* the joy of finding truth. This will be a far more effective tool than the Index, because the Index did not touch sin against the intellect, which is God's own created instrument for truth. There is a simony of the intellect as well as a simony of goods. We are at a point in history where this simony is the temptation of the educated man. To sell ones's mind for sordid gain, or for popularity, or for the coin of the mediocre achievement or the perversion of other minds — this is perhaps close to the ultimate simony, for reparation is almost impossible to make.

Are we ready for the increased tempo of the ecumenical motion of our day? This is not just a matter of seeing more good in the traditionally bad guys, or less good in ourselves. It is more than a question of campus conferences and goodwill gestures; it is more than overcoming the temptations to cut corners and skip over the rough parts. To be an ecumenical Catholic means finding the truth and holding it fast, but in the words of every ecumenist from St. Paul to Cardinal Bea, holding it in charity. The ecumenical Catholic is the man, well-informed and faithful to his trust, deeply aware of the fragmentation of Christianity, and ready to learn, to love and to live in less self-assurance, less pride, less complacency. How did it happen that so often we were willing in the past to cut the pattern of Christ's seamless garment to fit our own self-righteous frame? Slowly, painfully, we are coming back to the realization of what we have together: our common sacrament, Baptism; our common prayer, the Our Father; our common source-book, the Bible.

Yet for every step we take forward in ecumenical charity, there are a dozen pitfalls lest we lose ecumenical truth. It was perhaps easier (or rather, lazier) when we used to thank God that we were not like the rest of men. It is more difficult, because it demands more of us, now that our popes have opened the doors of St. Peter's to "the others," assuring them that they are in no stranger's house but in their own. The road to unity was more comfortable when it was crowded with Catholic motorists waving at Protestant pedestrians. Now it looks more like the road to Jericho where only the Catholic who stops and helps his brother is assured of reaching his destination. There are many mountains to be climbed and detours and speed traps to be avoided, but we must patiently move on with the Church. It will take courtesy and understanding, prayer and good will, hard work and probably discipline, correction and failure. But the twentieth-century Catholic has no other choice. We have plumbed the depths of St. Paul's remarkable sentence, "The eye cannot say to the hand, I have no need of thee."

And finally, how serious are we about the formation of students as respectable Catholic laymen? It is so easy to tick off the things that a chaplain must do: teach, counsel, warn and exhort, and bring the student to Christ in the sacraments and Mass. It is not so easy to face the things we must not do: stifle young initiative; repress what our experience tells us would be a risk; pamper by doing too much, ignore by doing too little. May I cite here the gain and the danger inherent in our present mood to emphasize the Newman Center and to de-emphasize the Newman Club? Certainly, it is high time that we broke out of the mentality of the Newman Club as a poor man's fraternity. Certainly, it is good to draw all Catholics, and indeed all students, to a truly Catholic center. It enshrines the intellectual and religious elements of our apostolate, and it prevents that strange brand of non-ecumenism found in the phrase, "But, he's not a Newman Club member," as if the subject were a Buddhist monk in present-day South Vietnam.

But are we the victims meanwhile of that odd human quirk of throwing out the card-carrying baby with the organizational bath-water? If the Club is to be downgraded, what will it become; a band of puppets responding to Father's strings, or a band of rebels responding to nothing? And if it has to go, what will replace it? Without the Newman Club what will be the testing-ground for leadership, the laboratory where student risks are still possible? There is a place, a very important place for the organizational structure of the Newman Club, at local, provincial and national levels. Not only can it assist the chaplain and the faculty member in religious education, in extension and external affairs, and in countless other ways; it engages the student at the existential level of politics, scheduling events, and the chemistry of interpersonal relationships. The conceptual level of Christian thought and the sacramental level of Christian sanctification must begin with the student as object. But organizational details of club programming require the student as subject. And it is a high probability that he will remain only an object in education and in spiritual formation unless he learns how to act creatively in the grubby, grabby, but familiar world of club activities. The Church needs a muscular, not a spoonfed laity, and it will grow only in appropriate soil. It will not grow in the antiseptic corridors of a center where every major decision is made by the professionals.

These three theses are not perhaps the most profound issues facing the Catholic world today, but unless they are honestly appraised, much of our talk about a renewal on the campus is just so much talk. The search for truth, with or without the Index of Forbidden Books, must replace the search for status, or security, or the fast buck. The ecumenical seed will bear campus fruit only after ample nourishment and careful pruning. And the supply of mature, lay Catholics will depend upon our willingness as priests to take the risks that always go with initiative and the creative act of building self-confidence. The Vatican Council is no panacea for our problems. But it is an invitation to use all the resources of our Catholic heritage in their solution. When the days of the Council are over and the decrees are in force, then the new age of Christianity will begin. It will be filled, as Newman said of an English spring, with keen blasts, and cold showers, and sudden storms — but also bright promise and budding hopes.

BLESSED DOMINIC BARBERI

In October, 1963, during the second session of the Second Vatican Council, the Passionist priest, Dominic Barberi, was beatified in Rome. One of the new Blessed's claims to fame was that he had received John Henry Newman into the Roman Catholic Church. Internationally known as a student and promoter of the cause of Cardinal Newman, the Archbishop was invited to deliver a sermon during the solemn triduum honoring the newly created Blessed Dominic. On 29 October, 1963, the Archbishop spoke in the Passionist church of Saints John and Paul in the Eternal City.

Christ sent me to preach the gospel; not with an orator's cleverness,
   for so the cross of Christ might be robbed of its force.
To those who court their own ruin, the message of the cross is but folly;
   to us who are on the way of salvation, it is the evidence of
   God's power.

1 Corinthians 1:17-18

In October, 1841, a young Italian priest went to England to establish the first house of the Passionist Fathers in that country. Eight years later, he died. It was an incredibly short apostolate, but Dominic Barberi was an incredible man. He has slipped into history by the back-door, as one writer has put it: it was he who received the great John Henry Newman into the Catholic Church. This was no mean claim to distinction, because Newman's conversion is one of the unmistakeable landmarks of English Catholicism. But if Dominic became famous only because of the accident of being the right man at the right time and place, then surely the Catholic world should ask, was it a mere accident? Why was he at Littlemore at the precise moment that Newman's will and the divine impulse of grace came together? Why was Dominic Barberi the right man?

We could start with the very name of the religious community that is now honored by his beatification. The Passionists take their name from the passion of Our Lord; their cross is the symbol of His suffering and death. But our language today gives an added meaning to the word passion, a meaning that goes beyond the acceptance of pain. We use the word to describe what happens in the heart of a man who suffers. Passion becomes an active flame, a burning desire, an overwhelming urge. We often speak of a passion for life or for love. But those are human. A divine passion is the flame and the urge in a man who has surrendered himself to the redemptive suffering of Christ on the cross. It leaps forward to conquer a soul, a neighborhood, a world, not for gain nor for face, but to bring back that world to Him who died for it. Dominic is now called Blessed by the Church he loved and served. He is blessed because he immersed himself in Christ, and identified himself with Christ's passion; but he is blessed too because this experience seized his soul, and poured itself out in a passionate burst of energy that was both perfectly disciplined and recklessly spent. He was totally resigned to the will of God, but he was almost hopelessly ambitious in his plans for the advancement of the Kingdom. This is the Passionist pattern. This was Dominic's pattern.

Those who knew him did not need to ask why he was the right man for England in the mid-nineteenth century. His novice master spoke of his "extraordinary humility." A Belgian priest who had attended his conferences later wrote, "For forty years and more, I have regarded him as a saint." And the most renowned of his converts, Newman himself, said this of Dominic: "His very look had about it something holy. When his form came into sight, I was moved to the depths in the strangest way."

Dominic's holiness was not achieved in a cloister. It bore the dreary marks of daily, petty, boring administrative details. It is one thing to carry, for twenty-eight years, the dream of becoming an apostle in a foreign country. It is quite another to have to spend those years directing novices, teaching philosophy, serving as superior and then provincial. He did all these things well. His words and actions seemed to merge into a perfect hymn of humility and zeal. The hymn was never serene, but it was always sublime. He never forgot the call he had received from God when he was only twenty-one. "I understood that I was to labor in northwest Europe, and especially in England." His health was very poor and deteriorating rapidly. One setback after another slowed up the plans for the proposed English mission. At the age of forty-eight, Dominic bravely began to learn the French language so that he could preach in Belgium. Two years later he tackled the English tongue. When he spoke to his first English listeners, he had to memorize the little sermon:

> I wish to say a few words for your edification, but I cannot do it because I am not yet able to speak English. However, I shall say

something – a very short sermon: My dearly beloved, let us love one another, because they who love their brothers accomplish perfectly the will of God. Let you love God, and man for God's sake, and you shall be perfectly happy forever. Amen.

If the words came haltingly, the message did not. His sentences were broken English, but it was holy eloquence to those who heard it. With a face and body shrunken by pain, he spoke to them from his heart. He was living now as St. Paul said, "Not I, but Christ lives in me." To the cultured groups at Oxford, and to the rough-and-ready people in the scattered Catholic missions of the Midlands, this was the voice of God, because it was quite evident that it was the voice of a man of God.

That he was kind and brave and spiritually resourceful, that he was an obedient religious, that he was full of God's fire – these marks are all in the record of his life. In part, they explain in those nine short years, Dominic's dream moved toward its fulfillment: sermons, retreats, missions; a hearing for the Catholic Church; respectful concern on the part of Protestants; converts by the hundreds. The present Archbishop of Birmingham, where Dominic once lived, has expressed it in this manner:

> He acted as a sort of catalytic agent between Protestants who were turning towards the Church, and Catholics who were suspicious of anything within the "Elizabethan Establishment."

But the surface record is not quite enough to explain the tremendous impact of the man. Now, decades after his death, the hidden record has come to light. *He was a man totally in love with God!*

The story of his life – quaint, picturesque and quixotic – does not tell it all. But the story of his soul goes deeper. It explains not only Dominic the man, but Dominic the saint. He wrote a great deal, but he set two formidable barriers against any revelation of his inner life. One was his own natural self-effacement, the other was a style of handwriting that challenged even his admirers. Because he was always in a hurry, his mystical writings, like everything else he wrote, were almost illegible. A mysterious shorthand obscured even those parts that can be made out. Because he was short-sighted, the ending of some words and lines were written not on the paper, but on the table. Now because of the great interest in his beatification, his spiritual life is being reexamined and freshly appraised. That he was a true mystic seems beyond question; his autobiography, a spiritual diary, and especially his *Commentary on the Canticle of Canticles* reveal a life intimately spent in loving God. True to his vocation as a Passionist, he found his own mystical death in Christ's death. He experienced the desolation of an interior purgatory in which he shared Christ's agony on the cross, and then the transforming union by which his life was spent more in heaven than on earth. If his collegues and his congregations did not know this, Dominic did.

Father Alfred Wilson, a fellow Passionist, corrects those who estimate Dominic's place in England only in human achievements and natural gains. "This long, drawn-out martyrdom," he has written, "and not Dominic's short ministry, was his major contribution to the Second Spring." The graces that his Oxford converts and hundreds of others received came not just because Dominic spoke to them. They came chiefly because he *suffered* for them.

It is an appropriate time to pay tribute to this body of men, the Passionist Fathers, whose community produced this holy priest. All over the world they follow, as Dominic himself did, the footsteps of their founder, St. Paul of the Cross. Their aim is to become "specialists in unfolding the lesson of the cross, relating the way of the cross to daily living, opening up to mankind a vision of the divine world." Those bishops among us who are privileged to have them serving our own dioceses would be the first to honor them, and to pray God to send us more Passonists, more men like Dominic Barberi.

The midst of the Second Vatican Council is a ripe time for the Church to recognize this early apostle of the ecumenical age. The humble Italian priest spoke to those not of our faith in accents we have ourselves heard in the voices of Pope John and Pope Paul. Dominic always assumed good faith in others; he refused to enter into empty controversy; he put a high value on tact and courtesy and, above all, charity. He went to England because he loved, in an amazing way, the people — all the people — of that great nation.

Three short sentences sum up the ecumenical approach that Dominic used. To a Protestant minister, he wrote, "If we seek the truth simply, we shall easily find it, and it will free us from our bonds." But he always carried truth in the vessel of charity. "Endless patience and charity, and above all, good example," he wrote to Rome, "these are the great needs." And while he plied his apostolic trade with truth and charity, he never missed the basic lesson of all ecumenical effort: "Anyhow, this is a work of God's own, and we have to let Him take His own way, having a care on our part to follow faithfully the path which the divine mercy lovingly points out to us." To speak the truth, to live in charity, and to trust in God — these are the real instruments of Christian unity today, in the 1960's, as well as in Dominic's time, the 1840's.

This is a man whom history barely knows, or knows only because he was John Henry Newman's first priest. When he met Newman, Dominic's life spoke far more eloquently to the sensitive Anglican clergyman than his halting words. He was the right man for Newman and for countless others, at the right time and right place. May God give us, in the twentieth-century manner, men like Dominic Barberi who can speak of Christ, and Christ's cross, and Christ's Church to a troubled world. The great fruits of the harvest of souls come not to those who are quick with words or ready with answers. The conversion of the world awaits those who are steeped in Christ's life, His sufferings as well as His glories, His cross as well as His words of consolation. May God provide, through the gracious intercession of his servant, Blessed Dominic of the Mother of God, this kind of men, this kind of priests, this kind of saints.

THE RENEWAL OF THE LITURGY

*Following in the footsteps of several great predecessors
— such as John England of Charleston and Aloysius
Muench of Fargo — Archbishop Hallinan knew very well
both the usefulness and effectiveness of pastoral letters.
Thus his Lenten pastoral of 1964 was as much a letter of
information as of preparation. In spite of the passage
of time, it remains a classic example of preparation for
liturgical renewal. It first appeared in the 20 February,
1964, issue of the* Georgia Bulletin.

When Pope John convoked the second Vatican Council, he almost immediately put liturgy in the first place for debate and decision. He wanted to give more vigor to Christian life, to adapt the Church to the needs of our times, and to help the whole of mankind (especially those who were baptized in Christ) into the household of the Church. This is what he meant by an *aggiornamento*, a renewal of the spirit of the Church, an updating of the ways of the Church. Thus far, the great conciliar Constitution on the Sacred Liturgy is the chief fruit of the Council. This is very fitting. And it is timely that our pastoral letter this Lent of 1964 should treat of this great theme, the liturgy, as it is termed, "The summit toward which the activity of the Church is directed; the fountain from which all her power flows."

The liturgy used to be thought of as a set of rubrics or rules for ceremonies. Spirituality used to be considered in the sentence, "I have a soul to save — by myself." Little connection was seen between the two. So the average Catholic *attended* Mass, *went* to Mass, *was present* at Mass, almost as a stranger or silent spectator. He took little part in either the reading of the Bible, or the liturgy of the Eucharist. The renewal calls for an entirely new concept: "A full and active participation by all the people is the aim to be considered before all else."

THE NEW MEANING OF LITURGY

The reasons for this are clear. First, liturgy is an action, a *community action;* second, it has *definite roles* — bishop, priest, layman, each restored to his proper task in public prayer; and third, *it has its pastoral and teaching part to play,* namely, to be simpler, more comprehensible. Action, then, definite roles, and a pastoral part. But foremost it is the action of Christ, our Head. God's goodness and holiness descends, and man's praise ascends. In fact, "to accomplish so great a work, Christ is always present in His Church, especially in her liturgical celebrations." It is the Mystical Body at work, or rather at prayer, where Christ the Head is joined to the members. A priest is not ordained for himself. His role at Mass is not a solitary one. He is simply the representative of the people.

INFLUENCE OF LITURGY

It is the people, God's holy people, that make up the Church, that *need* the liturgy. For the liturgy is not created nor made up by the Church. It is received from God, but it can exist only for the people. It will be helpful for us to examine this. There will be changes in it — English for Latin in some places, certain other changes, more Scripture. But the chief transformation will not be on the surface but rather in the fundamental things; the effect on *you personally,* on the *parish,* on the *Church,* and on those *separated from the Church* but still joined by baptism.

You are asked to come out from behind the pillar and put away your rosary. You are *asked to join with the priest in a community prayer and action,* first drawing in the riches of the Bible, then participating in the Eucharist, particularly by receiving Christ's Body and Blood. Your prayers, hymns, responses and gestures will be important. All the while, you will be more conscious of yourself, your family, your neighbor as part of this "holy people." Through the priest, who is Christ's representative, you are taking your part in the Mystical Body.

In the sacraments there is that same divine life at work. There has been the same mistake here, the misconception that the sacraments were simply signs or symbols. Baptism and confirmation of a child or adult now is more clearly seen as a true initiation into a new life; penance, although confidential, also partakes of one common vitality in Christ. Marriage and priesthood are not just "ways of life"; they are definite roles and tasks to carry out. The priest administers the parish; the parents the home and family. And the sacrament once called "extreme unction" is now called "annointing of the sick" to show that its chief purpose is to strengthen.

The sacraments, therefore, are to sanctify men, to build up the body of Christ, and to give worship to God. You are influenced each time you receive one of them, as you are when you take part in the Eucharist. Modern man is not content with abstractions. Concrete realities are essential today. In the Mass and the sacraments, as well as the Divine Office of the priests, the Church provides these realities.

Secondly, *what will the liturgical renewal do for the parish?* It has already been noted that liturgy exists for the people of God. That includes not only the Church, centered around the bishop in his cathedral church, but also those groupings of the faithful known as parishes. The Church is a living, pulsating thing but it exists here and now on the local level in our parishes. As one American priest, Father Joseph Connolly of Baltimore, has written, "Only when the Christian experiences that his coming to church is in response to God's call, that he is with his brothers . . ." then will he be able to sense himself and his parish as they are in the mind of God.

Thus the parish, each of us — priest, sister, brother, layman, child — has his role to play; some are more precisely liturgical, others more ordinary. In each of them, the liturgy strengthens the Christian's way of life. Otherwise, the great public worship of the Church is but a pageant, a show, a solemn drama. It was never intended to be such. It was intended to be for the increase of holiness of God's people. It is in the parish that this takes place for the average Catholic.

Thirdly, *the effect of the liturgical renewal on the Church itself*, of course, will be very great. In missionary countries, the principle of adaptation will allow for local usages and regional initiative; the vernacular will permit the old Latin rigidity to be relaxed. But in our own country too there will be a vast transformation. We have spoken of the effect on the person and the parish. Now, the Church will stress more vigorously the reading of the Scriptures, and in fact one commentator, Father Frederick McManus, a liturgical specialist of the Council, speaks of a real revolution in preaching — "the proclamation of God's wonderful works in the history of salvation."

Finally, in these urgent days of the ecumenical movement, with those not of our faith deeply interested in the *aggiornamento* of the Catholic Church, what effect will the liturgical renewal have *on the yearning for union between ourselves and those who are separated, but not formally set apart?* It will be indirect and gradual. It will be new and strange to Protestants to hear the Scriptures used with more familiarity in Catholic services. The vernacular, in our case English, can make them much more at home. Our new use of hymns, our common book, the Bible, and our mutual prayer, the Our Father, all become bonds of union.

PRACTICAL STEPS

What a theme for our Lenten meditation. In a short letter, this is what the new liturgy will mean to us. It is a key part of the updating, the renewal that Pope John held so vital for our times. The new liturgical transformation runs like a golden thread through Pope Paul's words to the Council: the need *for reforms; for the Church's awareness of herself;* for *union* with our separated brethren; and *for the bridge* to our modern world. In fact, up to this point the Constitution on the Liturgy is the great keystone of the arch of the Council. Soon will come the decisions on the role of the bishops, the part of the layman, on religious liberty and the ecumenical efforts. Right now, it is the public worship of the Church that is the key.

So now we ask the priests and people of our archdiocese to meditate on these things: that liturgy is a public community action, with definite roles and a pastoral, teaching part. It is Christ offering His Father the eucharistic sacrifice as Head of the Mystical Body. Its effect on each of us personally, on our parish, on the church, on our separated brethren, will be deep and vigorous.

Our pastors are urged to preach again and again the true meaning of the liturgy, and to follow each new move so that the new spirit will enliven our parishes. In our schools, our sisters and lay teachers and confraternity teachers are cautioned to explain the liturgy to our children, not in terms of rules and ceremonies, but of the new changes. Our parish societies should meet to discuss the new Constitution and the explanations of it.

It will not be an easy experience. It will be new and strenuous. But a year of it will bring the liturgy alive in our parishes.

The liturgy is "the public worship which Christ, the Head of the Church offers to His Heavenly Father, and which the community of the faithful — all of us — pay to its Founder, and through Him to the eternal Father." This means that it is divine, and yet it is human too. But as the French liturgist, Father Louis Bouyer, has written, "If it is the work of God, it is of a God who became man." That is our confidence. That is our assurance.

ROLE OF THE PUBLISHER
IN THE CATHOLIC PRESS FUNCTION

*In 1964, Mr. Gerard Sherry, then the editor of the
Georgia Bulletin, invited several representatives of the
Catholic Press (the editor of this volume included) to
voice their opinions in that publication. After a series
of such expressions, Archbishop Hallinan expressed his
own opinion as to what the role of the publisher should
be in relationship to his editor and readers. His statement, which appeared in the 21 May, 1964, issue of the
Georgia Bulletin, was recognized by editors as a major
breakthrough in the area of religious journalism.*

THE BISHOP AS PUBLISHER

It is not out of place to describe the diocesan newspaper in the
biblical words used to describe John the Baptist:

A journal shaken by wind of popular favor?
A newspaper clothed in the soft garments of costly advertisements,
an ample budget, and door-to-door subscribers?
Behold, these are the houses of the great daily press.
But what went you out to see? A *prophet* . . . a *messenger* who shall
make ready thy way before thy face.

What sort of "publisher" is a bishop who sends this modern John
the Baptist into our homes? The word itself suggests a vocation leading
to profits or to political power. But these are hardly the motives of
a bishop who assumes the title. If the paper can keep within its budget
and if those in politics (and elsewhere) will read it, the bishop utters
a quiet prayer of gratitude for the intercession of the press' patron,
Saint Francis de Sales.

The only profit the archdiocese seeks is a popular increase in
knowledge about the total God-man relationship. The only power
sought is the persuasion to move our people to make this knowledge
come alive in homes, parishes, the market-place and the whole community.

Yet the diocesan newspaper cannot exist in a purely spiritual or
even religious climate. Editor and staff must meet deadlines, pay

66

costs, and utilize new methods. They must keep a nice balance between local and worldwide news; between coverage and significance; between enough popularity to win wide acceptance and enough boldness to take a moral stance — and hold it.

John the Baptist won an audience, but to do it he lived austerely and eventually was martyred. In the course of conscience, the Christian press may have to live, as he did, on a diet of locusts and wild honey. It may even clash with 1964's copies of a brutal Herod. These hardships are but the hallmark of a true messenger, a genuine prophet. As Gerard Sherry, our editor, has put it, "The whole mystical body is called to be witnesses . . . to what He is . . . to His will as He has revealed it." Unless the Catholic newspaper opens for its readers this awareness, it is not a medium of communication at all. It is only a chronicle.

In this prophetic work of witnessing, the paper needs more than a mild loyalty and support. These can be earned. What is needed is alertness of staff, deep interest of priests and sisters, subscribers who read it, agree or disagree as it applies Christian principles to current issues — and then speak about it. Perhaps of all the Church's instruments, the Catholic press most needs involvement.

Involvement calls for more than passing acceptance. One has to be convinced and committed that a certain idea or object or person is important. We might contrast an automated machine and a competent workman as an illustration. The machine — accurate, impersonal and continuous — is like a church paper which simply records events and whose readers simply accept them. But the workman — human, thinking and feeling — is like the journal that takes sides, presents stimulating arguments, stirs discussion and possibly action. The Church needs this latter kind of involvement.

The staff must be involved, alive to the great issues and the small fascinations of the day, ready to put at least a journalistic toe into the apathy of a quiet pool.

The priests and sisters, as officers of the diocese, are key personnel in this involvement. They are co-workmen with the Catholic press in expressing Christian convictions. When they disagree with the paper's policy or techniques, they should speak up, not as special pleaders or defenders of the status quo, but as interested parties. Except in cases of conscience, their public support should be vocal and enthusiastic.

The laity is involved not only in the financial burden. This, in my opinion, is owed to every part of diocesan life. But an intelligent Catholic, aware of the need of a strong paper, measures the Catholic press not by the yardstick of his own private opinions, but by that of the teaching of Christ and His Church. When he cancels his subscription because the paper disagrees with him, the right question seems to be, "Why do I disagree with the paper?" Perhaps he is ending his involvement because he disagrees with a fundamental point in Christianity. The paper sometimes is made the scapegoat of his collision in the Church.

It was ever thus. Seventy-five years ago, Bishop Richard Gilmour, a staunch prelate who founded the *Universe* in Cleveland, said this of the paper and its lay editor:

> Readers may object to its views in matters of public interest; that is to be expected, and a paper that is not objected to will not have much that is worth commending.
> But no one can successfully maintain that the *Universe* has ever been other than loyal to Catholic truth and Catholic interests, and this when it requires some nerve to stand up for Catholic principles.

"Catholic interests" have broadened since 1889; they are less defensive, more apostolic. A Catholic press cannot draw back its skirts today and avoid the Christian stand on poverty, racial discrimination, freedom of conscience, the marriage code, organized crime, war and peace, world order, and a score of other subjects. The purpose was thus stated by the Fathers of Vatican Council II in these words:

> ... forming, supporting and advancing public opinion in accord with natural law and Catholic teaching and precepts.

This is involvement, by the paper and its readers. The bishop's role as publisher is to foster it, to limit clearly the "official" character of the paper to pronouncements within the area of the Church's teaching. When these principles are expressed, it is the bishop's duty to see that they are stated rightly. But beyond that, the editor, staff and readers must have elbow room to enjoy what Pope John called "the holy liberty" of the children of God.

In the exercise of that freedom the diocesan paper does not need to weigh mathematically all opposing views. Such neutralism is limited to the news column. Even here, the editor's judgment is often vital. But in the interpretative press — editorials, columns, letters — such a neutrality is foreign to the Church's mission in the world. She does not look with neutrality on degrading poverty and segregation, just as she does not blink at deceit, adultery or atheistic communism.

The popular Catholic mind must grow beyond yesterday's tendency to regard everything found in Catholic journals as "the Catholic position." They are free to present any Catholic position touching humanity and the social order. The debates of Vatican Council II led the way. If our newspapers evade this, they are not bridging that gulf that has too often separated Christian truth from everyday life.

When *Il Quotidiano,* Rome's Catholic daily for twenty-one years, folded this April, Pope Paul spoke of the reasons: "enormous liabilities and too little circulation." Then, comparing the modern newspaper to a "mirror," a "stimulator of judgment," and a "teacher," he stated bluntly, "It decides on the yes and no of the kingdom of God in our society."

Involvement? Full and alert support of a Catholic journal by a Catholic laity? Pope Paul speaks to every Catholic on this point:

> It is not possible to have this (contemporary) fund of thought aligned along Christian principles without the material, reminders and stimulus contained in the Catholic newspaper. . . . . the duty of every Catholic person, at least of every Catholic family, to be united by the spiritual and moral service which only such a vehicle of news and ideas can bring each day.

As I read the *Georgia Bulletin* and a dozen other diocesan papers each week, I have come to think of them as precision instruments of Christ and His Church. When Our Lord, as head of the Mystical Body, employs tools for His salvific craft, they must meet these two specifications: they must be forged in truth and applied in charity.

FORGED IN TRUTH

"Fear to offend it, to obscure it, to betray it." Pope John a year ago was repeating the traditional Catholic teaching about truth in the same tone that Leo XIII used when he opened the Vatican Archives to historians. But the practice of Catholics, clerical and lay, has not always followed the principle. We have often failed to grasp that the truth's purpose is not to project "a pretty picture," that truth is not a block of granite incapable of fresh insights, that it is not "finished" except in the mind of God.

There is much to recommend, especially today, in an awareness of public relations, the use of "the image." It does influence people, but what if the image is distorted and incomplete? What if it goes beyond "stressing the positive" and pointing up of progress (both of which are quite proper) to pretend that all is perfect? "Sweetness-and-light" has surely not been the watchword of the present Council. Both Pope John and Pope Paul have called for an honest examination of the Church today, and that is what the Fathers are doing. They are giving vigorous leadership to Catholics everywhere.

The diocesan newspaper should echo today the mind of one of America's most honest Catholic laymen, Orestes Brownson. He is quoted in Donald Thorman's fine book, *The Emerging Layman,* disagreeing strongly with the "image mentality" in 1860:

> There are persons, very excellent persons too, placed in positions of trust and influence, who think a Catholic publicist should resolutely defend everything Catholic . . . and studiously avoid agitating any question on which Catholics may differ among themselves, or which may lead to discussions, offensive or disagreeable to any portion of the Catholic community.

This was not Brownson's stand. Nor is it the stand of the Church.

> *Items:* In the *Georgia Bulletin,* we read of sharp disagreement between Cardinal Koening and Cardinal Siri on the significance of the Council, of theologians in conflict on the morality of contraceptive measures, of laymen expressing strong opposition on civil rights. These will disturb anyone who accepts the pleasant catch-phrase, "All Catholics think alike." But their presentation in a Catholic paper is a solid instance of honesty.

Again, truth is often the outcome of tensions generated in the life of the Church. No one who has read of the First Vatican Council can doubt this. And no one has portrayed the development of doctrinal truth more effectively than John Henry Newman. "If a great idea is duly to be understood . . . it is elicited and expounded by trial and battles into perfection and supremacy . . . . In a higher world it is otherwise, but here below, to live is to change, and to be perfect is to have changed often."

This change is never a shipwreck of truth; it is rather a true development of it. "The theology of the Church," writes Newman, "is no random combination of various opinions, but a diligent, patient working out of one doctrine from many materials. The conduct of Popes, Councils, Fathers betokens the slow, painful anxious taking up of new truths into an existing body of belief."

If this is true of doctrine, it is much more evident in the application of the truth to living, pulsing daily situations. Here the Catholic press is at home as it reports controversy, seeks new methods and probes a given condition with the Christian needle.

The tree that is the Church has been growing for nearly two thousand years, but it is still the same tree. Saint Peter faced conflict in the apostolic college itself. Out of it came the decision that the Gentiles must not be disadvantaged in the Church. Pope Paul recognized today the interplay of controversy in the shaping of Christian message. He has not hesitated to go beyond Pope John and the Council's decree on mass media in defending the very heart of controversy: the "right to objective information."

"It is," he said on April 17 of this year, "at once active and passive — the seeking of information, and the possibility for all to obtain it." The Catholic press, then, must make available the material for good judgment, with plenty of room for new insights and sharp discussion.

> *Items*: In the *Georgia Bulletin* we read, for example, of the current debate on Catholic schools. Because of tremendous progress, untold sacrifice, and rightful pride, there can be a bristling when they are criticized. Yet the criticism itself contributes to their progress. Although Archbishop Lawrence Shehan has noted that neither panic nor pessimism is warranted, he added "[criticism] will serve a good purpose if it spurs us to remove as soon as possible every cause of justifiable complaint." Our reading public has the right to information about the debate now going on. Out of it will come better Catholic education.

And finally, truth reaches out toward completion. There is reality in the statement, "Immoral films do harm to many people." But it is incomplete. The 1964 statement of the Bishops' Committee for Motion Picture, Radio and Television, headed by Archbishop John J. Krol, went farther. It called for "the responsible efforts of serious film artists to create meaningful work for the attention of mature viewers." The treatment of evil, "subject to moral restraint," can serve to bring about a deeper knowledge of humanity. A balance is achieved. Discourage what is patently harmful; encourage what develops a taste "for the good, the beautiful, the truly human."

Thus, the Christian grows, "testing all things, holding fast to that which is good" under the guidance of Christ and His Church. Sometimes the old formulas need a reexamination so that we may reach a larger truth.

> *Item*: The *Bulletin's* weekly movie and TV reviews tend toward a maturity suited to today's situation. In so doing, they lead readers to a fuller expression of the whole truth.

APPLIED IN CHARITY

The diocesan paper serves truth best when it works in charity. This "more excellent way," in St. Paul's words, does not inhibit truth nor falsify it. The genuine love of God and one's neighbor could hardly lead us to lie, distort or bury reality no matter what the apparent temporary good.

In selecting and interpreting news, the Catholic newspaper must be conscious of the common good, respectful of "privileged information," and obedient to the contemporary canons of journalistic good taste. In one sense, these are limitations on an absolute right to publish everything. In a deeper sense, their discipline is rooted in charity. So too, are the methods it can best use: persuasion, reasonable argument, and courtesy to all.

But to use the press in charity an editor sometimes faces delicate decisions. If the truth hurts, shall he print it? If it is necessary in this particular news, *yes*. If it is extraneous to the reader's right understanding, the answer is sometimes *no*. Only an editor equipped with a deep reverence for both truth and charity is competent to make such decisions.

Such reverence stems from humility, an honest quest of the mystery that rises when truth's call and charity's cry are mingled. It helps us to remember that the abuse of either damages both. An English scholar, Duncan Cloud, warns of cases when we "pretend that there is no *real* disagreement, that the fact is not *really* awkward . . . ." We need a reminder that not only truth is blurred. Charity is stunted, too. Daniel Callahan in a refreshing essay on "The Quest for Honesty" asks the Church to be patient with its interrogators:

> Before it dismisses them, let it put some charitable questions to them. Let it take their questions seriously. We desperately need such openness. That way both honesty and truth can be served.

Beyond the ordinary discipline of truth and charity, charity should stimulate our Catholic press to two responses: it must care and it must move. It can do neither without the other.

A Catholic driving through a slum should be shocked. If he is caught up in his own racial prejudice he should sense shame. When he thinks about the personal crises that can break in the married lives of his friends, or the wholesale agony of millions whose faith is under official persecution, the Christian cannot pretend to be an unaffected island. With the intellect's concern must go the heart's compassion. Mercy is a strong component of the virtue of love.

So the Catholic editor must reflect that care. Despite repetition, he must share something of the joy of every parish picnic, the sorrow of every funeral, the awakening of every child confirmed. On these simple things — homey, local, personal — he builds in his readers a wider concern about injustice in the Congo or the dream of world peace in the United Nations. To leave his readers unaware of the aspirations of society is a grave disservice. The paper must care deeply enough to maintain, week after week, a conscience sensitive to the needs and hopes of men.

Then, with whatever persuasive power at its command, the Catholic paper seeks to move its reader, to share this concern, and act upon it. It may do this simply by a clear call to action. Or it may show how others not of our faith are responding. It may point up alternatives or consequences. The "consecration of the world" is a long and arduous labor. Unless the press of the Catholic world alerts us to its potentials, this restoration to a sonship in God will slow down to its very opposite pole, Cain's apathetic question, "Am I my brother's keeper?"

AND THE BISHOP?

He has a unique relationship to the diocesan newspaper: reader and critic from one point of view; sponsor and supporter from another. But because he is teacher of his people, he stands as a guide to the paper. He is accessible to the staff for consultation, open to new ideas and methods, interested in the impact on the Catholic family and general public.

To keep wide open the area of freedom where truth can prevail, he exercises forbearance and patience, occasionally courage. Yet he cannot forget that Christ holds him responsible for the deposit of faith among His holy people. To insure that charity will co-exist with truth, he and his priests seek to exemplify always in their lives the love of God and fellow-man. Mindful of the trials of editors and the response of readers, the bishop asks for no utopian uniformity of opinion. He accepts Raissa Maritain's explanation of what a Christian is, "A man who forgives," whether he agrees or not.

When the new *Georgia Bulletin* first appeared, I asked that it enter the community "bearing light and courage — light to expose society's ills as well as its strengths; courage enough to inspire justice and charity in those who might falter along the path."

We are honestly examining our shortcomings and we invite candid criticism. But sixteen months later, there exists in my mind no imperative to change a word of that, nor any doubt that the *Bulletin* is bearing, week by week, the light and courage we all need.

FOOTSTEPS ON THE COUNCIL

This article is but one of many that the Archbishop wrote for the Georgia Bulletin *before, during and after the Second Vatican Council. It appeared in that publication on 24 September, 1964, and was but the "first in a series." It has been chosen for inclusion here as one of numerous articles he wrote in bringing "the spirit of the Council" to the people of the archdiocese.*

For two years, we have been conscious of changes in the old Church we know and love. It still stood there, sturdy and serviceable, rather grimy in the urban centers, rather glossy in the suburbs. The structure was basically the same one that our parents and grandparents knew. The laity was "under" the clergy in doctrine, morals and worship; the priests "under" the bishop; the bishops "under" the pope. All was well.

But was it really? In another country, France, the Archbishop of Paris had looked carefully at the Church of the war years and the world that lay around it. Then, in the 1940's, Emmanuel Suhard wrote a series of pastoral letters: "The Parish Community," "Growth or Decline," "The Meaning of God," "Priests Among Men." What he wrote pierced the hearts of many French Catholics; his influence spread through Europe and America. With the dreams of Christian priests and laymen and the pronouncements of Pope Pius XII, the Suhard thesis became the Catholic blueprint for a renewal of the Church. The Second Vatican Council, in its decrees, is energizing the ideals of Suhard and others.

Because all is not well. Why do some Catholics resent the efforts of their bishops and pastors to preach full equality and justice for the Negro? Why do scholarly Catholics feel that the Church is not interested in the intellectual questions of our times? Why do the faithful so often prefer private devotions to the public liturgy of the Mass? Why did it take so long for our schools to absorb the social guidelines of Leo XIII, the scriptural promptings of Pius XII, the ecumenical spirit of John XXIII?

In opening this third session of the Council, Pope Paul points to the reason: "The humiliating emptiness of our misery, and the crying need we have of His help and mercy." If the Church in the United

States is not understood by those of other faiths, as the presidential campaign of 1960 clearly showed, is it because it is not sufficiently understood by us who are its members?

The Schema on the Church opened the debate this third and decisive session. Pope Paul who put "awareness of the Church" first in his opening address of 1963 and in his first encyclical, *The Paths of the Church,* has called this Schema "the weightiest and most delicate of all." Cardinal Bea, who has come to be reckoned by Catholics, Protestants and Jews as a fatherly guide, explains the long debate on it by his insistence that it is the "most important document of Vatican II."

What questions does it involve? Paul VI has stated:

> The hour has sounded in history when the Church ... must say of herself what Christ intended and willed her to be .... The Church must give a definition of herself and bring out from her true consciousness the doctrine which the Holy Spirit teaches her.

The Holy Father in addressing the council members asked the Church "to study itself, or rather probe into the mind of Christ, its divine Founder" so that it may be an "even more fit instrument in the work of salvation for which it was founded." But it will not be a tight, inclusive, legalistic definition. Christ, who formed it for all men, on the one hand, and humanity, "to whose service it is committed," both forbid such a notion.

In the beginning, things were different. The concern of Christ and His apostles was first with the internal, spiritual development of the soul toward God. The Gospel of Christ is studded with passages which call for such interior dedication, the beatitudes, the two great commandments, the parables. "Seek you first the Kingdom, and all these other things will be added to you."

Likewise, St. Paul spoke of Christ's Mystical Body, not as a legal, external organization, but a body in unity of function and goal. The bishop, the priest, the layman were to serve in a ministry of love. Likewise, St. Gregory the Great, writing to an Egyptian bishop, said, "My honor is the honor of the Universal Church. My honor is the strength of my brothers." St. Thomas Aquinas called the Holy Eucharist the focal point, the sacrament of unity.

No one questioned the need of authority and obedience, the preservation of the Word and the necessity of the sacraments. But it was not until these were repudiated by some of the reformers of the sixteenth century that a shift in the definition of the Church became noticeable. St. Robert Bellarmine, to whom we owe much for the conservation of the Church's identity in the post-Reformation days, spoke from the beleaguered position of Catholicism in a chaotic Europe. His definition read:

> The one true Church is the Community of men gathered together by the profession of the true faith, communion in the same sacraments, and under the government of legitimate pastors, and principally the one Vicar of Christ on earth, the Roman Pontiff.

Every word of that is true, but it does not go far enough. It held the line against the attacks of heresy, but it does not serve today. It puts emphasis mainly on external conformity: outward profession, outward sanctification and outward obedience.

The new Schema on the Church has eight chapters:

The Mystery of the Church. Written in language rich in Scripture, this chapter places the Church in its proper relationship to God — Father, Son and Holy Spirit. The Mystical Body of Christ is beautifully and effectively described, starting with St. Paul and carrying us down to the encyclical of Pius XII on that subject. The whole chapter makes a little silly the expression, "I belong to the Catholic Church." As you read it, your response will probably be, "I am the Catholic Church, a part of it."

The People of God. Here the Fathers will dip into the Old Testament and God's covenant with His people. Members of the Church are defined in these terms, adding a clarification of the phrase, "the priesthood of the laity," and showing how the sacraments make possible and enhance this priesthood. The gift of charisms, special revelations possible to every order of the Church, will be carefully explained. The chapter closes with refreshing words on the place of non-Catholics and non-Christians in the overall use of the term, "the people of God."

The Hierarchy. Only in an abstract, textbook sort of manner will the old charts on the Church's government now survive. The whole sense of this debate will center on service and ministry, because the Son of Man came to minister, not to be ministered to. The sharing of the responsibility of the pope with the bishop is called "collegiality." This is examined in terms of Christ, Peter and the other apostles, then the application is made to the Church today, Christ, the pope and the bishop. The three-fold task of the episcopacy, teaching, sanctifying and ruling, is to be explored. At the urging of a number of bishops, notably Archbishop William Conway of Armagh, Ireland, a much-needed section on priests has been added.

The Laity. It used to be said that only two canons out of some 2200 in canon law referred to laymen, and the only available definition was "a person who is not a cleric." Articles 30-38 now spell out the all-important role of the laymen in the Church, defining him in much more positive terms, underlining his dignity as a member of the people of God. His apostolic life, his witness of Christ, his royal service of Christ the King, his relation to the hierarchy — all these topics are included. The older role of layman in the choir, classroom and collection basket (still very necessary) and his newer role as lector and commentator in the liturgy (even more necessary) will surely be enhanced as the decrees of Vatican Council II begin to take effect.

The Universal Vocation to Sanctify, Religious Orders, The Eschatology of the Church (her heavenly destiny), *The Blessed Virgin Mary in the Mystery of Christ and the Church.*

Each of these chapters has a logical place in this vital Schema, and the thinking Catholic will want to follow the debate and study carefully the final form of the decrees. In next week's article, a summary of some points of the debate will be given, with special attention to the interests of our people. Already, Cardinal Suenens has objected to the procedure for the beatification of saints: too long, too expensive and too centralized. Fathers of both the Eastern Rite and Latin Rite have claimed that the Holy Spirit is underemphasized. The cardinal said the chapter on eschatology enriched the whole Schema, but an archbishop said it should be totally omitted because it said nothing not already known. And although the chapter deals with the Church in heaven, two bishops thought it should include hell. The Church — in hell!

There are new procedures now, and more efficient presentations. Certain features of the session are disappointing: the restrictions of the United States press panel; the outside pressures and inside leaks about the statement on the Jews. But there are very encouraging signs: the opening concelebrated Mass of the Pope and twenty-four bishops, including our own Archbishops Shehan and Krol; Pope Paul's stress on collegiality; the new word against civil interference in concordats; the progressive work of the new liturgy consilium.

Only one topic seems to have earned the *non placet* of practically all the bishops. They don't like the new hour of opening the coffee bar, 11 a.m. In the earlier sessions, the counter provided all sorts of coffee, and (I was glad to note) Coca-Cola plus light pastries. It was a great place to gather and discuss the schemata, especially while one Council Father at the microphone was saying what had already been stated a dozen times.

Maybe the 11 a.m. opening is a move to discourage the bishops. We'll know, if this becomes the last session.

The Most Rev. Egidio Vagnozzi, D.D., Apostolic Delegate to the United States at the time, visits with Archbishop Hallinan in the Cathedral rectory.

Archbishop Hallinan dedicates a new Marist School on September 30, 1962. Left to right: Fr. Austin Verow, S.M., Marist Provincial, Fr. Vincent P. Brennan, Superior of the Marist Fathers, Archbishop Hallinan, and Fr. Paul Kelly.

An ecumenical breakfast at which Archbishop Hallinan was joined by Bishop Randolph Claiborne, Episcopal Bishop of Atlanta.

In St. Peter's Square at the time of the Second Vatican Council, Archbishop Hallinan visits with Bishop Robert Tracy of Baton Rouge.

Participants in the University of Notre Dame's 117th annual commencement exercises on June 3, 1962, were, left to right: Henry Cabot Lodge, former United States ambassador to the United Nations; Rev. Theodore Hesburgh, C.S.C., president of Notre Dame; Dr. Francis J. Braceland, Hartford, Conn., psychiatrist, who received the University's Laetare Medal for 1962; and Archbishop Hallinan, who delivered the baccalaureate sermon.

Father Hesburgh presents an honorary Doctor of Laws degree to Archbishop Hallinan, citing him as "an alumnus whom we cherish and of whom we are very proud . . . he realizes in the spirit of Cardinal Newman that no part of the Catholic inheritance is foreign to our country and that no place is too strange in our land for saints and angels to pitch their tabernacles."

OUR OWN AMERICAN TRADEMARK

This was an interview proposed by the editors of Con-
tinuum. The Archbishop wrote out the replies to the
questions proposed in longhand and dated his reply 31
October, 1964. For reasons unknown to this editor the
interview was never published. The record further shows
that no typewritten script of the interview was ever made.

There seems to have been a greater divergence of outlook among
the bishops at the turn of the century than there is today. Was
this a matter of personalities? Differences based on national origins?
So many problems still unresolved. Was this due to a less mono-
lithic Catholicism at that time?

A friend of mine has a favorite couplet:

The world will not be enticed,
By a cold, statistical Christ.

His second choice is:

There are many who lean on the myth
That the Church is a vast monolith.

The "single stone" metaphor is persistent although it appears to be a
misreading of our Lord's stern images of the stone rejected by the
builders and the rock on which His Church is built. Any stereotype
about husbands, human beings or hierarchies is apt to dissolve under
scrutiny. But generalization has a proper usage; let us apply it to the
American bishops of the 1890's and 1960's.

At least a dozen major issues of church polity faced that earlier
hierarchy, and a measurable conflict (although not a wide diversity)
existed within episcopal opinion. Attitudes on the assimilation of nationalities provoked the sharpest divergence, followed by the approach
to the public-parochial school issue, secret societies, labor unions and
a national Catholic university. The American relations with the Holy
See (an apostolic delegation, an American representation in Rome,
priests' appeals to the Holy See against their bishops) formed an area
of fairly tight episcopal agreement. Most of the bishops did not want
the first, preferred the second, and saw no need for the third.

78

The resolution of these problems was the *sine qua non* of an operative ecclesiastical policy. But it was more than an internal matter. It was sure to influence the image of the Church in the eyes of millions of fellow Americans, affecting the charge of "foreigners" and divided loyalty, as well as the hope of the conversion of Protestants, and an American contribution (the "sense of mission") to world Catholicism.

Eager to form an American spirit among Catholics, one group (Ireland, Gibbons, and their younger colleagues, John J. Keane and Denis O'Connell) was insistent on broad educational goals, lenient in judgment on such American institutions as the union, the public school, the fraternal society, and profoundly sensitive to the mutual mission of Church-to-nation and democracy-to-Catholicism. The most scholarly of the bishops (and the one least likely to respond to labels) was John Lancaster Spalding of Peoria. He was not in the inner circle, but generally approved instances of the liberal spirit at work. Less outspoken but sympathetic to it were Archbishops Kenrick and Kain of St. Louis, Riordan of San Francisco, Feehan of Chicago, Elder of Cincinnati, Gross of Oregon City, and Bishop Moore of St. Augustine.

Opposed to the liberal tendency, but often for varying reasons, were Archbishop Corrigan of New York, Bishop McQuaid of Rochester, and "the Germanizers," Archbishops Heiss and Katzer of Milwaukee. Their views were generally shared by such prelates as McDonnell of Brooklyn, Dwenger of Fort Wayne, and Chatard of Vincennes. There were, of course, "cross-overs." McQuaid, who fought Ireland's school plan and the Catholic University, was a staunch "Americanizer" with modern theories of seminary education; Spalding, on the other hand, inspired the struggle for the university and excellence in education, but opposed Ireland's view of the public school. The prelates of the two great Atlantic sees, Archbishops Williams of Boston and Ryan of Philadelphia, were not involved in the controversies of the 1890's.

There is a notable difference in American Catholicism at the turn of the century and in our time. It is reflected in episcopal thought, words and action. To understand it, one must be familiar with the changes in national life since 1890 (e.g. the end of the frontier and immigration, the awakening to our role in the world after two wars and a prolonged economic upheaval); but a summary knowledge of Catholic trends is needed too. In the first period, down to World War I, both the hopes of the progressive bishops and the fears of the intransigents were upset. Protestantism had not declined. Instead, the increasing momentum of secularism was being felt by Catholics, who experienced (although they took no lead in) the opening toward "manifest destiny" and the more critical Progressive Era. Catholic liberal optimism was consequently dimmed. But conservative pessimism proved inaccurate too. Nationalities were absorbed with benefits for the Church. The Catholic University of America became a reality, with a controverted but solid conservative influence. The parochial school continued to be the Catholic norm of elementary education.

The Church in the United States emerged from the confusion of "Americanism" puzzled by the obscurity of the charge, and from the Modernist crisis subdued by its tragic aftermath in Europe. A long period of theological docility set in. But if no theologians of note appeared until World War II, these decades prepared the Church in other ways. Progressive steps were taken to match the growing Catholic population with the physical complex of churches and schools needed to serve it.

In the second period, between the wars, these steps led to more collaboration: the issuance of the Bishops' Social Reconstruction program in 1919, and formation of the National Catholic Welfare Conference in 1922 with its subsequent annual meetings. Three streams of Catholic influence began to flow: one was the emergence of the Newman and Confraternity movements as a supplement to Catholic schooling, at least on a protective level; another was the necessary stimulation to Christian rural life; the third was the dynamic pioneering in the socioeconomic area by John A. Ryan and others at the Catholic University. It is interesting, in view of the assumption that all bishops come out of chanceries, to note that among the men prominent in these three significant movements were future bishops like Maurice Schexnayder, Robert E. Tracy, Lawrence F. Schott, Allen Babcock; Francis Haas and Robert E. Lucey; Edwin V. O'Hara, Paul P. Rhode and Francis Clement Kelley.

Aside from the bitter presidential campaign of 1928, the decades of the 1920's and 1930's were fairly unexciting. Cardinal O'Connell's encounters with Father John A. Ryan over the child labor amendment, and Father Charles E. Coughlin over the New Deal made headlines, but quiet action by Archbishop Curley in 1924 and Cardinal Mooney in 1937-38 preserved a considerable area of freedom with a degree of ecclesiastical dignity.

The third period in American Catholicism, 1945-1964, changed the Catholic complexion in the national scene. As Daniel Callahan aptly noted, the effects of World War II speeded up Americanization, mixed up religious groups into new living patterns, and supplied Catholics with an income that enabled them to compete culturally. A healthy self-criticism and a new chapter of the interrupted lay renaissance have begun. Our world is not that of sixty years ago. We can agree with Dr. Robert Cross that the bishops of the 1890's were "among the first to see the real meaning of the experience of the American Church." But we should also question, with Father Walter Ong, S.J., the wisdom of regarding the deeds or words of bishops like Gibbons and Ireland as "sources."

The battlefield — or if the metaphor is too polemic, the locale — has shifted. Gibbons' contemporaries dealt with concrete, manageable events and gave them a wider significance. Today the American bishops face more complex challenges, and they must apply them to concrete situations.

Item 1: In 1947, in 1958, and again in 1963, our official teaching on racial justice was made quite clear. But this had to be matched by such actions of integration as Cardinal Ritter provided in St. Louis in 1947, and Bishop Waters in North Carolina in 1953 — both before the Supreme Court reached its historic decision. The courageous efforts of Archbishop Rummel in New Orleans during the 1950's, against an anti-clericalism as vicious as this nation has ever seen, are part of southern history. The concrete cases continue: Archbishop O'Boyle's leadership in the Catholic part of the summer march of 1963; the steps taken by Archbishop Shehan in Baltimore; and the recent action of five California bishops (McGucken, Begin, Maher, Donohoe and Bell) against restrictive housing each applies the episcopal statements to real situations. They are dutifully warned by the fearful that these situations can be economically punitive and politically disturbing.

Item 2: All the bishops endorsed the social principles of *Rerum Novarum* in their National Pastoral of 1919. Then they spoke out frankly in their own dioceses (Muench in Fargo and Mooney in Detroit, both to be later honored as cardinals) and encouraged men like Ryan to act. His recent biographer, naming a dozen bishops friendly to him, concludes, "far from feeling hostility from the bishops, Ryan felt substantial support." Archbishop McNicholas spoke for the majority of the administrative board of the NCWC when he wished in 1934 that "we had a hundred John A. Ryans in the country to speak for the Church and for human beings." A clear-cut instance of an applied principle was the opposition of six Ohio bishops (Alter, Hoban, Walsh, Rehring, Mussio and Issenmann) to a "right-to-work" amendment to the state constitution in 1958.

Item 3: There is truth in the statement, "Immoral films harm many people." But it is incomplete. The old formulas often need re-statement so that we may reach a larger degree of truth. In 1964, the traditional policy of the Bishops' Committee for Motion Pictures, Radio and Television, was given a new, more positive dimension. The bishops, headed by Archbishop Krol of Philadelphia, called for "the responsible efforts of serious film artists to create meaningful work for the attention of mature viewers." The treatment of evil, subject to moral restraint, they added, can serve to bring about a deeper knowledge of humanity.

The myth of today's hierarchy being monolithic has been damaged by the clear divergence of our American bishops in Vatican Council II debates on liturgy and episcopal collegiality among a dozen other subjects. There is a difference between 1890 and 1960. A partial cause lies in our lack of knowledge regarding the inner debates, personal correspondence and chancery records of the contemporary scene. A historian of the next century will open up the archives to discover that these bishops held diverse views, expressed them and acted on them in an earnest effort to resolve them.

The annual bishops' meeting points to an intensification of the ways and means of translating principles into action. Back of the vigorous debate lie widely divergent views, self-criticism and self-analysis. Several years ago, the chairman tried to speed the agenda to an adjournment by starting to ask, "Do the bishops agree that . . ." He was met by a deafening roar as nearly 200 bishops, without waiting for the question, answered, "No!"

The manner as well as the content of today's issues differ sharply from the turn of the century. They involve demands of renewal and reform within the Church and profound questions of abundance–poverty, war–peace, freedom–authority, in the world in which the Church lives. With inspired vision, the bishops of an earlier day worked from local cases to broad conclusions, from particular means to ends acceptable to the majority But today, we not only must reverse ourselves and work from ends to given cases, we must constantly re-examine the ends themselves.

There has evolved, as a consequence, what might be called "the mid-twentieth century manner." Not only time, origin and temperament divide today's bishops from Gibbons, Spalding and McQuaid. The hour is later and the hour's *modus operandi* has changed — in government, education, welfare, the administration of justice as well as in the Church. Balance and restraint, study and testing, dialogue and the mature shouldering of responsibility — these are the ingredients of the modern way. If Bishop X appears today as the very antithesis of an Ireland or McQuaid, let us remember, with the historians, that the manner of an Eisenhower, a Kennedy, or a Johnson lacks something of the gusto of a Grover Cleveland, a William McKinley, and most certainly of a Theodore Roosevelt!

What has been the effect of the failure to convene national councils, such as those of Baltimore, on the American Church?

The Third Plenary Council of Baltimore was the result of several factors: the insistence of the "western bishops" (Gilmour, Heiss) that a national council was needed; the invitation to the American metropolitans, by the officials of the *Congregation de Propaganda Fide,* to come to Rome to prepare for the council; the convoking of the council by Leo XIII (January 4, 1884), who set November of that year as the time, and named Archbishop Gibbons as the Apostolic Delegate. The original demand, the preparation and the convocation were all essential to the event itself.

It is now prescribed by canon law that diocesan synods be held every ten years, provincial councils every twenty, and plenary councils "whenever the necessity arises." It is scarcely tenable that no necessity has occurred since 1884. Yet the law-making power of our national hierarchy has been held in abeyance for eighty years. It was used, in April, 1964, to implement the new Constitution on the Sacred Liturgy. If the genesis of Baltimore III is a guide, apparently neither western nor eastern bishops on the one hand, nor popes nor curia on the other have urged another plenary council in the United States. What has been the effect of this long, council-less gap in hierarchic legislation?

Suppose that, after 1884, the bishops had set a policy of plenary councils every twenty years: 1904, 1924, 1944 (or after World War II, 1947), and 1964 (or after the close of the Vatican Council II). In 1904, the most urgent matter on the agenda would have been a clear reply to the vague charge of "Americanism" that had emanated from a French misunderstanding of the American scene. The most practical items, however, would have dealt with the continuing disputes over nationalities, the Catholic University of America and the parochial schools. Concern for the Indians and Negroes could have been put on an adequate transdiocesan basis. College education for Catholic women was just starting; it needed a broader base. The agenda for a 1904 council would have been crowded, but effective laws and directives could have resulted.

World War I and its aftermath of the Ku Klux Klan, the communist scare, and the agitation for immigrant restriction would have provided contemporary material for a supposed council of 1924. The overhauling of Catholic missionary theory, explicit in Benedict XV's historic *Maximum Illud* (1919), was sharply pertinent to American Catholicism lest our own national problems obscure the universal dimensions of the Church. A tremendous start on these local problems was made within the coordinated framework of the NCWC, but this was incapable of legislation.

By 1924, however, a wealth of experience was available in many fields. Social reform, earlier advocated by the Federation of Catholic Societies, had now grown into the Conference on Industrial Problems. By 1924, the National Catholic Educational Association was twenty years old; the Extension Society (support for home missions), nineteen; the *Catholic Encyclopedia*, seventeen; the Holy Name Society, fifteen; the National Council of Catholic Charities, fourteen; Maryknoll (priests for foreign missions), thirteen; the National Newman movement, nine; and the Rural Life Bureau, three. Certainly this wide experience held conciliar possibilities: serious analysis of each movement, encouragement, coordination, pastoral directives and in some cases, national legislation.

Let us assume that World War II deferred the supposed council of 1944 until 1947. The nation had suffered the grim toll of depression and war, and besides, we had become a more citified, mobile, industrialized, and often anonymous people. Dangers inherent in these changes had been noted in the warnings of Pius XII when he greeted the American Church on the 150th anniversary of her hierarchy: materialism and excessive thirst for pleasure; the break-up in the family; the lost bonds between parents and children; and a "neglect of duty toward one's country and toward mankind." But Christian hope shone through the imperatives. Pius XII had encouraged collaboration with all those who acknowledge the supremacy of spirit over matter (1942), and inspired a whole new generation of thinking Catholics by the assurance of *Divino Afflante Spiritu* on the Bible, and *Mystici Corporis* on the Church (both in 1943). Liturgy's magna carta, *Mediator Dei*, was to come in 1947.

A groundswell of Catholic concern for God's worship and God's poor was beginning. The names of Dom Virgil Michel and Dorothy Day were known to those who searched, in the Church of the 1930's, for better answers to the persistent questions. Suburbanization, automation and prolific communication were post-war phenomena. The bishops were aware of their brave and struggling parallels in the new sociology of the parish, a growing Catholic voice in labor, and the birth of Catholic journals.

How much of all this spontaneity could be channelled through legislation, or should be, is quite debatable. John Cogley, in a recent column marked by his usual honesty, seems to think that the Church is healthier when bishops and experimenters (his word is "thinkers," which strikes me as rather exclusive) keep their distance. I do not agree. I do not think bishops, as successors of the apostles, should be insulated from personal contact with contemporary pioneers or critics. There is nothing in their role as pastor that inhibits involvement; on the contrary, it demands it. And their prophetical and priestly concerns will be more relevant to a needy world precisely to the extent that they are close to the "lay thinkers" as well as "lay leaders" of that world. Mr. Cogley prefers to keep the thinkers and the bishops in almost airtight compartments. I do not think it is quite that simple. As Carlyle wrote to the American historian, George Bancroft, after one of the latter's panegyrics on the United States, "All things have light and shadow."

The lights and shadows of 1947 could have supplied a fruitful agenda for a plenary council. Now, by hindsight, we know what a council can do that a conference does not. Vatican Council II has been a mighty event for the bishops:

— knowing each other better, and experiencing the unity of shared experiences;
— consulting learned specialists of every field in the Church's apostolate;
— broadening their visions of the Church catholic, beyond our own dioceses;
— bearing witness, before their fellow-citizens, to Catholicism as a spiritual force in the world;
— responding, as an episcopate, to the movement of the Holy Spirit.

National conferences became the custom after World War II. France, like the United States, began regular meetings at this time, but there only cardinals and archbishops met annually, the entire episcopate assembling only once every three years. Although the Latin American hierarchies held a plenary council in 1899, the new-style conferences began there only in 1955. Like our own NCWC, episcopal conferences have proved to be of tremendous help to the nations that held them. But only a true plenary council can provide the time, study and interaction needed for mature legislation. As in 1884, a council calls for work and courage. There will probably always linger in Rome the fear of a Gallican "nationalization" that would detract from papal power. And there will always be a few bishops resistant to collective action lest their own local autonomy be endangered.

It was the midwestern American bishops who insisted on Baltimore III in 1884. The stalwart prelate of Cleveland, Richard Gilmour, wrote to Gibbons: "The clergy need to be strengthened and protected against the people, and the people also against the irresponsible ways of the clergy, and the Bishop against them both." This aggressive approach, needed perhaps in the struggling 1880's, would not have recommended itself to a plenary council in 1947. Cardinal Suhard's great pastoral of that year, *Growth and Decline,* had given a new vision to the Church across the Atlantic: "Every day each one brings his stone to the common edifice." It was to be re-echoed two years later in Suhard's classic phrase, "The inseparable duality: priesthood-laity." An American plenary council could have given more impetus to the United States bishops' pastoral letter of 1947 on racial justice and perhaps evoked more response to the thought behind a small pamphlet published that year by the Catholic Association for International Peace: "Avoiding such a war [atomic] is the greatest moral obligation that lies on the countries of the world today."

Plenary councils in 1904, 1924 and 1947 would not have produced instant Utopia. But they could well have been a series of steps toward those "better and higher goals" to which Pius XII called America's bishops, priests and laity on their 150th birthday.

At the time of its establishment, many American bishops opposed the apostolic delegation. In the aftermath, how should the opposition be judged?

When the present apostolic delegate visited Charleston, South Carolina, for a Liturgical Week in 1960, we made a short tour of some missions, including "Catholic Hill" where the entire community is made up of third and fourth generation Negro Catholics. In introducing Archbishop Vagnozzi to Mr. Brown, the aging "patriarch," I explained that he was the apostolic delegate, but Mr. Brown did not grasp this. I tried again. "This is a representative of the Holy Father." Still no sign of recognition. Finally I said, "Joe, the archbishop works for the pope." A sudden light appeared in his eyes, and he said, nudging the Delegate, "Say, that's a good job you've got there."

The "job" has been held by a series of seven distinguished prelates since its inception in 1893. In the aftermath of Archbishop Satolli's part in the controversies of the 1890's, the position has called for continuing diplomacy. Its establishment was opposed by practically all the American bishops, whether progressive or conservative. Cardinal Gibbons had written the Holy See on January 3, 1893, through his "man in Rome," Monsignor Denis O'Connell, wanting to inform Rome that the American archbishops "with one exception, agreed that it would not serve the best interests of the Church, since the spirit of the people is not yet at a point where it would be favorably disposed to so great a benefit." But the letter was not delivered. O'Connell was told to withhold it; the apostolic delegation was established January 14, with Satolli as the first delegate.

Satolli's support of Archbishop Ireland encouraged the progressives, and John Conway, the editor of Ireland's newspaper, visualized the new arrangement as a kind of "ecclesiastical home rule" for the United States. But in 1895, Satolli reversed his support. The "Germanizers" adopted the new delegate and rejoiced with one of their historians, Reuben Parsons, when he said, "Faribaultism (has) ceased to flourish in Rome."

These judgments on Satolli, pro and con, arose from the highly emotional commitments of partisans. Any judicious analysis of the position itself was hardly possible in the furor of the 1890's. Gradually both sides came to live with the situation. The opinion of the American historian, John Tracy Ellis, on Cardinal Gibbon's feelings is worth quoting:

> Whatever misgiving the cardinal had entertained concerning the possible encroachment of the delegate upon the powers of the individual bishops had long since disappeared, and the valuable services which the papal representative rendered to bishops and priests in settling disputes and acting as a liaison man for their business with Rome convinced Gibbons of the worth of such an office.

The aftermath of the establishment has necessarily been a record of service in "settling disputes" and "business with Rome." As such, a great part of it has not been public. Changes in dioceses and provinces, to match the rapid Catholic growth, have required careful study by the delegate of every corner of American Catholicism. Necessary recommendations, after consultation with those concerned, are then made to the Holy See. This close attention to American needs, especially in such areas as the South and Southwest, goes largely unnoticed. More newsworthy, in the public eye, is the personal appearance of the Pope's representative at the installation of a new bishop or the erection of a new province.

Occasionally the voice of the delegate is heard in public affairs, in accents tuned to the American ear. Archbishop Satolli, at the World's Parliament of Religions in Chicago, 1893, urged his audience:

> Go forward, in one hand bearing the book of Christian truth, and in the other, the constitution of the United States. Christian truth and American liberty will make you free, happy and prosperous.

The same reassuring note was struck by the present delegate, Archbishop Vagnozzi, in a symposium honoring Leo XIII in 1960:

> As far as the United States is concerned, I feel that it is a true interpretation of the feelings of the hierarchy and of American Catholics in general to say that they are well-satisfied with their constitution and pleased with the fundamenal freedom enjoyed by their Church; in fact, they believe that this freedom is to a large extent responsible for the expansion and consolidation of the Church in this great country.
>
> Whether they remain a minority or become a majority, I am sure that American Catholics will not jeopardize their cherished religious freedom in exchange for a privileged position.

The bishops' opposition to an apostolic delegate in the early 1890's was launched by three fears: interference with their own episcopal rights; uncertainty as to which grouping of forces he would give support; and the anticipated anti-Catholic attacks against "Romanism." They were not opposed to authority as such. The American tradition has always been one of loyalty to the Holy See. As Dr. Robert D. Cross expressed it, they welcomed the delegate's authority "as a final check, but did not desire it as a tireless omnipresence."

This is characteristically American, and the solution of the "delegate question" has been a pragmatic one. The quiet and generally effective collaboration of seven delegates and hundreds of American bishops is a tribute to the skill, prudence and faith of both.

> *A number of bishops (in the early 1890's) expressed the need for a formal representative of the American Church in Rome rather than for a representative of the Pope in this country. Would such a proposal have any merit today? Had it been acted upon in the 1890's might it have affected the future of the American Church, particularly during the Americanist crisis?*

When Bishop Gilmour of Cleveland visited Rome in 1882, the question of an American episcopal representative in Rome or an apostolic delegate in the United States was very much on his mind. On his return from Rome, he wrote to Bishop McQuaid: "I much fear the intent is to send here, and not from here there." This succinct prophecy proved accurate. His displeasure was expressed again when he was sent to Rome to insure the approval of the Baltimore decrees of 1884:

> Why the American hierarchy should shrink from urging and insisting on their work being maintained, I do not see . . . What in God's name were we called together for? Was it to play lawmakers and then let our laws be thrown in the fire by Roman officials who but imperfectly understand our needs?

This was a widespread conviction among American bishops at that time. They wanted their own representative in Rome as England had theirs, Edward Cardinal Howard. Bishop Keane reported in 1883 that the Pope also wanted some similar arrangement and cited the three German cardinals in the Curia whom he consulted on matters German. For ten years, Denis J. O'Connell, while rector of the American College in Rome, did liaison work of this kind, informing the pope of American affairs and acting as intermediary for the American bishops. O'Connell's role was unofficial, however, with no formal recognition from the Holy See and no designation from the bishops.

This was precisely the flaw in the arrangement; it was not official. O'Connell was of the same mind as Gibbons, Ireland and Keane, and of course at odds with Corrigan of New York, his suffragans, McQuaid and McDonnell, and the German leaders. The liaison necessarily came to an end when O'Connell was forced to retire from the rectorship in 1895.

The selection of an American spokesman and intermediary, if conducted with due regard to the entire episcopate and the position of the apostolic delegate, could be quite beneficial. The choice should be a man thoroughly conversant with the Roman manner, yet thoroughly American in spirit; sympathetic to the majority of the bishops, yet not identified with a particular group; skilled in theology, history, canon law and languages. He would surely be as much help to the Holy See as to the Church in the United States. Selected and supported by our hierarchy, he would not be dependent upon an office or position in the central government of the Church. In many ways, he would complement the apostolic delegate so that the precise role of each would be preserved.

If this plan had been adopted in 1893, the Church could have been spared some of the bitterness of the school controversy caused by Satolli's turn-about. Certainly wise counsel by a representative American bishop in Rome could have calmed the fears of the Holy See about "Americanism" in 1897-98. As Gibbons wrote soon after

Pope Leo's letter about the errors doubtfully grouped under the term "Americanism": "It is very discouraging to us that the American Church is not understood abroad, and that its enemies are listened to, and that they can lie with impunity."

The cardinal was unquestionably wishing that the fear of his deceased friend, Bishop Gilmour, "to send here, and not from here there" had not proved true. A good man from here could have helped the Church there. The need is evident now, in the concern of Pope Paul and the council fathers, for a kind of "Apostolic Senate" in Rome. Its scope would, however, be more universal than particular, and the need of an American representative for American concerns would still exist. The spectrum of universals is more than the sum of all the particulars. But unless the particulars are attended to, the dream of universals may remain just that — a dream.

During the nineteenth-century controversies, Archbishop Corrigan constrained his suffragans to join him in criticism of Archbishop Ireland. Could this kind of pressure be exerted by a metropolitan today?

Archbishop Ireland was a midwestern, outspoken social reformer, a Republican, and not a prelate to feel constrained by diocesan boundaries. Archbishop Corrigan was an easterner, a Democrat tolerant to Tammany Hall, and opposed to the social betterment activities of priests like McGlynn and Ducey. They were vigorously at odds in the school controversy, but it was the congressional elections of 1894 that broke open their antipathy into a public scandal. Corrigan had already refused Ireland permission to speak on temperance at Chickering Hall in New York.

In the fall of 1894, Ireland appeared at Republican rallies in New York, speaking forcefully and aligning himself with party policies. The archbishop of New York was, understandably, furious. There was no need for him to line up his suffragans against the St. Paul prelate. Brooklyn's McDonnell was a protege of Corrigan, who in turn was a protege of Rochester's McQuaid. Both were of the same mind as the archbishop. McQuaid delivered a scathing, personal attack on Ireland in his cathedral on November 25.

Ireland's conduct in New York, in the words of one Catholic historian, had presented "an unbecoming spectacle before the general public." But McQuaid's attack was censured by Cardinal Rampolla on behalf of Pope Leo.

The authority of a metropolitan over a province is quite minimal in canon law today. Only the peculiar missionary status of American

Catholicism in the nineteenth century allowed the archbishops the influence exerted by Gibbons, Corrigan and others. In this incident, no pressure was needed. In any similar situation today it would not be permitted.

Dioceses in the early American Church were necessarily small. Is the immense size of many present American dioceses a hindrance to the mission of the bishops or is it a help?

The constant division of American dioceses since 1900 has rasied their number from seventy-seven to one hundred twenty in 1964. A diocese can be immense in two ways:

a) in size, with relatively few Catholics to support the needs; e.g. in many southern and western mountain states;

b) in numbers, with a relatively small area; e.g. the great metropolitan centers where close pastoral care is difficult.

The Church in the United States has valiantly tried to meet these difficulties. The large, sparsely Catholic diocese is helped generously by the American Board of Missions, the Catholic Church Extension Society, the Commission for Indians, the Catholic Missions among the Colored People, and the Missionary Cooperative program. Religious orders, both men and women, have been the willing collaborators with the bishops of many of these dioceses. To match a growing native clergy in these areas, diocesan seminarians and priests from more Catholic centers often volunteer to serve the Church where priests are few.

But the problems of "many Catholics, small area" in the big city complexes are equally pressing, and in the long range of Catholic history, far more acute. With thousands of members, a parish can easily tend to become institutionalized, rather than intensely pastoral. A diocese runs the same risk, centralization at the cost of a personal, diversified approach to its people.

One of the difficulties attached to the division of dioceses is a material one, the necessity of multiplying certain central facilities. A church can be converted into a cathedral, but a chancery and other administrative offices are needed. Interdiocesan coordination in training of priests, as in the provincial seminary of the Province of Detroit, will certainly increase quality while it decreases costs. But certain welfare institutions, as for example the care of dependent children or the aged, would seem to flourish in a more Christian and homelike manner on local grounds. There is no set pattern; rather, the field is open for imaginative planning and repeated testing.

The clergy in Germany have a popular saying that the best pastoral assignment is one "close to the railroad station, far from the throne (of the bishop)." An idealization of the new spirit in the Church might be attempted in this formula for priests: "Close to the people, near to brother priests, in touch with the bishop." *Mutatis mutandis*, the same might well be said of the bishop and the diocese.

> *Many American bishops in the nineteenth century believed themselves to have a mandate to introduce the Church universal to the benefits of liberal democracy. They saw this mandate in terms of bringing the Church into a more realistic relation with secular culture. Is there a similar sense of mission among the bishops today? Has the American Church made the contribution to world Catholicism which the nineteenth century bishops foresaw? If not, what are the reasons?*

A dream can be realized only when certain conditions are fulfilled: a) the ability of the dreamers to reproduce their kind, those who will understand and want the outcome of the dream; and b) the continuing validity of the dream's content in a new era.

Archbishop Ireland and the open-minded prelates of the late nineteenth century had a dream of the Church's mission to the world, to the age, and to the United States. Three times in Baltimore – in 1884, 1889, and 1893 – Ireland sketched its outline. In an elegant flow of rhetoric, he defined it: "I preach the new, the most glorious crusade. Church and Age! Unite them in the name of humanity, in the name of God!" The dream's essence was that the Church herself must be renewed, adapting herself to the new world in manner and method:

> The need of the world, the need of the Church, today as at other times, but today as never before, is men among men, men who see farther than others, rise higher than others, act more boldly than others . . . . Today, routine is fatal.

The unswerving faith and spiritual incentive of the Church, in Ireland's mind, could help the nation, but he was equally concerned that the open institutions of our country — schools, unions, societies, religious liberty, free speech and the concept of the state itself — should help the Church universal.

The dreamers did not, at least in the next generation, reproduce like-spirited bishops. Spalding commented in 1902, "Our great sees are largely in the hands of men who have lost their vigor of mind and body." The pioneers like Gibbons, Ireland, and Spalding himself were growing older. Younger men like the midwest's Muldoon, Schremb and O'Hara, sensed this mutual gift-giving of Church and nation, but

Ireland's phrase, "Routine is fatal," described in part the failure of many growing sees to take their part in the needed adaptation. Despite the increasing papal directives, the same hesitancy can be seen in the Catholic histories of almost every other nation.

Was the dream of the American progressives valid? Some items in it were fanciful: that Protestantism would eventually decline. Others were peripheral: that cardinals and archbishops should be the friends of presidents. Some parts of the dream were flamboyant, skirting the secular optimism of an Andrew Carnegie or a Russell Conwell. The brew of American nationalism in the years before 1914 was a heady draft, even for serious-minded prelates like Ireland.

But the heart of the dream was sound. And in the multiplication of schools and the awakening of the Catholic social conscience to the requisites of justice, it continued to beat. These two great movements owed much to the obvious growth and needs (both educational and economic) of the Catholic minority. They served as primary symptoms of health. That part of the liberal dream at least was being realized.

But Ireland had posed further direct challenges that called for an even more dynamic response:

> Go down in sympathy to the suffering multitude, bringing to them charity and, what is more rarely given, justice . . . Seek out social evils, and lead in movements that tend to rectify them . . . . The Church must regain the scepter of science which she wielded for ages . . . . Let us be the patrons of knowledge. Let us be the most erudite historians, the most experienced scientists, the most acute philosophers . . . . Layman need not wait for priest, nor priest for bishop, nor bishop for pope . . . . The Church has no fear of democracy . . . The Catholic Church will preserve as no human power, no human church can preserve, the liberties of the Republic.

He called for engagement, commitment, involvement. "To sing lovely anthems in cathedral stalls, and wear copes of broidered gold while no multitudes throng nave or aisle, and while the world outside is dying of spiritual and moral starvation — this is not the religion we need today!"

Well, there are multitudes today in the naves and aisles — despite the anthems and copes! — but Ireland's threats remind us that not all that needed doing was done! Certainly until the mid-forties, open demonstrations for justice, scientific and cultural challenges and clear-cut statements of the Christian case for democracy and liberty were not popular themes. Here and there, a bishop, a priest or a layman spoke out and acted, but the ferment did not really begin until World War II ended. From 1945 to 1962 it grew more urgent.

Then, in the debates of Vatican Council II, the wide fissures in American hierarchical thought became evident to the public — in liturgy, the sources of revelation, and collegiality, for example. A definite "sense of mission" was quite apparent: in the interventions on behalf of religious liberty and the Jews by Cardinals Cushing, Meyer and Ritter and Archbishops Alter, Shehan and O'Boyle. Bishop Primeau insisted on a wide area of lay responsibility; Bishop Tracy stood firmly on racial equality, and Bishop Helmsing accented ecumenical openings. Gibbons, Ireland and Spalding would have understood their concerns. So, in the earlier climate of Vatican Council I, would Purcell, Verot and Kenrick.

The American contribution to world Catholicism will not be quite what the enthusiastic bishops of the late nineteenth century imagined. This generation is making its own contribution, more in keeping with the tensions and crises of our times. It is a pastoral contribution, despite the current caricatures of "brick-and-mortar prelates," "real estate bishops," and "computer churchmen" so loosely made today. Caricatures can be useful, but they make rather dubious history, especially to describe a generation of bishops who for decades have been spending most of their hours administering the sacraments of confirmation and holy orders, counselling priests, and planning places to house God's people for the hearing of His Word and the partaking of His Body.

The contribution will be ecumenical as well as pastoral. No faster, but no slower, than the rest of the Catholic world, and in pursuance of the Holy See's directives, American bishops have become accustomed to moving easily among those of other faiths. Authentic ecumenism is more likely to advance in regions of two or three dominant churches than in the unplotted and undisciplined pluralism of hundreds of creeds. American steps toward unity have often faltered because of the mixture of secular and sacred objectives. Three earnest and intelligent churchmen with a genuine desire for dialogue have often found themselves thwarted in a panel by a bland chairman or "religious coordinator" who sums up their efforts with a triumphant, "Well, it doesn't really matter what a man believes as long as, etc." Yet in spite of our rampant pluralism and coexistent secularism, the ecumenical future of American Catholicism is reasonably bright.

But this Catholic contribution to the pastorate of the Church universal and the religious unity of the world will bear its own American trademark. Friends and critics alike acknowledge the activity of Catholic life in the United States. Scripturally, this is contained in our Lord's injunction: "Not everyone who says to me, 'Lord, Lord,' shall enter the Kingdom of heaven; but he who does the will of My Father in heaven shall enter the Kingdom of heaven." In blunt Texan language, Bishop Stephen Leven defended a true ecumenism against its critics in these words:

> It is not our people who miss Mass on Sundays, refuse the sacraments, and vote the Communist ticket.... We have not lost the working classes. Let us proceed in an orderly way with the examination and study of this providential movement called Ecumenism so that with patience and humility we may achieve that unity for which our Lord prayed at the Last Supper.

Theologically, activism is a bad word. But the ideology of the Kingdom, revealed and reasoned, must be actualized in the lives of Christians. The Church in the United States needs theologians, Scripture scholars, liturgists and canonists, but they will not replace the pastor. They can help him, opening his eyes to new facets of the truth, his lips to more effective catechetics, his heart to deeper theological concern for the world.

Both pastor and scholar have their roles. So does the bishop, bringing the two together not only for internal Christian dialogue but for a wider sense of mission, in the light of the American experience.

> *There were many more lay-edited journals in the Church of the nineteenth century than there are today. What are the major factors in this development: a different attitude on the part of the laity? a more authoritarian role by the bishops? greater expense involved in publications today? the existence of more secular channels for the lay voice than were open to the immigrants?*

Catholic journals of the last century offer a striking contrast to those today. Many of them began and continued as less religious and more nationalistic in tone and content; this was true of both Irish and German periodicals. But the more enduring ones, some begun by laymen, some by bishops, adopted a broad Catholic appeal. This was demonstrated, as one historian has noted, by their "courage to face abuse, the steadfastness to swim, as it were, against the national stream, and the daring to say what would inevitably be challenged."

These characteristics — a reasoned defense of Catholicism, an application of principles to the American scene — marked the best of the Catholic newspapers in the latter decades ·of the century. Included in such a list would be the *Pilot* of Boston, the *Catholic Universe* of Cleveland, the *Catholic Mirror* of Baltimore, the *Pittsburgh Catholic,* the *Catholic Telegraph* of Cincinnati, and the most famous of all, the *Freeman's Journal* of New York. Most of these were edited by laymen

who, whether liberal or conservative, felt free to take positions opposed
by their own or other bishops, as Daniel Callahan has observed. Cardinal Gibbons' policy of "general aloofness toward editorial policies"
was by no means universal, but the frequent protests of bishops that
the paper was not their official organ indicate a rather wide area of
freedom for the lay and priest editors.

By 1890, however, most of the outspoken editors of the century,
except Condé Pallen of St. Louis, had died or retired from journalism.
The list included Thomas D'Arcy McGee, James A. McMaster, John
Boyle O'Reilly, Manuel Tello and Maurice Francis Egan. With a few
exceptions, the diocesan press entered a long period of doldrums.
Unofficial journals usually found the financing too difficult to endure
for long. As in many other areas, the revitalization of the Catholic
press had to await the end of World War II; only a few independent
journals began in the 1930's the much-needed task of influencing
reader opinion.

The aims of a diocesan newspaper are so complicated and subject
to editorial stance and its coverage must be so diffuse that comparison
is a risky task. One decade's Pulitzer may become the next decade's
pot-boiler. Nor can Catholic journalism be practised in a world of
angelism. In our times, independent financial support is even harder
to come by than in the 1890's. That a diocese sets out to publish a
paper – launch it or buy it, finance it, house it and lend moral authority
to its circulation – is not surprising. That it should choose its editor
well, whether layman or priest, and then provide him with the tools
and freedom to do the job — this is not surprising either. Sometimes,
however, these two non-surprises collide in a surprisingly explosive
encounter. A preventative, if not a cure, for such a clash is fortunately
at hand: a special sense of responsibility for the truth on the part of
the publisher, and of responsibility toward the Church on the part
of the editor.

In reply to the specific questions, Are fewer laymen editing Catholic
journals today? Possibly, and I am not sure that a priest *qua* priest
is any better or worse editor than a layman *qua* layman. Are greater
expenses involved today? No question of that, but I am not sure of
its relevance to this question. Does the lay journalist's attitude differ
today? I suppose it does; every member of the Mystical Body should
have in our times a more discerning view of his role. This is true of
bishops too. Are they more authoritarian than in 1890? In my opinion
they are less so. The American hierarchy (except for two bishops)
carefully watched the two lay Catholic congresses, in 1889 and 1890,

with anxious eyebrows raised. Although the assemblies proved to be a remarkable outpouring of lay initiative and loyalty, the bishops did not encourage their continuation. But today's myriad conventions usually find laity, clergy and hierarchy working together over reasonably significant agenda.

The last named factor — more secular channels available for the lay voice today — is the most hopeful sign of all. We need lay spokesmen on diocesan papers, but even more we need Catholics raising their voices in accents that a secular society can appreciate in every worthy channel of communication: learned journals and popular magazines, books and lectures, classrooms and laboratories, government and community programs, all the arts and all the sciences. They must speak not specifically as Catholics but as highly skilled and accessible persons.

They enter this cultural mainstream not as propagandists but as men and women formed in Christ's image by baptism and confirmation, nourished by the other sacraments, versed in the Word of God and the mature theology of the Church. They are not apologists nor special pleaders, but intellectuals in the ancient and honorable Christian usage of the term.

If one of these laymen is also possessed of journalistic competence, he should have little trouble obtaining a position on a Catholic journal — if he and the publisher will both make the sacrifices that are needed.

CATHOLICISM IN A NEW SOUTH

On 24 April, 1965, Archbishop Hallinan delivered an address before the Archdiocesan Council of Catholic Women in Macon, Georgia. Although the address was intended to be of local interest only, it received national attention. This represents the major portion of that address; local references have been deleted.

The Ku Klux Klan and their collateral cousins who scorn Jews, resent Catholics, and oppress Negroes are in agony. Out of this grows their boldness and their desperation. Hate must have a focus, someone or some group to be feared and yet despised. But now, a new fact has blurred that focus; minority groups are losing their minority traits. The Jewish religious and cultural contributions to American life, the Negroes' refusal to accept a way of life that means "no voice, no vote, no veto," the world interest in Catholicism have changed the picture. The hate groups, long used to thinking of Jews, Negroes and Catholics as aliens and outsiders, find themselves frustrated to the point of fever and agonized to the point of violence. There must be laws to restrain this violence, and there must be a stronger public opinion to nullify their efforts, but we must pray for them too. They are often sick people and like Christ's persecutors, "they know not what they do."

Catholicism, at long last, finds itself in a new role in the changing South. We have been here a long time, but our numbers were small, and our cultural and social influence has not been great. Yet the South was settled by French and Spanish Catholics in the sixteenth and seventeenth centuries. The Church flourished in Savannah in the early 1800's. Despite swamps and rugged trails, cholera and malaria, Catholic laymen, with intrepid bishops and untiring priests, guarded the faith and worked together that God might give the increase. Still few in population, they wrote a glorious page in the 1920's and 1930's. The Georgia Catholic Laymen's Association fought ignorance and bigotry, firmly but courteously, intelligently and charitably, winning a wide respect for their courage. As late as 1955, Archbishop O'Hara and Rev. Dick Houston Hall, of the First Baptist Church in Decatur, engaged in a quiet, mannerly dialogue by letter. These tireless efforts slowly brought to the Catholic Church a gain in respect, a fair hearing in newspapers, radio and television, and in many other pulpits. The Catholics in Georgia a century ago can scarcely be called a minority group when a priest like Father O'Reilly prevented General Sherman from burning three government buildings and four Protestant churches as well as his own, and the city of Atlanta erected a monument in the 1940's to honor this priest and his early ecumenical vigor.

The new fact today is that the whole world is watching us. Catholicism has been emerging for seventy years, but this long process was personalized in Pope John XXIII and actualized in the present Vatican Council. Now all of us must sharpen our vision. Our prayer must be that of the man in the Gospel who was born blind, "Lord, that I might see!" We must make an honest and continuing effort to grasp the present scene, to reach out, take hold of, to grasp our present situation.

The Church is never chained to its past. Its characteristic marks are One, Holy, Universal and Apostolic, but not Rigid. Our founder, the Lord, built it upon a rock, but He referred to it as a vine. So all of today's changes, especially those related to divine worship, can be understood only if we learn and re-learn what the Church is. I recall the shock and sadness with which I once heard a family protest the presence of another racial group at their Mass, "This is our church — our grandfather built it!" As if it were a private club to which they belonged! What a far cry from the Scriptures and from the new Constitution on the Church! The Church is Christ's own mystical body, and the eye cannot say to the hand, "I have no need of you." The Church is God's holy people, united by the Spirit to each other and to God.

THOSE IN NEED

Besides our new look at the Church, we must open our eyes more clearly to the fact that our first mission as Christians is to the poor, those in need, the destitute, the dispossessed, the diseased, the disenchanted, both those we know, and the faceless, anonymous ones we often do not even see. This is not a problem for a vague humanity; it is a personal and corporate problem for us. The record of Catholicism in the southern states is encouraging: homes for the aged, for dependent children, for cancer victims and a dozen other areas where compassion is our duty. Despite the small percentage of Catholic population, the Church has gone out to the immigrant, the waves of Europeans in the nineteenth century, the Cubans and Puerto Ricans today.

The poor are those in need of jobs, homes and education, but the situation of the Negro in the South spotlights a far more basic need. Man can somehow live for a while without income or a home, but if he is not accorded human dignity, nor guaranteed equal opportunity, he cannot live as a child of God was meant by his Creator to live.

Slavery was an investment, but it was inhuman. Segregation was a legality, but it placed a stigma upon a whole people. The Catholic Church lived for decades with this legality because it had little choice to do anything else, but it never really bought it. There has never been a denominational body known as "the Negro Catholic Church." The Negro mission chapel or school was not intended to segregate him but to reach and teach the Negro wherever he was. If some Catholics, influenced by the customs of the community, called it a "Negro parish" to limit Negroes to it, they knew that they were contradicted by the words and spirit of the very Mass they were attending. We were slow in pioneering because we had neither the means nor the influence, but we were usually ahead of most other institutions. We went slowly because we had to co-exist in a culture we had never made. Sometimes the Catholic, speaking as a southerner, might take on the protective coloring of his white community and repeat its empty phrases, just as the Catholic, speaking as a city man in the North, might tolerate the rotten and corrupt government of these same cities. But both the northern and southern Catholic, speaking as a Catholic, knew in his heart that injustice is evil, and discrimination and corruption are unjust.

THOSE OF OTHER FAITHS

Finally, our eyes must open today to those of other faiths. We know them as relatives, neighbors, friends, co-workers, fellow-citizens. But we must seek to know them as children of God. Especially is this true of other Christians, marked as we are by the same baptism, formed as we are in the God-given wisdom of the Bible, and addressing themselves, as we do, to the one God whom we can call Our Father. This too is not new to Catholics in the South. Despite pockets of bigotry, a wide and honest fellowship has flourished. Now it must be nourished in this new climate of ecumenical understanding, enlivened by prayer, and given common tasks to do in the public welfare. There is here no abandonment of our precious heritage; the doctrine and worship of the Church is not changing, as Pope John said, only its spirit and its forms. This deposit of faith must be guarded carefully, but we must study how other churches have come to regard it. Every man's conscience must be his guide, but it must be an enlightened conscience, alive to truth wherever it may be found. We must be careful, prudent, obedient, or we will make a mockery of our faith and a setback to genuine unity. But we must at the same time be open, courageous and charitable, or we will betray that trust our Lord placed in us at the Last Supper when He prayed that all may be one.

As we begin to see with eyes more fully opened, we will find that we must strain them to see clearly, as we do when we enter a partly-lighted room. The changing history of the Church has been one of full light and dark shadows, but it has never been totally in the dark. Christ, our Master, is after all "the Light of the World." For the past several centuries, the forces of history have dimmed the full light of Catholicism. Our popes and bishops have taught faithfully, and our priests and laity, those beloved pastors and parents of our early memories, have struggled to believe and to live as loyal, courageous members of the Church. There may have been much routine in our catechisms, but they held the line. If we thought of "going" to confession, or "getting" to Mass, these were unfortunate expressions that did not diminish our sorrow over sin, or our joy in receiving the Eucharist. Although we often joined others in using the Bible as a private stock of texts to throw at each other, we rejoiced to hear those Gospel narratives over and over again. The sacraments were our means of grace, even though marriage had become pretty much of a fashion-show, and the sacrament that was intended as a source of strength for the sick was thought of as a farewell to the dying. Spiritually, these past generations, now the subject of so much foolish pity or even scorn, grew mightily. Out of their faith has come the new vigor of the Catholic Church today. Pope John, the apostle of the *aggiornamento*, came from peasant stock and simple faith, not unlike that of our own ancestors. A real renewal, such as the Church is living today, cannot come out of a vacuum. It is formed by present needs and fresh insights, but it must draw its strength chiefly from the God-guaranteed treasures of the centuries since He said, "I will be with you all days."

DAWN IN GEORGIA

Now we are at the dawn, and our eyes strain to see the old realities in the new light. Dawn in Georgia is a very beautiful time of day. The red clay takes on a richer, more variegated hue; the pines stand no longer as specters of the night but as sentinels to the beauty of God's world of nature. The Church has been at home here a long time. Now it is asking us to grasp more fully, as dawn gives way to daylight, what we are and what we are for. We are a part of the Church. God's own holy people. We are the Church of the poor, of all those who are in need — of food, or help, or human dignity. And we are the Church universal, praying that we may take those steps marked for us in God's providential plan, the steps toward the unity of all men who love God, are formed in Christ and moved by the Holy Spirit.

THE CHURCH IN SOCIETY

During the closing days of July, 1965, the leaders of the Catholic Church in the South met in Atlanta for the first Southern Catholic Leaders' Conference on Social Change and Christian Response. On 29 July, 1965, Archbishop Hallinan delivered this keynote address.

The Catholic Church in every age has been faced with issues which are universal in scope and moral in their solution: lust, injustice and blasphemy, for example. Her judgments have been clear and the record of Christianity is there for all to see. She has fostered the Christian home against lust, the dignity of man against injustice, and the majesty of God against blasphemy. But at given moments, she has faced problems that are particularized in time and place. As she applies the moral law to these problems, she moves out of the pulpit into the existential marketplace of everyday realities. Sometimes her teachers and her disciples have misread the times and misapplied the pure teachings of the Gospel and the *magisterium*. It is easier to judge these instances by hindsight than at their given moment.

We are now engaged in Vatican Council II in fixing the Church's role in the society of the twentieth century. The schema, *The Church in the Modern World,* reads like a healthy commentary on the hopes and anguish of our world and a spiritual prognosis for its improvement. In the spirit of Popes John and Paul, it is contemporary and open in a way that the *Syllabus of Errors* of Pius IX never was.

The times and temporalities are never easy to read. We have only to think back to St. Augustine's sincere conviction that the world is totally hostile, or to the theologians of the eighteenth century who favored the state as a royal patron of the Church, or to those nineteenth-century writers who feared and denounced the progress of modern thought and science.

For a century, the Church has seemed to a restless world that she was speaking from a beleaguered bastion. But this appearance was deceptive. Seeds of inquiry and experimentation were being carefully nurtured. No decade since 1870 has been devoid of internal criticism

103

and patient observation of the fantastic advances in science and technology. Those who today betray a syndrome of impatience ("Nothing ever happened until Pope John and I came along!"), need to study more Church history, especially recent Church history. They will be far less impatient and more ready for mature reflection and action.

In the transformation now indicated by the changing role of the Southern Negro leader, the Northern liberal, and the white community, what is the proper function for the Catholic Church, for religion in general? Economics and politics, pressures and structures of power are far more evident than in the pioneer phase of racial improvement. These changes at first glance seem to lean toward a secularization of those earlier ideals of "witnessing one's faith" and "creating communities of forgiveness." But this is a superficial reading. There has been no evidence that the biblical injunction is now invalid: "Unless the Lord builds the house, they labor in vain who build it."

Dr. Martin Luther King told the Chicago Conference in 1963: "The ultimate solution to race problems lies in the willingness of men to obey the unenforceable." He added, "Here, then, is the hard challenge and sublime opportunity: to let God work in our hearts toward fashioning a truly great nation." In a paper on "True Believers in the Movement," Dr. August Meier of Roosevelt University reported the resentment of many Negroes against the middle-class Northerner and his radical and beatnik colleagues. Now he sees some hope because a different type of white is coming from the North, youth deeply committed to the religious and national ideals, as the bulk of the Negroes themselves are. Bayard Rustin finds religious bodies as natural allies with Negroes, labor and liberals, and points out that especially in rural areas they were most effective in rallying support for the civil rights bill.

To clarify the thinking of those, both white and Negro, Catholics and those of other faiths, who see the entrance of clergy and sisters only as a showpiece or as protective coloration or as an irritant to a town or a community, the Church's role must be defined more clearly. A Negro leader who boasted last week that he would call up priests and nuns to demonstrate has lost the perspective of the extraordinary confrontation at Selma. Priests, nuns and bishops — and I would include ministers and rabbis, too — are not shock-troops to be exploited. They are witnesses to justice and love, giving their presence to communities where justice and love have been diminished. They have served well as witnesses of the Church's concern. Now when they come, they come as co-workers with the Negro in the great social development that is in process.

Another mistake is rooted in the old notion that the Church must be clerically composed and clerically committed. The laity's function (from Pope Pius XII's "You do not belong to the Church — you are the Church," down to the definition in the new Constitution on the Church — the people of God) is inspiring an entirely new grasp of what the Church means. Catholic institutions must, of course, share responsibility for moral leadership in racial justice, but laymen in their own secular professions and trades and work, their homes and neighborhoods, share an equal burden. Theirs is the work, as popes and the council have clearly stated, of the *consecratio mundi,* the consecration of the world.

The Church (bishops, priests, sisters, laity) must be, at the ordinary level of community life, a catalyst. Guided in moral deliberations of those commissioned to teach, sharing in the tedious as well as the imaginative areas of everyday life, God's people must initiate and quicken the Christian response as a catalyst accelerates the change in a chemical process.

What is needed here? First, dialogue constantly, conversational and formal, with other Christians and Jews, with Negroes and whites, with professionals and volunteers, with government at every level. Out of this will flow a twofold good: the ordained ministry can give moral direction at crucial points; the laity can give themselves to every practical and proper venture. These will include voter registration, Operation Headstart, steps toward education, job and housing progress. We cannot do everything at once, nor can we think of this grave and urgent task as the only task before us. But as the Southern bishops said recently, "The Catholic Church in the past has done in racial relationships what she could. Now she can do more." The chemical catalyst immerses itself to get the right reaction, yet it emerges unhurt and ready for more work. The Church will not do less.

Second, the Church (again, all of us) must bear the burden of conscience. The news media, colleges and government have their own reasons for interracial concern. Often these are high-minded and sincere. But sometimes they are more economic or political; sometimes it is to create the right image. These cannot be the motives of the Church. It is not to obtain power or a fine image that religion appeared on the picket lines. It is because religion has relevance to the tragic circumstance that called forth that demonstration. The Church must stand on moral ground when it leads the conscience of its followers. She should not wait for pressures of any kind, from whites or Negroes, from defenders of the status quo or spokesmen for this or that particular solution. The Church must speak with the same clarity she used in 1958: "Legal or compulsory segregation in itself and by its very nature imposes a stigma of inferiority upon the segregated people . . . . It is vital that we act now and act decisively . . . to seize the mantle of leadership from the agitator and the racist . . . . The heart of the race question is moral and religious."

The Church can do a real service here in redefining words that have slipped their theological moorings. "Prudence" is a good example. Rightly used, this is a virtue that inclines us to view problems in their proper perspective, to use proper means to secure our aim. But how often has this poor virtue been drained of meaning? It has been used as an excuse for our failure to face facts, as a form of "gradualism that is merely a cloak for inaction," to cite the bishops' statement again. Certainly we must avoid "a rash impetuosity that would sacrifice the achievements of decades in ill-timed and ill-considered ventures." The bishops proposed this question as a test of prudence: Are we sincerely and earnestly acting to solve these problems? Both the ragged segregationist and rugged agitator should find common sense in that. It is a litmus test for all. Is it the status quo, or power, or justice that we really want?

The Church is serving as a catalyst in the community, as the conscience of society. But no member of the living faith is content to stop there. As one of God's people, he enters the streets and stores and factories as a bearer of Christ. Marked by baptism and confirmation he must be in the world but not of it. St. Paul cautions us especially not to come to terms with it. What does this mean? It means that we must use our own strength as we have received it, a gift from Christ. We must follow in His footsteps and conform ourselves to His image, seeking the will of the Father in all things.

The spiritual effect of Christians who bear Christ in their lives upon the secular society of today would be tremendous. In the difficult and delicate field of interracial living it could change the angry tone, the fearful give-and-take, the structured format that our nation has tolerated since 1864.

Last year the author of *Our Faces, Our Words*, Lillian Smith, wrote that a terrible choice rests upon us:

> We, as a people, could be confronted soon by a series of catastrophes. Whether this happens depends on the wisdom of responsible Negroes, but more, much more on what every responsible white American does next. One thing is certain in a plexus of uncertainties, and that is, our encounter with the future cannot be evaded; it must be met by both the artist and the scientist in us, by our deep intuitions and

our vigorously proved knowledge — and by the human being in us, too, that creature who knows the power of compassion, the potency of a strange love that keeps reaching out to bind one man to another.

Certainly the Church — both teaching and taught, both sanctifying and sanctified, both laity and clergy — can never evade the future. She lives in pilgrimage, and her goal is the destiny of God's people in eternity. Now we are His people by grace, but then our fulfillment will be in the glory of His Son.

This conference is counter-posing two things: social change and Christian response. As serving Christians we must carefully scrutinize and analyze the change, and then help to activate the response. It is reasonable to say that we came here to do that. It must be just as reasonable to presume that we go home as those who enkindle the fire that Christ cast upon the earth. As catalysts, we can share in directing and hastening the change. As witnesses of a united conscience we must always measure these changes against the eternal truths. And as Christ-bearers we commit ourselves to the promise and the trust so integral to the mind and heart of the great apostle Paul:

All things are yours, and you are Christ's and Christ is God's.

THE MAN WHO HAS EVERYTHING—AND NOTHING

Every year, at least at Christmas and Easter, Archbishop Hallinan addressed a pastoral letter to the people of the archdiocese. This pastoral was chosen as another example of the Archbishop's pastoral concerns. This letter appeared in the 23 December, 1965, issue of the Georgia Bulletin.

My dear people in Christ:

Winter can be a cold and lonely time. And midnight is an hour of shadows, silence and solitude. Deep in the troubled human spirit, walking through a disjointed and turmoiled forest, the loneliness eats its malignant way. It lies like a funeral pall heavy on our brave, little thrusts toward freedom, our fresh ideas, even on our profound loves.

In December, in the dark of night, we pick our careful way. There is nothing of lively April in our step, no quiet assurance of the harvest so familiar to September. We fall, we rise, we plod along without joy.

What are we searching for? It is holy, but it is not a grail. It promises beyond a grail's satisfaction. It is a Being, a Being enough to satisfy our faint hopes and lift our uneasy hearts to the full measure of their loving. We seem to seek an unknown God. He seemed to be present in the brisk buoyancy of April and the fulfillment of September.

December has blacked out His presence in us. For December is the end of the year, the symbol of all that can go wrong with our lives. It signifies the drabness of a greenless dusty road, or a home, an office or a school corridor. It is a sign for the cruelty of an unkind cut, the failures we didn't deserve, the successes we didn't really want, the defiance of friends and the contempt of enemies.

But we have known in other years the guiding hand of God's fatherhood, and so we doggedly struggle on. We have seen His Spirit orbiting our world and lifting us out of our restless moods. And finally there is branded in the grooves of our awareness the memory of His Son.

We might, but for a quirk of genealogy, have been with Zachary and Elizabeth, walked with Joseph and Mary, listened to John, the solitary percursor, and Simeon who just waited for the glory of his God. In those pre-Christian times, our stubborn onward push through the forest would have been lit by the comforting flashes of the old prophecies. They are still our little lights, beckoning us on, warning us not to abandon the great Light ahead.

We might have been the apostles or the holy women of the first century or the scholars and peasants of the high Middle Ages, the confused and bitter Christians of the Reformation, the little saints and big sinners of any century. Their steps were more sure because life was simpler for them than for the prophets. We would have pushed on with them in greater trust. For a new reality was loose in the world. Not a prophet; not a god unknown and unloved. What is new and real and all-important in the Christian years was The Light of the World, so clear and radiant that any sense of unknownness can lie only in us, not in Him. The knowing rests in His spreading Word, and we have heard it.

Tonight we seek Him still. It is still a lonely journey for the man who thinks of himself alone. God is in history, but has that part of our history grown dim and distant? We call to Him now in the familiar old prayers, but only an echo comes back. We rap at the usual doors our spirit used to know so well. There seems to be no answer.

For one stark, shocking moment we gasp. He is no more. He is not in His heaven, and modern men who are wise in texts and legends assure us that He is dead. We cannot reach him in our prayers. He is not found in the limited loves of our tightly private society. Where is He?

We do not want to take the word of his learned undertakers that He is dead. But shouldn't He be at home at least on the night of His birth in time? The shepherds found Him. The wise men of an earlier day found Him, too. It took them longer because, perhaps like some of the wise men of our times, they had to come a greater distance.

Could the apparent failure lie in us? The thick scales of our blindness must be pierced with care. We are accustomed to the flickering candles of our facts. Dimly we are aware that the Light of man's history might blind us as we peer through the scales of our commonplaces. To tinker with the eyes is dangerous. And the letters of the apostles warn us that even perfect vision cannot really bring into our focus the meaning of the Child of Bethlehem.

No, it won't do. Faith must come by hearing, not by seeing. Slowly we stop our complaints and listen. We hear words out of the forest's density, words that have made men fall to their knees and bow their heads with unaccounted wonder:

The Word was made flesh, and dwelled among us.

That is why He seemed not to be at His home. In a sense, He had changed His address; He had taken a new residence on earth without ever taking leave of His Father in Heaven. That is why our dunning prayers raised no echo but their own. There is the reason for December's midnight cold and isolation. We thought we had to keep pushing. We forgot to be still and listen and learn that He was coming. We should have been waiting for Someone, but we didn't know it. The Son of God was on His way to us. He was coming to keep His rendezvous with mankind.

Our Brother, who is Christ the Lord, is on pilgrimage. He did not wait for us to come all the way to Him. Our seeking God is turned inside out. Now it is God that comes to man. The whole adventure of our life, loaded with destiny, is turned around. Now we are pilgrims too, but our Brother is our guide. We still know loneliness and fear, but now it is different. The root of Jesse has sprouted and grown and blossomed — Jesus is here. The key of David has opened the tight little prisons we built for ourselves. The dismal failures and fallen hopes of the past seem now like phantoms. Emmanuel, God with us, is the reality.

Now our consciousness catches fire. We look around. If Christ is my Brother, then He is your Brother too. You (whoever you are) and I (whoever I am) must be of the same family. No one is alone. We are one in Christ — on His Mother's side!

The pulsing of our hearts, lifted up, is heard in our voices. We do not sleep tonight; we sing! We find that the happy greeting, "Merry Christmas," can ill afford to be mumbled. A strange and bright expectancy rides upon our lips. Family and friends and neighbors come closer; even the unpleasant ones can evoke a new warmth. The circle widens. There are thousands in our city, millions in our world.

These are our brothers, too: the families of the four workmen who plunged to their deaths while they built a skyscraper in our city; little children too young to worry about civil rights and human dignity, but who want and need a little more to eat, something to hope for, a Christmas gift with some brightness to it; and the men who are leaving Georgia this week to fight in Vietnam.

Can we help them? Can we press their case before God in our prayers? Can we at least share enough humanity with them to think about them? Do we care whether another man exists or not?

Christmas brings joy, but it does not bring a narrow security. We sense that a great decision is being settled in our Christmas liturgy as it was in our Christmas history. But it will be settled not in my favor, but in ours. Christ lives in every man's circle of existence, sometimes at the center, sometimes on the periphery, but always in the totality of the People of God.

Can we share the blessings of this presence with other men? Only if we share ourselves. Christ has bought out our empty loneliness by His bounty. When I looked for Him in vain, it was because He had made His home in the souls of men. I could have easily found Him there. He became incarnate not in Peter, or in Paul, or even in His Blessed Mother. He became incarnate in all mankind.

No one is alone who shares the presence of God by sharing himself. A feeble, hungry old man in his wheelchair is not always the one who is lonely. He may have memories, a prayer or a good word for others. But the lonely man may well be the bouncy, boisterous host at the Christmas party, surrounded by attractive and admiring people, happily drowsy with food and drink, the man who has everything.

He has everything but God in his life and others in his heart. The old man in the wheelchair, solitary and abandoned, with his memories and his prayers and a good word for others now and then, he is the one who has everything — beloved by His God and loving every man.

God bless you all this Christmas night, your families and friends, our brethren of other faiths and of other nations, the children, the sick and the oppressed. May He bless you through the year!

PROBLEMS OF PRIESTS TODAY

Ironically, the bishop that most priests in the United States admired the most had very little to say about the problems of the priestly ministry. Perhaps it was because he lived so deeply the priestly vocation that he could not understand why other priests could have problems in their vocation. He did not, however, ignore the problems of his brother priests; he preferred to deal with them personally. In his sermon at the dedication of the major seminary of St. Vincent de Paul, Boynton Beach, Florida, on 25 January, 1966, he took the occasion to address his brothers in the priesthood.

Last Pentecost, bishops of the southeast joined in a pastoral letter. Probing into the 400-year missionary tradition of the southern colonies (later states), the bishops saw "a second springtime of Catholicism in this warm and gracious land."

> The Church is at home in the South. The majority of persons of other faiths share with us a genuine sense of God, a love for the Bible, a tradition of church membership, a courteous and gentle approach to others.

Racial strife and religious disunity have in the past betrayed this religious sense. But there are signs today that the South has learned her lesson, that in the social and ecumenical ventures of our churches the Catholic Church is "a hardy base on which Catholic laymen, side by side with those of other faiths, are raising a wiser, stronger, better society."

In this panorama of contemporary history, the dedication of a major Catholic Seminary is an event of the greatest importance. It is a bold apostolic move by Bishop Coleman Carroll. It is a tribute to the Vincentian Fathers who have always pioneered in seminary development. For the layman's formation the priest is of the essence, and for the training of the priest the seminary is the indispensable instrument. It is "a family" of students and teachers, "a closely-knit community" whose spirit and activity reflect the bishop's fatherhood, and to all the priests it is "the heart of the diocese."

The renewal of the living Church is noted in every document of the Second Vatican Council. With it go the series of reforms: liturgy, scriptural study, ecumenism, missions, and the two fundamental re-assessments, On the Church and On the Church in the World Today. This renewal and reform is of the highest *magisterium*: Pope and Council Fathers acting in their role of lawmakers of the Church Universal.

But the documents will be nothing but paper texts unless we read them in their context, make the changes called for, and a new context for tomorrow's Church. The context of Christ's message and mission does not change, but the manner and approach must be adapted to the needs of today. One of the most urgent demands today is the complete priest. He should ask why his predecessors, the priests who first inspired his vocation, his pastors, were hard-working, unselfish, loyal sons of the Church. He stands on their shoulders today not that he may lessen their stature, but that he might increase his own. The new approaches and resources lead him now to deeper insights. The new knowledge points to a vision possible only through faith. The pressing needs of the poor and the oppressed, the ordinary people and the intellectual, open the young priest's hands so that grace may flow through them. The complete priest does not resent change, because it multiplies his opportunities. Yet he loves the liturgy, the poor, the separated brethren too much to make hobbies of them. He sees each special service as a part of the priestly apostolate. His role is pastoral, not particularized. He is first of all an apostle and only secondarily a specialist in prophecy, evangelism, or other roles enumerated by Saint Paul or any added since.

The priest of today faces tremendous problems matched with a shocking personal responsibility. Of all the reforms called for in the Decree on Priestly Formation, the most urgent is to stop fragmentation. "You are one body with a single Spirit, each of you when he was called, called in the same hope; with the same Lord, the same faith, the same baptism." Instead the training of the priest has been split up so that his life is lived on several levels. Karl Adam warned us of this separation thirty years ago. It has been echoed by contemporary theologians, like Karl Rahner and Yves Congar. And Archbishop Garrone of Toulouse summed it up:

> Living in a seminary, I have always been struck by the way in which the technical differentiation of scholastic disciplines is calcu-

lated to set up compartments in the mind of the young priest. These may well nullify in his ministry the simple power of the word that nourishes and saves.

At the root of all the words, dogmatic and moral, canonical and historical, lies the Word itself: Christ incarnate in our flesh, in our manhood and mankind, and in the Church. Out of this unity the young priest grows and matures. It is here that the Council has advice for the perplexed candidate and the world he has lived in and will live in. The bridge between these two worlds must be carefully built. Formed of the Word of God, designed by His Spirit, it must be free enough not to be a rut, yet sure enough not to be a detour.

If a seminary training is truly integrated (in the dynamic, not racial sense of the word), its graduates will find that "to the extent he loves the Church of Christ, to that extent does he possess the Holy Spirit," in the words of Augustine.

In an open society — whether it be the Athens of Plato, the universities of the high Middle Ages, or the affluent society of our western world today — only the Complete Man can make his way. He need not be brilliant, but he must have good sound judgment. He need not be a crusader, but he must insist on justice. Taken from among men, today's priest must measure up to a dimension unheard of in the time of Leo XIII, John Henry Newman, Cardinal Gibbons. These three stood out because they were mature. Today every priest must have that dimension. Is today's candidate ready for the rugged, complex life ahead? Is today's seminary prepared to get him ready?

The Second Vatican Council provided the texts. It is now our task to fashion the context in which they will be heard and read. The job can be broken down into three questions.

First, how much does it mean to the candidate to be honored and popular, to be financially secure and socially accepted? The Decree gives him a criterion for this: ". . . a simple way of life, a spirit of self-denial . . . ." Does a priest or bishop, guaranteed his keep and his good name, really need more? The Church and her servants must be the Church of the Poor. But who is to be the judge of poverty? Which priest, for example, serves the Church better: the one who uses whatever he has doing good, as the Master did; or rather, the one who gazes coldly at the first, and criticizes him bitterly for his possessions? His is the charge made by the Pharisee in the temple. In the context of money and prestige, poverty can be a mean trap. We seldom judge others as we judge ourselves.

The second context to be formed for priestly training is the development (in charity) of the proper tension between freedom and authority. The Church here has an almost impossible job to do: produce priests who can think for themselves, and simultaneously obey their bishop or live with a domineering pastor. Following the rules of the Second Vatican Council, seminaries all over the world, and bishops and pastors too, are examining their own conscience, not hesitating to offer reasons for regulations, and not multiplying the phrase, "God's will," to describe every rule, every bell, every command. Out of all this is coming a human, humble, reasonable approach. Since obedience is a two-way street, I would presume that thousands of seminarians are examining their conscience too. They are trying to see what the common good means, what duties go with the freedom of responsibility, what great good (both personal and social) is possible when the root lies in a true motive of conscience. The Council points the way to a context in which the crisis of obedience is eased because the tension is made to flow on both sides.

And finally, a new context is needed for the privileged state of life through which a young man is called by a precious gift of God and to which he responds by his free and mature vow of celibacy. There are many practical reasons why the unmarried life better suits the priesthood in our Western society; the best one is named by the Decree, that "perfect charity whereby they can become all things to all men." And there are many forms of personal fulfillment; one is the union of husband and wife, another "the undivided love with which man can embrace the Lord." The priest who finds fulfillment in his work, teaching a child, a 3:00 a.m. sick call, a talk on racial justice, the endless ministry of the sacraments and the Eucharist — this priest is not likely to start thinking that conjugal love is the only fulfillment. Most priests are enriched, not deprived, by celibacy. After all, an adult, free choice made in the form of a vow can hardly be flicked aside like the dream-wish of a child.

The texts for the updating of Christ's Church are available. It is the new context into which they must fit that needs immediate care. One of your own seminary leaders, the Vincentian teacher, Father Stafford Poole, summed up the burden ahead:

> All this means that everything in the seminary must have a real, but not necessarily immediate, relevance to the priesthood.

> It must lead to the priesthood, and it must help in some way to form the student for the particular work in the Church that he is going to be charged with.

It adds up to a great task, one vital to the very life of God's people. It is a task worthy of a family, and here is the family: Archbishop Vagnozzi, representative of the Holy Father; Bishop Carroll, successor of the apostles in the diocese of Miami; other distinguished prelates; your own administration and faculty; and you the students. You can be sure that the bishops present are at work in this urgent and noble field, the traininng of priests. What I invite you to, in the spirit of the Second Vatican Council, is the harmony and unity of seminarians and priests as they pray and study, discuss and experiment in the shaping of this new context, finally reaching a true commitment, which in turn may need to be revised from time to time.

No priest was ever built by a piece of paper. Many have been formed by a good priest they knew in their youth. But every priest is ultimately made of mind and will and heart, by the imposition of a bishop's hands, and the grace of God that is sufficient for us.

TWO TASKS UNFINISHED

In February, 1966, Archbishop Hallinan was invited to address the "Hungry Club" of Atlanta. The text of his address was duly recorded in the Georgia Bulletin *on 3 February, 1966. This major excerpt of the address is significant because of the Archbishop's position on ecumenical activity and civil rights.*

There is so much going on inside the Catholic Church today that nearly everybody is curious. Instead of Latin, much of the Mass is in English. Instead of ignoring Protestants, we now say the Lord's Prayer with them, and on certain occasions join in Bible services in their churches. Instead of a silent laity, our people are singing out, speaking out, giving advice and criticism to their priests and bishops when needed. No wonder that Protestants are puzzled, and uninformed Catholics are confused.

When all the bishops of the Catholic world — some 2400 from all the continents — left for Rome four years ago, they had many things on their mind, but few thought that Pope John's revolution would turn the Church in a new direction, towards new horizons. Now, as we look back, the changes are tremendous. Like an iceberg, only a small part is visible to many Catholics: the English at Mass, the increased friendship with Protestants, the "emerging layman." These things have entered into their lives. Now comes the real beginning. It is the hour and the burden of informed and responsible Catholics, of priests and bishops.

It is our task to open up new approaches to Protestant and Orthodox churches, and especially to the Jews, and to other non-Christians. We admit our share of the blame for the Christian division, and we pledge a genuine cooperation with them as we explore the bond that holds us to Christ. In a recent TV interview I was asked by a friendly minister, "How can we be sure? Could this be another Catholic trick?" I replied that if I were a Protestant, I might ask the same question. But, as Al Smith used to say, "Let's look at the record." I asked him to look at the record since the Second Vatican Council began. Pope

Paul has joined with Protestant and Orthodox observers in a deeply spiritual Bible service in St. Paul's Basilica in Rome. Here in Atlanta we have doubled our ecumenical efforts by helping to initiate a unity octave, eight days of prayer in which we all attended each others' churches. Guidelines for religious unity have been issued, and we are now working on an ecumenical center, for the use of all faiths, in our new building project at Baker and Ivy Streets. We see Jews more clearly as our brothers, Moslems as believers in one God, people of many faiths and no faith as sincere persons looking for answers.

But the Christian also is a part of our human society, a spokesman to the world of government, industry, labor, education, science and the arts. "The Church must speak," Pope Paul has often said, "because she has something to say." That is why there are Catholic schools and organizations, a Catholic press. The Church speaks from a central core of divine facts and moral law, guaranteed by Christ, but these must be applied to a thousand new situations, all in the spirit of the Gospel. Has a man (or a nation) lost the faith? The Church must have compassion on him. Have states and nations shut their eyes to God's law? Patiently, firmly, consistently, the Church, like John the Baptist, must protest. Is a family in need, of food or housing or a decent wage, or an equal share in education? The Church must take its part. Is a whole people deprived of the inalienable rights of their citizenship, and worse, their very dignity itself? The Church cannot remain silent.

Now is there an "official Catholic stand" on each and every issue? Obviously, no. There is one body of truths transmitted by Christ, but as these are applied to cases, there can be dozens of "Catholic responses" possible within that framework. In its long history, Christianity has never been monolithic because its members differ in background, temperament and taste. But it is the unfinished task of a Catholic today to search out his own opinions and behavior, and square them with that central core of Christian truth. And it is our unfinished task (bishops, priests, teachers) to relate these given personal and local situations to Christ's Word and the authentic teaching of His Church.

If you are a reader of my favorite newspaper, the *Georgia Bulletin*, you are well aware that almost any editorial will find a dissenting reply in one of our syndicated columns and especially in the Letters to the Editor. But it is our job to take a stand, to provide Christian clarity as well as charity. It is to point out the element of justice in unionism, of purity and decency in movies and paperbacks, of peace in support of the United Nations, and of freedom, equality and fraternity in the treatment of race.

The council spoke on race too. In the document on the Church itself, the bishops spoke clearly:

> At all times and in every race, God has given welcome to those who fear Him and do what is right . . .
>
> There is in Christ and in the Church no inequality on the basis of race or nationality, social condition or sex . . .
>
> All men are called to belong to the new people of God.

And in another document, the Council, looking beyond the Church itself at a human society that is flaunting human rights, proclaimed:

> With regard to the fundamental rights of the person, every type of discrimination, whether based on sex, race, color, social condition, language or religion, is to be overcome and rooted out because it is against God's law.

The Vatican Council has ended, but the work has only begun. Catholics must awaken to a new awareness of what the Church is; the renewal and the reforms must go on; the movement toward Christian unity must rise above the difficulties of 400 years; efforts to permeate the work with justice, the mercy, the unity and the peace of Jesus Christ must receive a mighty thrust.

There is something of a parallel between the Catholic renewal and the American awakening to the urgency of civil and social rights, human dignity and fulfillment for all citizens, regardless of color. It took Catholic prophets like Pope John XXIII, and American prophets (both Negro and white) to alert an isolated people to action. As Lillian Smith said recently, we must put away our efforts "to change the situation without changing ourselves, our deeper natures, our second and third layers of mind." From 1962 to 1965, the Catholic Council and its examination of conscience continued, the struggle and the setbacks. From 1954 to 1965, the American struggle went on, north and south, black and white, and some found guilt and others found agony and death. As of the beginning of 1966, the victory for right seems to be won, releasing for the Church the liberating forces of faith, and for our nation the mighty dynamic of justice.

Is the victory really won? Can Americans, white or Negro, become complacent again over the Negro's rights? Will the work of the churches underscore man's need of his "inalienable rights?" Can the Catholic Church rest now, having spoken through her bishops, acted through her schools and hospitals, opened her door wider to the Negro layman, the Negro nun, the Negro priest (like the excellent young priest teaching now in one of our high schools, fully integrated), the Negro bishop like Bishop Harold Perry of New Orleans? To help throw some light on these questions, and point up our other unfinished task, let me ask several more, and give my honest, personal replies as an Archbishop of the Church:

(1) Has the Christian church a duty to proclaim, in season, out of season, justice for the Negro? Yes. By a courageous Sunday sermon in a northern Georgia town the day after Lemuel Penn was murdered, by the frequent voice of the *Georgia Bulletin,* spotlighting the ugly incidents of discrimination and violence, by sermons and school instruction, by interracial meetings and neighborhood projects, by conferences and pastoral letters. The answer is, Yes.

(2) Has the Church a role to play in direct action? Yes. By six of our priests witnessing their moral convictions on the streets of Selma, with the approval of our own church authorities, by programs of voter registration such as one priest undertook in the lonely area around Crawfordsville, by integrating all our schools not by token placement, but across the board, by opening our hospitals on the basis of need, not race or creed.

(3) Should the Church speak out in matters of controversy? Yes, if the case is clearly moral, and the facts are on the table. Most contemporary problems are complex, and the current issue of an elected member refused his seat in our Legislature certainly is. Like many Negro citizens, including a prominent Negro newspaper, like some legislators, and like Lillian Smith, I totally disagree with this man's statements, his whole point of view on our nation's foreign policy, and his reflections on this country's honor.

But I disagree, with convictions just as strong, with those who voted to exclude him from the place he won in our Legislature. He almost certainly hurt the civil rights movement here in the United States; he may well have given comfort to the foreign enemy. But he was duly elected, and he should have been sworn in. I regret that this has become in the minds of white and Negro extremists a racial question. Too, I regret even more that the majority of our legislators have pushed our progressive state backward and served the old unchangeables with another round of racial moonshine.

(4) Finally, with much of the civil rights legislation in shape, can the churches retire to the quiet sanctuary, and let the government and individuals do the rest. Laws are necessary. So is good education in racial justice. Direct action with due care and proper timing is

needed too. But where in this picture is the unique contribution of Christianity, the brotherhood, the love, the charity that is the greatest of the virtues? This is our responsibility. And we are just beginning.

I invite you to look into the results of Vatican Council II and the earnest work of other great church assemblies. They have given a menu for a hungry people. Your name as an organization has a double, indeed a triple meaning. You meet to eat with the elite, because you are hungry for food after a morning's work. But secondly, you are hungry, too, for information and for facts and new insights and for truth. What is the third meaning? We know it from the Gospel. The place was a mountainside; the speaker was the Lord: "Blessed are those who hunger and thirst for holiness; they shall have their fill" (Matthew 5:6).

DIALOGUE WITHIN THE CHURCH

At a time when "dialogue" was one of the key words within the post-conciliar Church, Archbishop Hallinan issued this pastoral letter at the beginning of Lent, 1966. It appeared in the 17 February, 1966, issue of the Georgia Bulletin.

A father and his son, arguing over the use of the family car, are a homely echo of today's tensions. Words fly between the haves and the have-nots, the East and West, whites and non-whites, persistent laymen and resistant clergymen. Voices are amplified with emotion. Neither side listens. There is a breakdown in communications.

The theater is alert to this, frequently complaining that words by themselves just won't do. Shakespeare wrote in *Othello*, "Words, words, mere words. No matter from the heart?" and four centuries later Liza Doolittle sings with scorn in *My Fair Lady*, "Words, words, words, I'm so sick of words!" Society's frequent failure to communicate simply reflects the picture offered by the playwright.

In Catholicism today, we cannot afford any such breakdown of communication. So much of our conversation is like cocktail chatter about nuclear war or birth control. "To be sociable — to talk merely because convention forbids silence, to rub against one another in order to create the illusion of intimacy and contact." This is what Dag Hammarskjold of the United Nations called, "the human condition." But it should never be "the Catholic condition." Newman's description of "viewiness" comes to mind: full of "views" on all subjects of philosophy, on all matters of the day, a view at a moment's notice. The religious world, the profound English thinker said, generally holds that religion consists not in knowledge, but in feeling and sentiment. Expressions of these feelings can be put into words, even into a pretended dialogue, but words without true ideas and real consequences can only betray us.

In our archdiocese, we have considered and acted upon ecumenical dialogue. Our theme, in this Lenten Pastoral of 1966, is a different dialogue, one carried on within the Church as we seek the Word of

122

God and then respond to it. It occurs at many levels and uses many techniques. Only three are considered here:

     I. THE WORD IN PRINT — the Christian Journal
    II. THE WORD IN TEACHING — The Christian Teacher
   III. THE WORD IN THE LITURGY — the Christian Homily

Our conversation with God is carried on by prayer, meditation and public worship. These are the private and social channels by which we communicate intimately with our God, but they do not exhaust the dialogue of a Christian. We must recall that "large, floating body of Catholic truth," in Newman's phrase. God first of all speaks to us through *Creation,* which Dante called "the scattered sheaves of all the world, bound by love in one great volume." Then through the *Prophets* in the fragmentary and quite diverse revelation of the Old Testament. And finally through *Christ,* the Word Himself in our midst, the image of the Father speaking of our saving destiny and so acting as to insure it for us.

That is the Christian core. But the teaching Church guards and explains it, church fathers and theologians explore it, bishops and priests apply it, and the laity earns that noble name of "faithful" by their steadfast loyalty to it. The Word was made man, and a modern poet has posed a question:

> God's own descent
> Into flesh was meant
> As a demonstration
> That the supreme merit
> Lay in risking spirit
> In substantiation.
>   — Robert Frost

God's "demonstrations" do not fail. The spirit became substance without ceasing to be spirit.

The excellent scripture scholar, Father Barnabas Ahern, C.P., quotes from St. Paul and then comments: "In Christ Jesus, 'the goodness and kindness of God our Savior appeared' in human flesh. He died and rose again, not merely as an individual but as the true Israel. If only man says Yes to what Christ has done and becomes united to Him in Baptism, he becomes one with the Savior."

But if our reply is No, we lose His Word and our own become scrambled. A sensitive modern man saw the failure, not "to focus our strength into one pencil of light pointing to the Name up through the darkness," but rather to dissipate "our strength in a moss-fire where nothing is consumed, but all life is suffocated." Hammarskjold wrote this years before his death.

I. THE WORD IN PRINT

> The Catholic press lives and works upon, as it were, a border line, between the clergy and the laity, and more particularly between the Church and the world. The Catholic press occupies an exposed place, and therefore a perilous place.
>
> — Father John C. Murray, 1965

There is a growing market for books, pamphlets and magazines dealing with Catholic affairs. By and large, our good secular press handles such news profusely and competently. Here attention is called to the Catholic press, and in particular to our own archdiocesan newspaper, the *Georgia Bulletin.*

Its forty-year history parallels Catholic growth in Georgia. In the 1920's, it was a fighting crusader against raw anti-Catholic bigotry. For several decades it mirrored other diocesan papers in the recording of parish and diocesan events. When Atlanta became an archdiocese in 1962, the times called for a vigorous, modern newspaper, covering not only our own affairs, but a good cross-section of everything Catholic.

The *Georgia Bulletin* does many things for our archdiocese. It teaches straight Catholic doctrine and answers questions. It tells of the joys and sorrows of weddings, funerals, graduations, meetings, sports, and confirmation classes. It highlights our own part in the ecumenical, liturgical and social movements spurred on by Vatican Council II. It provides ample "documentation," important Church decrees, messages and addresses. The columns are quite varied and the letters to the editor are quite spirited. And best of all it speaks up on the issues of the day.

Not everyone approves all this, especially its clear stand on controversial issues. Much of this criticism is healthy, but those who discriminate against Negroes do not want their paper to call this an un-Christian practice. Those who want to keep America isolated do not like editorials on the United Nations or other world bodies praised by recent popes. Birth control advocates, conniving politicians, as well as slum landlords and pornographers resent the *Georgia Bulletin's* opposition. So do those who are anti-ecumenism or anti-academic freedom. When a recent protester was asked just what sort of paper he wanted the *Bulletin* to be, his reply was definite:

> It ought to carry first communions, confirmations and the funerals of priests.

It can be presumed that all Catholics are in favor of the first two, but those who enjoy reading about the clergy being buried might well be suspected of a rather morbid anti-clericalism!

Our newspaper works humbly in the Christian spirit once defined by the present pope:

> It is not possible to align the body of contemporary thought along Christian principles unless we have the material, reminders and stimuli contained in the Catholic newspaper.

Three modern Catholic writers affirm this. The press has the opportunity of being "a vehicle of dialogue between clergy and laity, among the laity itself, and between local churches across national boundaries" (John Courtney Murray) . . . of "forming Catholic public opinion" (George H. Tavard) . . . and "showing the application of Vatican Council II to Main Street" (Douglas Roche).

This is a major assignment, and the archdiocese has provided an editor, staff, newspaper and support worthy of the job. From the beginning, the *Georgia Bulletin* has gained prestige as a vigorous and brave paper. Gradually those whose ideological toes were occasionally stepped on, were saying, "I don't agree with it, but I wouldn't miss it." After three years, it is possible to say that responsible Catholics, both laymen and priests, are proud of the paper, read it, discuss it. Further, it is quoted from coast to coast, and followed closely by many Atlantans not of our faith.

This cooperation must increase as our numbers, news, influence and opportunities grow. Every parish and institution should submit news regularly. Every pastor should regard the communication of Catholic thought through the *Georgia Bulletin* as one of the most vital marks of the parish. Every Catholic should be a potential reporter, advertiser and circulation-builder for it. Dissenters should write to the editor. Supporters should make their support vocal.

He who cancels the *Georgia Bulletin* because the paper disagrees with him should ask, "Have I a right to cancel out a medium which stimulates such thoughts?" Perhaps disagreement with the *Bulletin* does not mean disagreement with the Church; perhaps it does.

The *Georgia Bulletin* can and should be the voice of the Catholic South. It will be if every family (1) reads and discusses it; (2) subscribes and gets other subscriptions for it; (3) recommends it to business firms for their advertisements. Priests and Sisters are urged to use the *Bulletin* as a Catholic voice in their parishes and classrooms. They will find that, used constructively, it will be a meaningful voice. It is one of our best diocesan papers. It could be the finest.

II. THE WORD IN TEACHING

> If a teacher loves only the persons to be taught, he is a sentimentalist ... if he loves only the things of his mind, he is a robot.
> — Sister M. Joselyn, 1951

"We have to use words," said Canon F. H. Drinkwater, English teacher and administrator, referring to the many forms of Catholic teaching: the kindergarten school, college, and university; the classes identified as "Confraternity," "Newman" and adult; the instructions to Sunday congregations, those interested in the faith, or planning to get married.

The final responsibility for proclaiming the word of God is the teaching of Christ, the *magisterium*, popes and bishops "to preach the gospel to the whole of creation." An individual bishop uses pastoral letters, the pulpit (especially the cathedral), newspapers, radio and television; but chiefly he relies on his priests, brothers, sisters and laymen. There must be dialogue here too; Catholic education must never become a "treadmill" or a "foundry" as Newman warned. The Catholic teaching body must be a cherished mother, an *Alma Mater*, in a family where the deposit of faith is sure, ideas are free, manners are respectful, the atmosphere is open, and the unchangeable law is charity. In this picture, the path of knowledge is always a two-way street.

The key to this is the teacher. In a summary of religious education, excellent for 1929, Pius XI wrote:

> Perfect schools are the result not so much of good methods, as of good teachers ....

Such teachers are thoroughly prepared and well-grounded, with the necessary intellectual and moral qualifications, cherishing the youths confided to them because they love Jesus Christ and His Church, having sincerely at heart the true good of family and society. These indeed are the heroes and heroines of the unsung frontier against religious ignorance.

Our parents should judge their schools, and especially their religious teachers, in the modern manner. Just as there is a new math and a new liturgy, so is there a new catechetics. It speaks more warmly of the Scripture; it teaches the layman's changing role in this new, involved age of the Church. The aim is to dissolve "the film of familiarity" that makes divine things routine. This done, we must not hide them again, either in the jargon of the old school (*supernatural, perfect society, beatitude*) or of the new (*kerygma, encounter, the mystery of the economy of salvation*).

Catholic catechists today are going back to the English critic and poet, William Wordsworth, who wrote in 1800, "The heart is reached by the language of ordinary life, warm and simple, not by academic or scientific or bookish language." *Note*: Do you recall the catechism answer, "God made me to know Him, to love Him and to serve Him in this world, and to be happy with Him forever in the next?" Most Catholics do remember its simple words, and, what is more, they try their honest best to follow them.

In our archdiocese, three quiet revolutions are under way. Our people should know about them.

(a) Total reorganization of the Confraternity of Christian Doctrine to provide good lay teachers for the thousands not in Catholic schools. KEY: This is now part of the Department of Education.

(b) Coordination of the work of sisters and lay teachers in all our schools in a modern, integrated, progressive program. KEY: Fresh responsibility for the school board in the matter of religious education.

(c) The evolution of the "Catholic Center" at our colleges and universities with a wide offering of classes, lectures and discussions. KEY: Gradual dropping of the old "Newman Club" atmosphere in favor of a religious and educational program, broad and deep enough to attract the majority of Catholics as well as those of other faiths, particularly the leaders.

III. THE WORD IN THE LITURGY

The sermon should draw its content mainly from the sacred scriptures and liturgical sources, and its character should be that of a proclamation of God's wonderful work of salvation, the mystery of Christ ever made present and active within us, especially in the celebration of the liturgy.
— Vatican Council II, Constitution On the Sacred Liturgy, 1963

Now that the sermon has a new name, the homily, and has been defined and made obligatory for Sunday Masses, it is time that we who preach consult with those who are to listen. What kind of homilies best explain the Gospel truths? What style is preferred by our congregations? What is the minimum preparation by the priest? How

long should a homily be? What is the minimum preparation the layman should make? What can he reasonably take home? Priests will
welcome suggestions if they are honestly and respectfully made. Familiarity and warmth help too. Only the humorless layman or priest is
likely to break down the dialogue at this point.

Canon Drinkwater has pointed out what every priest knows: "The
congregation at Mass is the final and most severe test of teaching
ability simply because the ordinary congregation is so very mixed,
of all ages and sexes and educational levels. And at Mass there is so
much that needs to be said, and so short a time in which to say it."

Criticizing the homily, a favorite Sunday breakfast pastime, should
take these points into consideration. The homily proclaims both the
word of God and the human words of the writers. The psalms, for
example, are filled with the urgency of God's word, a lamp for our
feet, a light for our revelation. God speaks, "Incline your ear . . . hear
my word . . . be not deaf to me," and Israel responds, "My part is to
keep your words . . . I hope in your word which endures forever." Then
we move into the New Testament. And ever since, the Christian's
response has been the same as that of the frustrated fishermen-apostles:
"Nevertheless, at your word, we will let down the nets."

The Church is a community of hearers. It was thus with Mary
who replied to the angel, "Be it done to me according to your word."
It was thus with the apostles as they listened to Christ's words on the
mountain, from the boat, at the Last Supper, and after His rising from
the dead. No theme is more dominant in the letters of St. Paul than
the word of God, preached, listened to and lived. Between the word
and the Eucharist, the word and a moral life, he saw no conflict. Without the word we would not have known this new life of grace.

Our priests all over the world are going back to school, reading
and discussing the old truths and the modern manner of speech. It is
a manner new to our generation, but far more venerable than the old
sermons, the denunciations and the hurried gospel commentaries we
had come to expect. In the spirit of the Vatican Council renewal,
our priests are pointing the way for a Scripture-reading laity. Then
will come the truly Christian conversation.

CONCLUSION

Thus in 1966, the archdiocese of Atlanta is working hard to build
finer dialogue, to prevent a breakdown in communications. It is urgent.
We are caught in a web of cables and tubes which stifles us with

mediocrity, often delivered with a glib, flippant style easy to listen to. The situation is completed by the sordid paperback, the plays of angry frustration and the over-exposure of sex in spy stories, popular singers and the selling of cars, beer and detergents. In this wasteland, the homily must sound crystal clear. Only the man who listens to God's word can break through his own web and brighten his own desert.

On the other side of the dialogue are the powerful sounds of renewal given us by Vatican Council II. Any Catholic today would hardly call himself mature until he has read most of the Council decrees, at least one good book for background, and followed the post-conciliar spirit in Catholic journals like the *Georgia Bulletin.*

There is much to improve in our Catholic press, education and preaching. But the continued interest of our people indicates that dialogue will not run dry. We are making real the dream of Cardinal Newman when he wrote:

> Christianity is no theory of the study or cloister. Its 'sound has gone out into all lands' and its 'words unto the end of the world.' Its home is in the world, and to know what it is we must seek it in the world, and hear the world's witness to it.

The Church must speak, says Pope Paul VI, because the Church has something to say. But the church is all of us. How can we be Christ's spokesmen in northern Georgia unless we support our Catholic press, stimulate the best in religious education, and join with priests and laymen in the dialogue of the homily, the parish study group, and the conversation at home.

Robert Frost once wrote:

> Nature within her inmost self divides
> To trouble men with having to take sides.

We have chosen our side, the mystery of God-made-man. Now we are called, more clearly than ever before, "to give an account of the hope which we cherish." (1 Peter 3:15). The dialogue *with the others,* baptized or not, is the duty of ecumenism. The dialogue *within the Church* is the duty of Christian formation.

The word-in-print is ours to support and criticize. The word-in-teaching is ours to help and improve. And the word-in-liturgy is ours to hear and answer, to adopt and follow. God speaks through His prophets, but He also speaks through His editors, His teachers and His preachers.

When we say with the psalmist, "I called and the Lord answered me," we cannot close any channel. Love and dialogue blend into one.

As an old Scottish saying went, "Bare words make no bargain." But actions grow purposeless unless they have God as their highest source, and the dialogue as their daily channel. May God bless your dialogue — in church and school, in home and society. And in blessing this, may He bless you too.

A GREAT TIME TO BE ALIVE

Christianity is a life of hope. No single speech of Archbishop Hallinan expressed this conviction more than this simple and modest address to the National Conference of Catholic Scout leaders held in Atlanta on 14 April, 1966. Again he employed his frequently used metaphor of going up the down escalator and down the up escalator to manifest a sense of hope and joy.

Sometimes, in the Church of today, one gets the impression that he is trying to *go up* the down-escalator (or worse, *go down* the up-escalator). The new breed is rushing past you three steps at a time trying to get off. And the old breed keeps standing pat, right on the top step, determined not to get off at all. A Catholic these days (and need I add, a bishop?) has plenty to do just trying to keep his footing.

In studying your splendid brochure on Catholic Scouter Development (just one year old) I suppose I was prepared to page through the old ideas, the familiar warnings, good advice, etc. It has been some time since I was chaplain and Mr. Louis Novak was scout-leader of the troop at St. Aloysius parish in Cleveland, more than twenty-five years. I haven't, like my younger and more vigorous brother-bishop, William Connare, had much direct association with scouting except following reports while I was in the Youth Department, and occasionally, as a bishop, rubbing several priests together to produce live, dedicated scout chaplains. Fr. Morrow and Fr. Danneker have kept warning me that Catholic Scouting, too, had been touched by the magic wand of the beloved Pope John XXIII, but I guess I was skeptical until I waded into your brochure and found myself holster-deep in the ideas of Pius XII and Paul VI, Cardinal Suenens, Yves Congar, Léon Bloy, Andrew Greeley, with liberal portions of the Constitution on the Church lapping in waves all around on alternate pages. The climax of my conversion came when I read a short, blunt statement, "Today, things are different."

In the quaint slang of my younger days (before there were monsignors in the Scout chaplaincy!), I said as I read that sentence, "You can say that again!" It's a wonderful time to be alive in the Church, as exhilarating as it is sometimes nerve-wracking, as joyous as it is sometimes anxious. We are dusting off some good old American proverbs like, "Religion, like politics, is a private affair. I never discuss it." Now we are rediscovering that these are not private affairs at all, especially religion. If two or three can be gathered in Christ's name and have Him in their midst, what must be going on in a full family of parents and children? Indeed, what must be going on during Sunday Mass in our parishes with two or three hundred, or maybe eight or nine hundred gathered in the same way? We are revising our old picture of a "pyramid Church" with that sharp line between clergy and laity, and finding that the Church is recovering her apostolic diagram of concentric circles, with the source of authority in God, its channels designated by the Church, and its use and exercise determined by charity service. The thread running through every document of Vatican Council II is the ministry and its proper distribution of roles. If we are seeking earnestly, not only in church, but in homes and neighborhoods, cities and nations and the world to be servant-members of the Servant Church, then not only the words of the Council but the Holy Spirit of the Council will be at work renewing our lives. Pope Paul said this in his words to the World Scout Jamboree: "May you know how to recognize this breath of the Spirit, and be inspired by it."

In this *aggiornamento* of Scouting, those planning the program outlined in the brochure — Mr. Griffin and Mr. Kirk, Msgr. Earl Whelan and Msgr. Gregory Mooney, Bishop Connare and many others — are as conciliar in their thoughts and work as the Council Fathers. We are still in the "frontier days," as Father Congar wrote in *The Laity, the Church and the World*:

> Lay people stand on the frontier where the Church meets the world, and their own particular mission is to bring Christian influence to bear on secular life.

But it's a different frontier these past five years. The present enemy is not necessarily the villains of secularism, naturalism or communism. The good guys are not uniquely represented by the clerical Matt Dillons nor the lay Chesters. We are not fighting the world in which we live. We are fighting our own complacency, our own ignorance, our own resistance to change. It is to ready our young men to fight this creeping apathy that you invite them to become scouts, meet with them, instruct and train them, motivate them, and share with them nature's rigors as well as nature's joys. You don't tell them to go on an overnight hike; you lead them, sometimes when you'd sooner be watching TV from your easy chair, just listening to rain instead of fighting it. At the core, scouting in the Christian manner is a fresh adaptation of the old theological axiom, "Grace transcends nature." Nature is our heritage of God's creation, and it is our human instinct to deal with it, enjoying it, using it, sometimes overcoming it. But grace is the fruit of the Son of God's Incarnation, lifting nature to a new level. It can transform a boy's sense of fair play into a man's restless search for Christian justice; it can transform a simple act of helpfulness into a man's share in the loving of neightbor, and thereby loving God.

This used to be classified top-secret material for priests. But Pius XII righted all that in his words, "You are the Church," all of you, all of us. This is precisely the value of your program. The activities of a Catholic scout leader are "a part of, not apart from his pursuit of the Catholic way of life." Scouting is not a man's profession, trade or business; it goes deeper. It is not his role as father and husband, though it is an extension of the values of a Christian home. It is not a hobby, because it is far nobler than that. It is a significant part of his vocation, his calling by God, his divine assignment. Scout leaders (of the laity) and chaplains (of the clergy), understanding that, join in God's tasks, and we can almost invoke the solemn scriptural words of Our Lord, spoken in another situation: "What God has joined together, let no man put asunder."

Another post-conciliar thought: we are all engaged in a vast movement of mutual understanding, prayer and work. Strictly called ecumenical, it really goes beyond the family of baptized believers to include those of other religions. Here in the United States, the Catholic scouters, along with the Newman chaplains and the Armed Service chaplains, have been practical, card-carrying ecumenists long before it was respectable. Beginning early in our century and assured in the 1930's, this mutual sharing with the magnificent program of the Boy Scouts of America has flourished. The declaration of principle (Article IV, Section 1) of the national constitution puts the recognition of God and the acknowledgment of His blessings right where they belong, in the center of life for every citizen, indeed for every man. We are all grateful for the manner in which Catholic scouting has cooperated with the Boy Scouts of America, and all the more grateful for the hand of friendship and mutual sharing extended by the national body. We are united, not because of weakness, but because of strength.

Catholic scouting, just as Protestant and Jewish, has, besides its core of scouting activities, its own distinctive motives and characteristics. These are not simply "pluses." They build upon the natural foundation, transforming this by forming, informing and reforming the natural boy in the image of Christ according to Catholic truths and principles and practices. You are restudying this aspect of your program. The *Ad Altare Dei* award is a good symbol of this. It can inspire the Catholic boy to be a top-rate Boy Scout and a top-rate Catholic, just as the Protestant or Jewish boy will be a better scout insofar as he is a better Protestant or better Jew.

It is in this spirit that I am grateful to receive this award tonight, even though it's been a long time since I've tied any knots (except for marriage), or helped an elderly lady across the street. If I have anything of my own that I could put forward as a claim it is simply this: I have a sure confidence and a Christian hope in the whole program of Catholic scouting and in the past, present, and future of the Boy Scouts of America.

WANTED: VALIANT WOMEN

At least four years before Americans caught on to the program of "women's lib," the Archbishop was talking about the role of women in the Church. He also brought the subject up in an intervention before the Second Vatican Council. This address, delivered before the Omaha Archdiocesan Council of Catholic Women, on 20 September, 1966, bears witness to his interest in the subject.

WOMEN IN THE CHURCH TRADITION

On a bright, October day in 1965, during the last session of the Second Vatican Council, I submitted two proposals, or interventions as they were called. One was on "Racial Injustice," the other on the "Equality of Women in the Church." I thought that the subject of race was fresh and relevant — big, as we say today — whereas the subject of women is as old as Eve and has been fairly exhausted by Miss America, Queen for a Day, and the sex symbols of Hollywood.

But I was wrong. No one has ever again referred to my proposal on race, but the intervention on women is still being quoted. Many wives and single women appreciated my efforts to include them as acolytes, lectors and theological consultants. Nuns liked my insistence that they be represented on the Roman Congregation for Religious. (After all, it is rather absurd to have celibate prelates, some of them seventy years old, judging the styles of sisters' habits.) Even the more belligerent Catholic feminists who want women priests have applauded my speech, even though I don't want women priests.

Now, I am aware that millions of Catholic women do not want to be lectors, acolytes, deaconesses or theologians. They want to be wives and mothers, and they have a sacrament to prove it. Some want to be nuns, and they have their vows of consecration to prove it. Some live single lives — by choice or the lack of it, by death or by separation — and a life of sacrifice and compassion are the marks of their mysterious vocation, as Pope Pius XII called it. These are the marks of the external feminine. The French writer, Leon Bloy, puts it pointedly: "The holier a woman is, the more she is a woman." Bloy's description can describe any one of the three: wife, nun or single woman. But it would be hard to stretch it to cover the dehumanized, unhappy women of the American version of *La Dolce Vita.*

In spite of the strange, almost anti-feminine strain in Catholicism traced from Saint Paul through Saints Augustine and Thomas Aquinas, there has always been a rich treasure of womanhood in both the Jewish and Christian traditions. Before Sarah was loyal, before Rebekah was wise, before Rachel was beloved of her husband there were, first of all, women.

In the gospels, Elizabeth prophesied and women of Samaria and Canaan professed their faith; the woman at the temple gave all the money she had, two small coins, and the widow at Naim mourned for her only son; Martha and Simon's mother-in-law prepared the meals, and the Magdalen wept for her sins. Each was a woman — some wives, some single women, some widows, and one divorced.

In the apostolic generation, Priscilla and her husband offered Saint Paul the hospitality of their home; the charitable Dorcas made dresses and cloaks for those in need; Phoebe was a deaconess "who gave great help to the apostles." Wife, widow and single they were, but their names are now immortalized in the book of life.

The highest praise of woman is in the last page of the book of Proverbs. In an age dominated by household agriculture and trade, she is honored by her husband, children and servants. Every biblical detail is applicable today:

> She opens her mouth to wisdom; the law of mercy is on her tongue.

Her daily actions are good reasons why "her husband trusts his heart to her." She is generous to those in need, reaching out "her hands to the poor and her arms to the needy." She takes care of her staff, clothing them warmly and rising at night to feed them. She is skillful in making her own clothes, and prudent when she invests in a vineyard. She doesn't read *Charm* or *Glamor,* nor buy fragrant chemicals guaranteed to soften her skin, hair and dishwater. She knows, as most women do, that "charm deceives and beauty passes on," but we praise the woman whose fear of God is love and mercy, not social know-who and kitchen know-how.

Then there is Mary the Virgin who stands for innocence and integrity, and Mary the Mother who stands for love of her husband and care of her Son. Beyond Rachel, Elizabeth and Priscilla, Mary

"opens her mouth to wisdom, and the law of mercy is on her tongue."
The human nature of all men is hers, but so is the feminine personality.
She is "the model of the Church," as Saint Ambrose writes; "Mother
of the members of Christ," according to Saint Augustine; "the sign of
certain hope and solace for the pilgrim People of God," in the words
of Vatican Council II. Let Mary be at home in every home, present
at every table, tending every nursery, presiding at every gathering.

MY QUALIFICATIONS

By now, you have settled back in your chairs edified, but not
exactly excited, by a topic that sounds like a want ad from the classified
job section of the Bible *Bulletin*. My qualifications are quite limited:
I did speak up at the Vatican Council. I have also studied such books
as Stern's *The Flight from Women*, which is psychiatry that sounds
like poetry; von de Fort's *The Eternal Woman*, mysticism that reads
like philosophy; and Friedan's *The Feminine Mystique*, which her publisher calls "the Year's Most Controversial Bestseller." I did not have
time to read three others: Mead's *Male and Female*, de Beauvoir's
The Second Sex, and Deutisch's *The Psychology of Women*.

I must confess, however, that my opinions about women are much
like those of Henry Higgins in *My Fair Lady* when he sang:

> Why can't a woman - be more like a man?
> Men are so honest - so thoroughly square,
> Eternally noble - historically fair.*

Prejudiced? Hostile? Anti-feminist? Not at all. After all, women make
up one half of the People of God entrusted to me as a bishop. My
attitude rather is something like Tolstoy's. Once, the three Russian
novelists, Tolstoy, Chekov and Gorki, were sitting in a garden, talking
about women. Tolstoy finally said:

> I am going to tell the truth about women only
> when I am standing in the grave. I shall
> say it, jump into the coffin, pull the lid and then
> I'll say, "Do with me whatever you want!"

A wise man realizes that the other sex is a mystery. And besides,
whatever knowledge man has got had best be kept confidential. After
all, women cast the majority of votes and spend about ninety percent
of the family incomes. As Clare Boothe Luce noted in 1947, "In case

---

* Copyright © 1956 by Alan J. Lerner and Frederick Loewe. Used
by permission of Chappell & Co., Inc.

anyone doubts that they have a man's world well by the throat, they buy seventy-three percent of all men's neckties!"

So I am not proposing any radical ideas, pro or con, about women. I will simply submit these three theses:

(a) Women are really people.
(b) Women are certainly different.
(c) Women are here to stay.

Women are "children of God with a God-given nature and task" under Mary's protection, on their way toward their Father Who is in heaven.

WOMEN ARE REALLY PEOPLE

But not every woman is Mary, just as she is not the busy Martha nor the sinful Magdalen. Women are really people; they are really human.

As Barbra Streisand sings, sometimes they are acting

More like children than children,
Letting our grown-up pride hide all the need inside.

But there are other times when they are

People who need people . . .
No more hunger and thirst, but first,
People who need people.*

Happiness is need that is fulfilled, and unhappiness is need that is hidden and frustrated. But these are human, not feminine, qualities. There is a need in the spirit of us all, men and women. And we will never grasp woman's role until we see that she is a person with human needs, not a biological deviation, a social appendage, or an economic competitor.

It's an old saying that "It's a man's world!" Contemplating its present messed-up state, what woman would ever claim it? More likely she would say, "He can have it!" Society was meant to be human, but we have dehumanized it. Both men and women are made for God, both here and hereafter. But if we watch women's faces, we come to suspect that their image and likeness is not of God but of animals. She is tired of describing her role as "just a housewife," tired of living in a "thing-ridden house," tired of moving slowly from femininity to full human identity. The "road from Freud to Frigidaire has turned out to be a bumpy one," as Betty Friedan notes in the *New York Times* of June 28, 1960.

---

* Copyright © 1963 and 1964 by Bob Merrill & Jule Styne. Used by permission of Chappell & Co., Inc.

For many a married woman, the chief barrier to her femininity is her husband's company. It is a terrifying threat to hear IBM's president, Thomas Watson, say, "Our wives are all part of the business." As *Fortune* magazine summed it up, "The husband belongs to the corporation." The wife has become the company's ally. She sees the corporation consuming her husband. What a far cry from the Christian imperative, "All earthly activities should be bathed in the light of the Gospel."

Friedan calls for women to compete in the business and political arenas not as a woman, but as a human being. She must pursue academic degrees, part-time reading programs, and educational home projects. She has a place in business and politics not as a housewife, but as a citizen, demanding leaves and sabbaticals for maternity, and nurseries paid for by the company. If we stop dehumanizing, depersonalizing and defeminizing women, they will emerge as free, rational human persons. They are women, yes. But they are people, too.

WOMEN ARE DIFFERENT

But they are people with a difference. They don't write books and articles about men; they write about women. It was Gertrud von de Fort who wrote, "The world can be moved by the strength of man, but it can be blessed, in the real sense of the Word, only in the sign of woman." The comment that women can "rinse an idea in the waters of the heart before hanging it to dry on the tight rope of the mind," was made by Mary-Angela Harper. And it was Phyllis McGinley who commented, "If we have not man's compassion, we also lack his gullibility."

In religious matters, the essence of holiness is the perfection of a double love, of God and of one's fellow men. Father Joseph Donceel tells us that man's knowledge is more logical, more conceptual, while woman's is more direct and intuitive. He is at home in the world of ideas, she in the realities of everyday life and social contacts. Men, like Our Lord, preached. Women healed. Christ's life and teaching can be summed up in humility and charity. The average woman demonstrates both of these virtues more naturally than the average man.

Have we obscured the need for a basic difference of women? Is not their honesty evident in instances, as when you ask if she likes your hairdo and she tells you? Would it be better, Henry Higgins to the contrary, if a man were more like a woman? The other sex may have the same human nature, but it is her feminine difference (as the French know!) that makes life worthwhile.

WOMEN ARE HERE TO STAY

Genesis was right. "It is not good that man is alone." The world knows it and Christianity knows it. In three modern novels women emerge as living persons, not as fictional characters. It was a woman, Caterina, who pleaded, "Come back and build them a school," in *The Secret of Santa Vittoria*. It was a woman who was accorded the role of ministering to the dying in Charles Percy's *The Last Gentleman*. To enlighten, to heal, the teacher and the nurse, woman's traditional roles. Women give themselves to men; men in return give women a reason to live. Thus does Peggy, in John Updike's *Of the Farm*, describe her attitude. And it is Paul Claudel, in his sensitive *The Tidings Brought to Mary*, who makes a vital distinction: "Man is the active power in the Church . . . . Woman's privilege is to sacrifice herself."

The teaching and the healing, the giving and the sacrifice mark woman's personality in our contemporary fiction. And the world and the Church reflect this sad reality. It is man who dominates history, but it is woman who stands not for history, but for the generation. Peoples and nations need good mothers as much as children do. And von de Fort's plea is even more urgent: "It is only a motherless time that cries out for a mother."

So much for the dismal secular situation. What about the religious?

Women play a rather insignificant part in Catholic thought and life. Although they teach and nurse and to some extent engage in social programs, they do very little in liturgy and theology or politics within or outside the structure of the Church. Yet Vatican Council II states that our era needs more wisdom, and the chapter on the laity says that "each individual layman must stand before the world as a witness to the Lord Jesus and as a sign that God lives." Woman's place among the People of God must be free, vital and dynamic, marked by sacrifice and compassion. If it is not, then her dignity is diminished, and worse, the Church's vigor is impaired.

THE VALIANT WOMAN

We have quoted the Scriptures and the Vatican Council; anthropologists, novelists, and philosophers, writers both Catholic and otherwise; Henry Higgins and Barbra Streisand. All agree that a problem exists, but hardly any of them agree on its solution.

Beatrice Lillie used to sing a mournful lament, called "Waiting at the Church," about a bride-to-be who remained just that, a bride-to-be. There she was:

Waiting at the church,
He left me in the lurch,
Oh, how it did upset me!

That was the Catholic woman prior to Vatican Council II, silent and passive, unseen, unheard, and unknown. But in the new liturgy and catechetics, the new ecumenism and the new renewal of the laymen, she has found her way.

She is marching now, head high and heart pulsing to the vibrant, fast-stepping song of that old rascal, Eliza's father. The tone is dynamic, the tempo martial, and the song is "Get me to the church on time!" It is urgent that she get there because there is so much to do and there is no time for waiting at the church.

Miss America, Queen for a Day or Hollywood's sex symbol? Or Rachel, Magdalen or Priscilla? Which will it be? Modern woman — married or single, nun or widow — can find the best image of womanhood in the valiant woman of the book of Proverbs. The word valiant is related to valor and to value. Her courage is certified in the high praise, "She is clothed with strength," and her value is attested by her "proven worth." Tender and thoughtful, she is dressed in strength and dignity. This is the kind of woman that the world and society require, that the Church and religion need.

That is why the word must go out to homes and to convents, to lay associations and to civic groups, to choirs, factories, offices and colleges: "Wanted — Valiant Women." Particularly, the message must go to councils of women like your own. It is the reason why you are present and why I am here.

May God, Who seeks witnesses to Christ and signs that God lives, inspire and bless you! May the Church count you as a certain hope and solace for the pilgrims of the People of God!

Archbishop Hallinan welcomes the new Auxiliary Bishop Joseph L. Bernardin to Atlanta from Charleston on May 3, 1966.

*Archbishop Hallinan
introduces Bishop Bernardin
to some of the
priests of the
archdiocese at
the airport terminal
in Atlanta.*

At the United States Bishops' Conference in Chicago, May, 1967, Archbishop Hallinan and Bishop Bernardin are joined by Monsignor James Walsh of Miami, Florida.

Abbot Walter Coggins, O.S.B.
Belmont Abbey, N.C.,
Patriarch Peter Paul Meouchi,
and Archbishop Hallinan
visit the Piazzo de Pietro
at the entrance to the
Lebanese College
during a council session,
October 3, 1965.

Archbishop John Cody, Chicago, and Lawrence Cardinal Shehan of Balti-more visit Archbishop Hallinan in Atlanta.

Friends from the Second Vatican Council are reunited at the Atlanta airport in May, 1965, when Archbishop Guilford Young, Hobart, Tasmania, stops to visit Archbishop Hallinan.

WAR AND PEACE

Before delivering his address to Detroit's Continuing Education Institute, the Archbishop, joined by his auxiliary bishop, Joseph L. Bernardin, issued a pastoral letter that appeared in the 13 October, 1966, issue of the Georgia Bulletin. *This pastoral letter reflects the remarks he made subsequently in Detroit.*

The slaughter of men and the death of villages are certainly not new to the history of mankind. Yet the passionate desire for true peace has never died in men's hearts. The tension created by the desire for peace and the realities of war has been brought into sharp focus by the current conflict in Viet Nam. But as Pope Paul reminded us in his encyclical two weeks ago, this war is just one of many tragedies which severely threaten the peace and stability of the human family. "For instance," he stated, "there are the increasing race for nuclear weapons, the unscrupulous efforts for the expansion of one's nation, the excessive glorification of one's race, the obsession for revolution, the segregations enforced on citizens, the iniquitous plotting, the murder of the innocent."

THE FIVE QUESTIONS

The Church cannot remain silent in the face of these grave disorders. True peace will not be brought about solely by military victory; it will not be achieved by maintaining a balance of power between enemies. Reflecting the thinking of Pope John XXIII as expressed in *Peace on Earth,* the Second Vatican Council has stated very clearly that "peace results from the harmony built into human society by its Divine Founder and actualized by men as they thirst after ever greater justice." All action and all talk about peace will be irrelevant unless it is cast in a moral context.

The Church, then, as the living voice of Christ must speak out. It must give an effective witness to the gospel message which provides a sure framework for universal brotherhood. This must be based on

142

mutual respect and love so essential to the establishment of peace. For this reason an American Catholic who has lost his moral perspective on war can hardly be considered a true Christian patriot.

As the great debate on war and peace gathers momentum, certain urgent questions demand that we respond:

1. What are the demands of true patriotism?
2. Is it possible to speak of a just war today as we did in the past?
3. On a broader level, should nations try to maintain peace by a balance of terror?
4. Does universal disarmament (all sides) differ morally from unilateral disarmament (one side)?
5. What are our obligations in contributing toward a genuinely moral consensus regarding American involvement in Viet Nam?

WHO IS THE PATRIOT?

The well-being of every nation depends on the patriotism of its citizens. The American Catholic — citizens, soldier, pacifist — has held an honorable place in our country's history side by side with those of other faiths. The bishops of Vatican Council II, however, clearly point out that there is a significant difference between *true patriotism*, which is "living for God and Christ by following the honorable customs of one's own nation," and *false patriotism*, which stems from "a narrowing of mind . . . racial prejudice and bitter nationalism." True patriotism, in other words, does not end at a nation's borders. That American is truly patriotic who, while devoting himself to the legitimate needs and concerns of his country, also seeks "the welfare of the whole human family . . . a universal love for mankind." As Pope John stated in his last encyclical, *Peace on Earth*, "Individual countries cannot rightly seek their own interests and develop in isolation from the rest."

This is not to say, of course, that a country cannot defend itself. While making it clear that all means short of force must first be employed, the Council restates the traditional teaching of the Church regarding the right of self-defense: "As long as the danger of war remains and there is no competent and sufficiently powerful authority at the international level, government cannot be denied the right to legitimate defense . . . ." Moreover, the Council Fathers commend those in the military forces who serve as "agents of security and freedom on behalf of their people" as long as they fulfill this role properly.

In the light of our duty to examine the moral position of our country, another question remains, that of the right of a conscientious objector. The Church, after a brief warning that peace cannot exist "unless personal values are safeguarded," states clearly:

> It seems right that laws make humane provisions for the case of those who (for reasons of conscience) refuse to bear arms, provided however, that they accept some other form of service to the human community.

LIMITS AND ILLUSIONS

If men are to remain human, there must be definite limits to the conduct of any war. The Council clearly defines these limits:

1. Any act of war aimed *indiscriminately at the destruction* of entire cities or of extensive areas along with their population is a crime against God and man himself. It merits unequivocal and unhesitating condemnation.

2. Those actions designed for the *methodical extermination* of an entire people, nation or ethnic minority must be vehemently condemned as horrendous crimes . . . . Blind obedience cannot excuse those who yield to [orders calling for such actions].

The Council also debated the massing of arms as a means of avoiding war. It pronounced such a method of deterrence a "treacherous trap for humanity." It is a trap because it is, without question, a dangerous way of maintaining peace. Moreover, the causes of war are actually intensified because the vast sums used for stockpiling weapons make it extremely difficult, if not totally impossible in some cases, to give attention to the human misery which is usually the root cause of war. For this reason the bishops made an urgent plea for disarmament. But they realized that disarmament is a two-sided coin; it would have little meaning unless all sides agreed on it and unless there were effective means of enforcing it.

What bearing do these general principles have on our involvement in Vietnam? What implications do they have generally for our efforts to promote world-wide peace?

THE ONLY ALTERNATIVE?

As in every great human problem, there is no simple solution. American Catholics can put faith in the integrity of our government's aims in Vietnam. There is surely abundant evidence of it in a number of areas: the recent large vote in South Vietnam opening the door to local civilian government; the aid we have given to get such projects as the Mekong Delta improvements underway in Southeastern Asia;

the support of the United States voiced in Washington last month by President Ferdinand Marcos of the Philippines; the total withdrawal of American troops from the Dominican Republic, leading the way to a constitutional government free of extremists, both left and right.

In the light of events rather than slogans, then, it can be argued that to the present course of action in Vietnam there may be no visible alternative.

But we cannot stop here. It is the Christian duty to keep looking for *other alternatives.* We must know as much about the factual situation as possible in order that these alternatives be realistic. To a limited extent, our national security requires secrecy. Except for that, however, we must keep insisting that our leaders fully inform us of the facts and issues involved in the Vietnam war.

We must help to enlarge the new climate of thought, based on Pope John's principle: in an age which prides itself on its atomic energy, it is unreasonable to hold that war is still a suitable way to restore violated rights. We can help by conversation, study, example, discussion groups and lectures.

Christians should advocate what they believe is the best way to bring about disarmament: mutual agreements, safeguards and inspection; world federalism; the creation of a public authority empowered to negotiate toward peace.

We have the obligation to make sure that our government pursues, vigorously, wholeheartedly and repeatedly, every opening which has even the slightest hope of peaceful settlement. Ambassador Arthur Goldberg's recent summary of the present American policy was such an opening. To the United Nations, he stated that we were ready to join in a phased withdrawal of all external forces and a halt to bombing upon the assurance from North Vietnam that it would halt its war effort.

As Cardinal Lawrence Shehan of Baltimore recently said in his splendid pastoral:

> Those who argue against restraint and against keeping a nation's war-making acts within moral bounds are likely to win an even greater hearing ... (But) if our means become immoral, our cause will have been betrayed.

We must protest, therefore, whenever there is danger that our conduct of the war will exceed moral limits. A Christian simply cannot approve indiscriminate bombing, methodical extermination of people, nuclear arms designed for "overkill" or disregard for noncombatants.

In short, our dedication to the cause of peace must become so evident, so intense, so convincing that the old balance of mutual terror will be phased out to make way for a new balance of mutual trust. In Christian confidence, we can hope that if many nations come to trust each other, those who instead rely on war will re-evaluate their own positions.

On a broader level, we must give our leaders a mandate to pursue the problem of disarmament. While no Catholic teaching demands that a nation disarm by itself, the whole Catholic momentum today is toward a disarmament that is complete, thorough and international, resting on mutual agreement and workable safeguards. We cannot stand aside because such a solution is hard to visualize or difficult to achieve.

Moreover, we must never cease to do everything in our power to help make it possible for the poorer nations of the world to give their people what they need, educationally, culturally, materially, and socially, to live in a way that squares with their God-given human dignity. We must be strong for the working out of the social and economic programs that will heal, not inflame, the causes of war.

"NEVER WAR AGAIN!"

Mankind longs for peace and has tragically sought it through the inhuman process of war. The Church calls us all, especially parents, teachers and those who form public opinion, to make known "fresh sentiments of peace." Pope Paul, speaking of the purpose of his recent encyclical, asked, "What is the use of it?" and answered that all Christians should "speak out and pray."

We must speak out; we cannot remain silent. In his novel, *War and Peace*, Tolstoy asks how men can ignore the continued disasters in which "Christians, professing the law of love, murder one another." Christian consciences and voices must be raised against the savagery and terror of war. We must speak out — for justice, for truth, for freedom and for peace.

And we must pray with Christian minds and hearts until hope replaces anxiety, and love crowds out hatred. On October 11, we observe the Motherhood of Our Lady, mother of the Son of God and of all His brothers. Do we love them as brothers? The month ends with the Feast of Christ the King, patron of our Cathedral. The preface for that feast describes a world not stained with the blood of men, but marked by the blood of Christ, the Lamb of God, "a Kingdom of truth and life, of holiness and grace, a Kingdom of justice, of love and peace."

Through the courage and the prayers of each of us, may our country and every other sovereign state "beat their swords into plowshares, and their spears into pruning books. One nation shall not raise the sword against another, nor shall they train for war again" (Isaiah 2:4).

As people of God, let us reaffirm what Paul VI, his vicar on earth, said a year age to the United Nations: "Never war again!"

ECUMENISM IN THE NEW SOUTH

Few observers of the 1960's would doubt the fact that Archbishop Hallinan's efforts were a "major breakthrough" in the ecumenical work of the churches in the South. A future historian will recount these endeavors in greater detail. This address has been chosen to illustrate one of the many activities he engaged in during his years in Atlanta. It was delivered at St. Bernard's College, Cullman, Alabama, on 26 January. 1967. The Archbishop's introductory remarks, referring to his friend, Monsignor Bernard Law, have been omitted from this text.

The subject chosen is large, complicated and not well researched. It touches on the phenomenon of revivalism, the tensions of slavery, secession, strife and segregation. At two extremes, both Baptists and Catholics have shown a hard intransigence hardly worthy of Christ's followers. Yet the streams have run close together as well as far apart, and in them all has walked the man we call the "Southerner" with his own basic religious character. Does 1967 present the picture of a new wave as the streams converge, or a backing up of old water in the dark eddies of a thousand camp-meetings and a million broken dreams of glory and Armageddon?

Many churches, both traditional and spontaneous, make up the church-going Southern Christian. But we must, in following the mainstream, put aside such Catholic landmarks as the Florida missions, the New Orleans' French and Spanish settlements, and the thoroughly American instance of Bishop John England's program of lay and democratic usage in Charleston (1820-1842). The Anglicans emanated from their establishment in Virginia; the Lutherans out of southern Pennsylvania; and other sects were born, or cross-fertilized, dissected or died in the land south of the Potomac, Delaware and the Ohio rivers. But the three great currents were in this order: Presbyterian, Methodist and Baptist. All came south in the latter part of the eighteenth century There had been a Presbyterian church in western Virginia in 1738; John Wesley had been in Georgia in 1735, but this was before the founding of Methodism; there was a Baptist church in Charleston in 1684. Not until the years 1755 to 1775, however, did the three great evangelical churches organize with sufficient strength to cover the South. By that time they had become, in spite of their Anglican and Calvinist beginnings, authentically American.

The South is really many Souths, geographically as well as culturally. There is Appalachia — Tennessee and Kentucky, present West Virginia and the northern, mountainous parts of North Carolina, Georgia and Alabama. Here the religious mainstream was staunch Presbyterianism. There is the Deep South — South Carolina, and most of Georgia, Alabama and Mississippi and the upper part of Louisiana — where the three denominations, Methodist, Presbyterian and Baptist, predominate. Then there are such exotic Souths as southern Florida, cosmopolitan New Orleans, and the technologically-orientated settlements at Chapel Hill, North Carolina; Oak Ridge, Tennessee; and Cape Kennedy, Florida. In these centers of transplanted Yankees, all faiths and forms can be found.

Despite generous exceptions, the religious current has been Calvinist, plus the Dissenters' moral code of the seventeenth century. This enabled the fixed and static teachings of predestination to bear fruit in a stern way of life. It was every-man-in-his-proper-place, a status quo of the social order. But the code of dissent put a high value on autonomy (as in the Presbyterian and, even more, the Baptist tenets) and emotional individualism (as in the Methodist).

Compensating factors included a devotion of a very profound nature and emphasis on the Bible, the home and the local church. The awareness of God (true, it was the Jehovah of Sinai and the prophets) ran through the South in a degree equalled only by the New England faith of the Great Awakening of the 1740's. It was during the Second Awaking in the 1760's that the three sects made their indelible imprint on Appalachia and the Deep South.

These are the primary streams. They affect the "leaders," the "led," and the "lost." They lie deep in the narratives of such diverse southern writers as William Faulkner, Flannery O'Connor and Robert Penn Warren. They have inspired such great schools as Duke and Emory Universities; they have been evoked in white citizen councils, lynchings, legislation to search Catholic convents, and the cross-burnings of the Ku Klux Klan.

UPS AND DOWNS OF UNITY MOVEMENTS

When the gentle but powerful evangelist, John Wesley, said to another Christian, "If thy heart be as my heart, then give me thy hand," he touched on one of faith's most dynamic instincts: the desire for unity with others in God. A Baptist historian, Dr. Theron D. Price, recently put it this way:

> Our natures seem to require the displacement of chaos by the realization of unity and continuity in the order of existence. In this sense, unity is primarily an instinct or drive.... Apart from such instinct and struggle there would be for us no conquest of chaos and therefore no cosmos and no culture. (*Christian Unity in North America*, 1958, "A Southern Baptist Views Christian Unity," p. 81.)

How well has Wesley's invitation and this Baptist "instinct for unity" worked out in Southern churches? No ready answer is available. Nearly two centuries have been filled with what Dr. Walter B. Posey, church historian of Agnes Scott College in Decatur, Georgia, has termed "Religious Strife on the Southern Frontier" (1965). The very chapter headings of his book are signs of controversy: Protestants against Protestants (that is, Baptists, Methodists and Presbyterians); Against a New Sect (the Disciples of Christ); Against Catholics, especially after Lyman Beecher's *Plea for the West*, in 1832, for an end to a "system of ignorance, priestcraft and superstition." This last movement might be called polarized ecumenism. That is, souls uniting to fight a common Christian enemy, or even, in the light of Our Lord's counter-plea "That they all may be one," ecumenism-in-reverse.

Granted a certain instinct for unity, the American experience has been corroborated by such foreign visitors as Alexis de Tocqueville in the 1840's and Philip Schaff in the 1850's. To cite but two observations:

> All the sects are comprised within the great unity of Christianity, and Christian morality is everywhere the same. (de Tocqueville, *Democracy in America*, p. 314)

> We need no new sects; there are already too many.... America, to fulfill her mission, has only to present in its unity and beauty the old and eternally young church of Christ... embodied in so many denominational sects, yet united in a common national life. (Schaff, *America*, pp. 203-04)

Toward the end of the century, James Bryce of England again oversimplified American ecumenism: "Proposals for union... witness to a growing good feeling among the clergy, and a growing indifference to minor points of doctrine and church government." (Bryce, *The American Commonwealth*, II, p. 580)

But religious unity was not as simple nor as near as these foreign prophets saw it. Cooperation between denominations was not widespread, but antagonism was. "They found strength," writes Dr. Posey, "in exclusiveness, individualism, and eventually divisiveness." (Posey, *Religious Strife on Southern Frontiers,* p. 18) An old preacher summed it all up. "What must they come amongst us for? If we allow them to come into our churches, the people will all go to hear 'em preach, and won't go to hear us preach, and we shall all be put down."

It is discouraging to the honest ecumenist to hear a highly placed prelate, Bishop James Cannon, Jr., repeat almost the same thought in the 1930's when the "organic union" of the Northern and Southern Methodist Episcopal churches was being discussed. He wrote, "The Methodist Episcopal Church, South, would not agree to that plan because it would be swallowed up, and be a minority of one-third." (Cannon, *The Present Status of Methodist Unification,* p. 19)

The Catholic position, although that of a decided minority, rooted its exclusivenes in the doctrine of the true Church and its historical continuity. Seen with the vision of faith, or even with the human eyes of history, it represented both a fidelity that fickle America could well learn, and an intransigence that our pluralistic society could well forego. Unwanted and uninvited to the shifting table of religious union, Catholics generally stayed close together, provided their own schools, societies and journals. When they discussed Protestantism, it was usually by way of reply to the ancient charges of "ignorance, priestcraft and superstition." Whatever the Catholic response to an invitation to union would have been, there are few instances of such a Protestant invitation ever being proffered.

In the South, perhaps even more than the East or Midwest, the denominations "shoved and pushed, attracted and repelled each other like children." (Posey, p. 23) The coming of foreign and home missionary societies, Sunday schools and tract-distributors led the Apple Creek Baptist Association to invent a new word, unfellowship, with all such foreign groups. One reason was their fear that these groups would insist on an educated clergy; another, equally strong, was that the missioners were more concerned with new-fangled ideas that were broader in scope than the parochialism of the separate churches.

Roughly summarizing, it may safely be said that four factors brought the quarreling Protestants together. (1) The revivalism of 1805-1806 when all forces joined in the truly phenomenal camp-meetings and wholesale conversions. (2) The anti-Catholic campaign starting in the 1850's with the heavy Irish and German immigration and contining well into the twentieth century. In reality, this union against the common enemy never ceased, it just rose and fell. (3) The crisis of the War of 1861-1865 which brought Southern churches (except the

Catholic and the Episcopalian) together, and separated them from their Northern counterparts. (4) The union against science and the new philosophies, when Dr. J. H. Thornwell, soon to be the president of the College of South Carolina, accused his old teacher of "infidelity." From southern pulpits, the word went out that this infidelity and a new paganism called Science was sweeping the world. "Christianity and atheism are the combatants," added Dr. Thornwell, "and the atheists, socialists, communists, red republicans and jacobins are all on one side." (W. J. Cash, *The Mind of the South,* p. 92)

It is certainly true that in better men the nobler instinct of a true religious harmony persisted. In 1858, a prominent Methodist preacher, Augustus Longstreet, asked his colleagues to drop their anti-Catholicism and bind all the South, all foreigners, Catholics and Democrats, against nativism. The Episcopal Bishop of Kentucky about the same time accused the sects of wasting their time with "paltry distinctions, to the sad neglect of the weightier matters of our common Christianity." (Posey, p. 13)

At the First Vatican Council, Bishop Augustin Verot of Savannah argued against the timing of the decree on papal infallibility in these words: "I live among Protestants, and I have a pretty good opportunity to see how they conduct themselves . . . . It is not accurate to hold that among them there is increasing hostility toward the Holy See. (If the exposition of certain points is softened and moderated by the council, as far as truth will bear) then at least the door will be opened." (Michael V. Gannon, *Rebel Bishop,* p. 215.)

Probably many clergymen of all faiths and certainly their intelligent laymen looked forward to a day in which these sentiments could be realized. As Robert E. Speer, the Presbyterian president of the Federal Council of Churches, said in 1924, "We are coming to a common recognition of the elemental unity of life and experience among Christians. There is no Presbyterian type of sin with which only the Presbyterian Church can deal." (*United in Service,* Report of Federal Council of the Churches of Christ in America, 1920-1924, p. 14)

But the nineteenth-century American experience left us a sad heritage of discord and division. It still exists today. Since the humble beginnings of the World Council at Edingburgh in 1910, the movement toward unity has gained momentum. Recent events, most especially the late and highly significant Vatican Council (1962-1965), have increased this momentum. If it was true, as was stated in the 1930's, that there was "much interest, less understanding," today there is surely much more interest and the beginnings of a sound understanding.

ECUMENICAL DEVELOPMENTS SINCE 1910

In our times, H. Richard Niebuhr has said, "Denominationalism represents the moral failure of Christianity." (*Social Sources of Denominationalism,* p. 25) The Vatican decree on ecumenism contains this pregnant sentence. "In recent times more than ever before, the Lord of Ages has been rousing divided Christians to remorse over their divisions and to a longing for unity."

Perhaps the two World Wars have forced our generation to re-examine the power of the old instinct for religious unity. Lives spent cheaply, nations crushed, supplies and money rising in clouds of waste, personal despair and group frustration — these are expensive ways of maintaining the peace. Technology without a conscience, security without cost, and pleasure without effort have added to the human condition. America is wealthy, weary and misunderstood. The South is wracked by the death pains of an ancient slavery and contemporary injustice. Can the churches today offer us a unity that politics, economics and science have failed to provide?

A religious profile of the Southerner does not necessarily encourage our quest. In Appalachia and in the Deep South, the dogma of Calvin, the cult of violence and a faded individualism vie for mastery with brighter, more vital, more Christian qualities. Why is liturgical renewal so rare in the major evangelical churches of the mainstream? Why has the restless questing of the human intellect so seldom linked with God? Why has an emotional storm more meaning than a true understanding? Why has the social gospel, with its demands of economic justice, of living wages, and racial equality of non-discrimination, been so little recognized? The churches have been slow to help the worker and the Negro, but the body of the denominations has been even more resistant. In 1955, Robert Crawford, a hard-shell segregationist, told a Virginia audience, "The worst obstacle we face in the fight to preserve segregated schools in the South is the white preacher. The patriots of Reconstruction had the preachers praying for them instead of working against them." (James McB. Dabbs, *The Southern Heritage,* pp. 252-53.)

All these factors — isolated worship of God, a suspicion of the human intellect, racial and economic sectarianism — have worked against religious unity. They have been based not on love, but on fear. In a survey made in 1934, the Southern Evangelical churches were shown to favor the present denominational system, and being thus conservative, disapproved any strong impetus toward genuine union. In the quadrennial meeting of the Federal Council (1924), one Methodist layman,

Mr. M. M. Davies of Atlanta, said clearly, "I began to realize the narrowness, the bigotry of denominationalism, and the value of cooperation .... The coming of the Kingdom is delayed because His followers are in so many different groups." (*op. cit.* p. 24)

The Catholic bishops of the Carolinas, Georgia and Florida would agree with Mr. Davies in their recent pastoral letter. They wrote, "History reveals a splintered Christianity; centuries have failed to heal it. But on this Pentecost [1965] our hopes are higher. In the presence of a growing dialogue and a hearty cooperation, one can hardly deny that the Holy Spirit, breathing over an anxious world, is inspiring men of all beliefs to meet together to talk and pray together."

Emory University, Methodist-orientated, is growing into a truly ecumenical center in Atlanta. Last week, a significant unity service was held there with all the major faiths represented, and the university awarded honorary degrees to its own Bishop Frederick Pierce Corson and to the distinguished world religious leader, Leo Josef Cardinal Suenens.

Similar examples abound today. Catholics have come out of their non-ecumenical shells, and Protestants — both leaders and led — are becoming much more aware of the great work of the Council of Churches. There is evidence of ferment at the pastoral, and especially the academic level. There is even considerable leadership from many bishops and other officers and administrators. But perhaps it is the layman who is most interested, even though his understanding may not be too mature. After all, Baptists have worked and lived with, socialized and argued with, even married and bore children with Catholics, and vice versa. Why cannot both begin the simple steps up the ecumenical ladder together? Laymen, it might be said, can rush in where bishops and theologians fear to tread.

THE FUTURE — WAVE OR EBB-TIDE?

Among the wiser aphorisms of Karl Marx was his comment that history repeats itself, once as tragedy, then as farce. How neatly that epigram fits the South! There was something of glory in the Rebel generals, perhaps even in the Confederate leaders. There is only a pale shadow (with a loud-speaker) in today's southern governors with their sheriff-bullies and ragged editors.

Can we fit the Church unity movement into this world of tragedy/ farce? When one of three churches located side-by-side in a row refuses to share in an exchange-collection to be given to the church next door to help its needy children, just where are we? When a bi-racial committee fails to get the largest church-body in the city to provide a single representative, where do we stand? We are very probably on time for the curtain to rise on the twentieth century's most ironic farce.

Ecumenism has received a bad press since the sixteenth century and nowhere with less need than in the American South. With a common Bible and the Lord's Prayer to start with, an awareness of the presence of God in our lives, a moderate degree of commitment to and mission in the world — we should have been more prepared for the ecumenists than we were. Christians should not have shuddered, or worse, turned away, when a Methodist, Rupert E. Davies, said in 1962, "Denominational evangelism has ceased to be of any great value at all. There is no longer a receptive audience for those who teach as Methodists or Anglicans in isolation from their fellow-Christians . . . ." (*Methodists and Unity*, p. 98) A Baptist, Dr. Theron D. Price, also wrote in 1958: "Our ecclesiastical divisions *per se* are less serious than lukewarm faith and feeble love . . . . The Southern Baptists are in much greater danger at present of failing to make our witness to the Whole Church by isolation than of losing the distinctiveness of that witness by association." (*Christian Unity in North America*, "A Southern Baptist Views Christian Unity," p. 88)

On the ecumenical roadway there are detours, roadblocks, soft shoulders and pot-holes. But as in every human endeavor, God works in His own good time. We must trust that His Son's prayer, "That they all may be one," will be realized either with, without or alongside our puny efforts. The ladder of religious unity has many steps, and there is no place to begin except at the bottom rung.

In order, we might start with *Preliminary Ecumenism*: conversions and contacts, and always courtesy and kindness. This is what Catholics and Protestants should have been doing for the past four centuries. Our time-lag can be compensated for only by the honesty and charity of our present approach.

Second, *Praying Ecumenically*: this stage engages us in public and private prayer for unity. Here we pray with Our Lord.

Third, *Acting Ecumenically*: every mutual effort toward the common good, from a bowl of hot soup for a convalescent Baptist to an elaborate cooperative program of racial justice.

Fourth, *Understanding Ecumenically*: now the work really starts. To learn about other churches, to hold them in reverence, to stress similarities and to examine and honestly explain the dissimilarities.

Good will and trust, of course, are necessary on both sides, but without the hard work of study they will issue in nothing but superficiality.

Fifth, *Doctrinal Ecumenism*: at highest levels, in the study and comparison of religious concepts, their history and their development. The finest minds must be linked to honesty, and the unity instinct must be rooted in charity. This is the work now going on between members of the Bishops' Commission on Unity and their opposite numbers in the Council of Churches.

Finally, *Full Ecumenism*: actual sharing of beliefs and common participation in the liturgy. We must view this phase in the light of four centuries of strife, and countless sects, denominations, and churches. But it is of far more importance to think of this achieved unity as God's work needing man's best efforts.

"If I were a mystic, I would attribute the change in the South's situation to fate," historian Walter Prescott Webb recently said. "If I were a minister, I would say that the Lord Himself, after permitting the people to suffer much, has finally come over on the side of the South." (Webb, *The Idea of the South,* "The South's Future Prospect," pp. 71-2.)

Perhaps, He has. If this is true — that He has spurred on our instinct for religious unity and corked the bottles of venom and violence distilled from our peculiar grapes of wrath — we *can* look upon a second springtime. We are located in time on the eve of a verdant April. When Stephen Vincent Benét wrote *John Brown's Body* he envisioned the "little New Year, the weakling one blowing the fluff from a turkey-wing at skies already haunted with Spring." Our Southern skies have been haunted all right. They lie heavy over our heads like the steamy night of a Georgia camp-meeting. We have walked along the three great streams of Baptists, Presbyterians and Methodists. We have watched them sweat together on the "anxious seat," then rise in anger against each other because of dissension. Then we saw them fight together a new claimant, the Disciples, or an old enemy, Romanism.

Secession from the Union brought them into a union of their own, and disunion from their Northern co-religionists. Thus united, the Southerners were ready to meet the eighteenth-century enemy — rationalism — in the 1900's, and the nineteenth-century foes — science and socialism — in the twentieth.

Out of it all, the ugliness and glory, the boasts and humble prayers, we inherit once again what we have called before a new South. We are haunted with Spring. If we stay apart in sectarian isolation, it will be a cruel, deceptive Spring. But if we climb unity's ladder, step by step, with courage and patience, it will be a Spring of Christian hope.

The God of Calvin — stern, alone, forbidding, exclusive. Or the God of Jesus — father as well as judge, gentle as well as firm, all-embracing and all-forgiving. Which God will the South adore in our time? If we are content to float with the ebb-tide, we will lose our living faith in the backwash of history. But if we strike out together, then Christians will ride on the future's wave. It is a wave of trust and hope and the unity of all God's People in Christ Our Lord.

PEACE IS PRETTY POOR READING

For the average American today, 6 May, 1967, appears to be ancient history regarding the Vietnam War. On that day, however, it was a burning issue and revealed the prophetic insight of the Archbishop of Atlanta. He was the first ranking American Catholic prelate to voice disapproval and dissent with American involvement in Vietnam. In this address, delivered before the Institute for Continuing Education in Detroit, he simply entitled his speech "Remarks on War and Peace." The editor has changed the title to incorporate a quotation the Archbishop used from the works of Thomas Hardy: "War makes rattling good history. Peace is pretty poor reading." And again, "The man of peace shall sing of victory."

The man who must have breathed and lived the double subject of *War and Peace* was Count Leo Tolstoy, who wrote a huge book about it. But he did not solve the dilemma: why war, not peace? He finally asked the ultimate question, "Why do Christians, professing the law of love, murder one another?" Nobody has answered that one.

An Englishman of the nineteenth century, Thomas Hardy, gives us a clue: "War makes rattling good history. Peace is pretty poor reading." Walt Whitman, the big, broad American poet, went further; "The real war will never get in the books."

A large measure of the fault lies not in those who write books, but those war leaders they write about who inspire them. A verse about the sword-rattling Theodore Roosevelt pinpointed his personality:

Our hero is a man of peace,
Preparedness he implores
His sword within his scabbard sleeps,
But, good Lord, how it snores!

It is often, however, the warrior who has given us the best definition of war. General William Tecumseh Sherman of the Union Army told the city fathers of Atlanta early in 1864, "War is cruel, and you can't refine it." Later, in a letter to an old Army buddy, General Steele, he added, "War at its best is barbarism." And a dozen years after Appomattox he told the graduates of Michigan Military Academy:

> I am tired and sick of war. Its glory is all moonshine. It is only those who have neither fired a shot nor heard the shrieks and groans of the wounded who cry aloud for blood, more vengeance, more desolation ... [Then in the shortest definition on record, he concluded:] War is hell!

Were it not for an unearned gift of humor, and an even more unmerited gift of Christian faith, I could well be a man torn with anguish. Even humor and faith, on their respective levels, can be clouded today by the obscurities and complexities in which we walk. So I am a "clergyman concerned about Vietnam," to use the name adopted by one peace group. My concern is merged with theirs, with that of a growing number of ministers, priests, rabbis and bodies of religious leaders. Our moral focus is being sharpened. Our concern is being deepened.

I certainly do not mean that we are concerned about Vietnam with the old romantic attitude, "Let's bless the weapons, and get on with the killing, the winning of the war!" We cannot forget that thoughtful "marking" of Dag Hammarskjold: "Your cravings as a human animal do not become prayers just because it is God you ask to attend to them." The chaplain's role in war is not to sing, "Praise the Lord and pass the ammunition!" If he is to be a good chaplain, realistic and reverent of human life, he cannot go beyond the teaching of war as a duty, and a sordid, ugly and inhuman duty at that.

Nor do I mean concerned because I have been touched personally by some danger or inconvenience, or because of some fixed commitment to a conservative or liberal position. By concerned I mean just what the Catholic bishops of the United States said in their statement of November, 1966: "It is clearly our duty to insist that all the issues involved in the Vietnam crisis be kept under constant moral scrutiny .... It is our duty to magnify the moral voice of our nation." In an eloquence born of his own past discouragements and of Christian hope, Pope Paul VI, on October 4, 1965, spoke for all men of good will when he cried out "No more war, war never again!"

In the agonizing dilemma of war and peace, we should not be surprised to find a wide divergence of opinion among Christians, Jews, Moslems and those of other faiths. Some of these opinions rise not out of moral, but out of political soil: the detailed questions of armament and negotiations, bombing and withdrawal. On these we can and must debate. But other issues are fundamentally moral: the indiscriminate destruction and/or methodical extermination of cities and peoples; the acknowledgement of the courage and honesty of the honest soldier and the honest pacifist; escalation and overkill; full access to all necessary facts from civil and military leaders; the use of international bodies working for peace like the United Nations. Here there is very little room for debate.

I believe that the first group, those essentially political in nature, are debatable in the full light of religious liberty and the open freedom of the American conscience. There is not just one answer to any of these questions: when to arm, when to negotiate, when to bomb, and when to withdraw? These are political and military means to an end. A hundred intentions and circumstances enter in. We must as citizens judge them carefully, and we must respect the sincerity of those who hold different judgments from our own.

The moral judgments on the other hand differ in kind. I beg leave to sum up the authentic Catholic position, authentic, because it can be found in the Vatican Council, the pleas of John XXIII and Paul VI, and the statement of the National Conference of Catholic Bishops in November, 1966. It is set in the full context of Christian faith, well expressed by Hammarskjold when he wrote, "I am the vessel. The draught is God's, and God is the thirsty one." In great part this is the Catholic position: that God desires and loves His children. From love flows basic principles of moral law. In understanding that law there could well be important differences. In substance, I do not believe there are.

1. We hold that it is morally evil to destroy indiscriminately whole cities or areas with their people. This is a crime against God and man himself. In this same category of condemnation would be any plan for the methodical extermination of an entire people. Blind obedience to such orders cannot excuse those who carry out these evil actions.

2. We hold that the stockpiling of weapons with its underlying philosophy of overkill is a treacherous trap for mankind. It is a false deterrent, not only because it is loaded with danger but because it exhausts the resources that should be used to alleviate the needs and misery which cause war.

3. We believe that it is unworthy of a great nation to withhold from its citizens those facts and issues which are involved in a war. True, there is always a minimal area where national security must be insured. This imposes certain necessary, but quite limited restrictions on the release of information. It does not throw a blanket of secrecy over subjects as serious as the bombing of civilian targets.

4. The man who in good conscience refuses to bear arms, and instead performs some other service to the human community, deserves the protection of the law, and it may be that history will accord him a worthy role in the keeping of the peace. Those, on the other hand, who defend their own nation or another people in the struggle against aggression merit the traditional honor of those who, in Gospel style, demonstrate their love for their fellowmen by giving their lives for them.

5. We must summon up all possible support when our government makes efforts to negotiate a workable formula for real disarmament. This should proceed at an equal pace for those involved, and be backed up by authentic and workable safeguards.

6. We must support the work of international bodies working for peace, especially the United Nations. Basic to this is our willingness to accept honorable decisions that may cost us some inconvenience or loss. As Paul VI said last fall, "The settlement may have to be made later in the train of bitter slaughter, and involve greater loss."

If churches — and we are the churches — are to magnify the moral voice of our nation, they must teach better than they do now that man must love his neighbor. Charity must guide the judgments we make on friend or foe, on presidents and foreign leaders, on senators and editors. The hawk has no right to hate the Vietnamese, north or south; the dove has no right to speak of presidents or generals with ridicule and insult.

There are alternatives to war. Every nation, of course, has the right to defend itself and other peoples who are victims of aggression. All the means short of force are to be used first, but we hold with the bishops of Vatican Council II: "As long as the danger of war remains, and there is no competent and sufficiently powerful authority at the international level, government cannot be denied the right to legitimate defense."

The world's championship of peace must become so evident, so intense, so convincing that the old balance of mutual terror will be phased out to make way for a new balance of mutual trust. We must all walk the second mile; we must continue to cry out in a hope born of our faith in God. If many nations come to trust each other, those who instead rely on war may re-evaluate their own positions.

Demonstrations and petitions have their place. Sometimes they can add decibels to the squeaky voice of the national conscience. But full-page ads and mobilizations often perform only the limited task of reassuring those who already agree, or almost agree. Selma was different. In the bitter war of civil rights, Selma challenged Americans to stop talking about racial justice and do something about it. It worked and is working, despite the ancient maunderings of rightists who are wrong and the inflammatory jargon of the leftists who are neurotic.

The movement for peace urgently needs its own Selma to serve as a ferment within the national conscience. This new Selma will cut through the peace talk, and convince our people that justice, freedom, human compassion, as well as peace are at stake. Until a major event like the second Selma happens, we all have work to do.

To move from smooth principles to the raw tasks ahead of us is like transferring from a jet to wheelbarrow — and just about as exciting. But the tasks remain and multiply and irritate.

Enlarge this new climate of thought that makes peace not just desirable, but possible. Our age prides itself upon science, technology and power; it is unreasonable to argue today that war is still the right way to restore violated rights. We have at hand many channels of influence: ordinary conversation, lectures, books and pamphlets, thinking and discussion groups. The Christian must be truly a channel of peace.

Urge in detail a particular course of action. This requires study and prayer, a cleansing of old prejudices, an insight into new approaches, a will to go beyond the knee-jerks of the hawk and the dove. Surely there is nothing incongruous in a Catholic advocating mutual agreements, inspections and safeguards. If he works to bolster an international body for peace, is he doing anything more exotic than following the words of Christ, "Blessed are the peacemakers, for they shall be called the sons of God" (Matthew 5:9)?

These are a few practical moves that he can rightfully make and nobly encourage. The Christian must be an advocate of peace.

Finally, we can insist that our government pursue, wholeheartedly and repeatedly, every opening that has even the slightest hope of a peaceful settlement. We must insist that our allies do the same thing, and our enemy and his allies do it too. America's past sins and present errors should not produce a myopia that lets us see only the opposition as the victims. The Christian must be the persistent and probably the unpopular seeker after peace, a peace arrived at by the road of justice.

The immediate victims of war are the people of Vietnam, the wounded or dead fighting men on both sides. But there are millions more unsung victims. Some are in Southeast Asia, millions more are in Africa, India, impoverished China and Latin America. Our slum-filled cities and impoverished countryside shame and torment our own America. Their only clothing is their anonymity. Their only shelter is the lonely shell into which they have withdrawn. The supplies, money, skills and techniques that are feeding the war in Vietnam are not feeding the poor there and here.

Our generation will have to answer to God's Word. His prophet Amos and His disciple James warned the complacent leaders of their times that God would judge sternly because "men persecuted their brothers with a sword, stifling pity," and "trampled on the heads of ordinary men."

There are so few valid reasons for war. We should appeal to history to learn the futility of battles; but it is dangerous to use history to form judgments on the half-formed perspectives of other centuries. We appeal to the God of peace, remembering Tolstoy's words in *War and Peace*, "How can Christians professing the law of love, murder one another?"

Our conscience and our voice must be raised against the savagery and terror of war. But we must do more than speak and hold meetings and issue declarations. These are only directional lights. On the road that leads to lasting peace, they are needed, but they are not enough. We must run that second mile. We must trudge when we cannot run; we must stumble when we cannot even walk.

This history of mankind, stained with the blood of our wars, has in spite of itself been a history of man's search for peace. Other civilizations foolishly thought they had secured it when they had only achieved the terror of an armed *Pax Romana* or the trading power of a *Pax Brittanica*. The nations of our age — bitter, bloody and alienated — do not paint a very good portrait of true peace. But no one can deny that there is a new power alive in the world, the acknowledgement of guilt because we have done what we should not have. Guilt can prepare the human patient for the catharsis of repentance. And only with repentance can our social well-being be restored.

War is exciting, peace is dull. War is romance, peace is routine. But war's normal habitat is hell, while peace abounds only in God and the pilgrimage we make to Him in heaven. In the Psalms that we all love there is a significant comparison of the warrior and the man of peace:

> I saw a wicked man, fierce and stalwart as a flourishing
> > age-old tree.
> Yet as I passed by, lo, he was no more; I sought him, but he
> > could not be found.
> Watch the wholehearted man, and mark the upright.
> > There is a future for the man of peace.
> > > (Psalm 36)

Which man will we preach, the fierce one or the wholehearted? What destiny will we seek, "Lo, he was no more," or "There is a future for the man of peace?" The answers are clearer now than they were in 1941, or 1917, or 1861, or 1775. There can be only one Christian type, the man who is whole of heart. There must be one human destiny, the future of the man of peace.

THE CHURCH LOOKS AT THE COURTS

This address, delivered before the district jurists and members of the Bar of Louisiana and Georgia, was given 10 May, 1967. It represents the Archbishop's concern for all aspects of the pastoral ministry. Although not included in the address, in his own handwriting he jotted down some introductory remarks (as was generally his custom). The five notations he made deserve mentioning. The first states, "My first brush with the law was at the age of ten, known as 'Hallinan vs. Sisters of St. Mary's School.' I was apprehended for throwing icy snowballs at some fourth grade girls. I was brought before Sister Escobeda." The second notation: "I had no counsel; interrogation took place without warning that I had a right to presence and aid of counsel during questioning." Third item: "I was charged with felonious assault and battery by Sister (ironically) Justina. No witness. No evidence. When asked direct question, 'Did you throw?' Reply, 'I did.' 'Anything to say in your defense?' 'Yes, I did not hit anybody." Fourth item: "Sister Justina was a great baseball coach and she turned away in disgust as she said, 'Ten blows in each hand and write SNOWBALL 500 times." Fifth item: "Since I have subsequently had advice of counsel and learned that had I admitted only 'intent to strike' and got a negotiated plea of guilty I could have got the rap reduced to five blows and only fifty words on the blackboard — SNOWBALL!"

Our generation remembers well the intriguing story by Thornton Wilder, *The Bridge of San Luis Rey*. I do not cite it this morning as a preacher with a moral — the inexorable play of an impersonal force over the lives of ordinary people. And because I have no competence in the law (either criminal or civil), I do not propose to analyze the interaction of liability or evidence. It is introduced as a melancholy example of today's dilemma. The man of the courts and the man of the sanctuary are simply two contemporary figures, at once the proponents and the victims of today's moral crisis.

Wilder used the device of the crashing bridge to end the lives of his passengers and then to study the causes that brought them to this

165

destiny. It would be melancholy for society to watch the Church and the Courts go tumbling into the gorge, wearing our miters and our coifs at dizzy angles; our books, our experience, the ancient wisdom of our crafts lost. I am enough of a Christian optimist not to think we are nearing that bridge, but I hope our trust in the abiding presence of the law (yours and mine) will be treated with realism, not with romance.

One need go no farther than the latest conference on religious morality or the closest book on our moral crisis to realize that all is not well in the Kingdom. The pulpit is muted, the cross is covered up. Large vacuums loom, somewhat like the empty seas on our photographs of the moon. And since theology is preoccupied with many other matters, then psychology and sociology, with their focus on man, rush in to fill the gap. Cardinal Newman warned a century ago that this would happen.

In the university curriculum, theology eventually disappeared and now it is allowed in only by the side door of such subjects as Comparative Religion, or God in the Modern Novel. As a student once said to me, "God has been reduced to the status of an elective, and as the college catalogue says, he is not offered this year!" Anthropology and economics have the answers.

God is sidetracked in the university, travestied in movies and TV as the "man upstairs," and confined to a Religion Page (between the want-ads and the funnies) in our modern newspapers. God has come upon lean years. And as in Nietzsche's time, there are always present in the wings those who would bury Him. In a way, Christians can thank these dour undertakers who are presiding at the death of God. In a perverse sort of way they have lit up the dead-end of the tunnel down which militant atheists and mock-up atheists as well as the secular humanists have led us. The undertaker and the pallbearers of God have forced us to a stark choice: to go their way hugging their own tiny transcendence, or to go His way opening ourselves to the brilliance of His Word, the treasures of His compassion, and the rich vigor of life shared with Him. But these are not popular ideas today. "Take up your cross and follow me" has emerged in the idiom of today, reworded and reworked: "Take up your credit card and follow me." Or in a spiritual version, "Fly now, pray later."

I speak more hesitantly of your profession because of my own reverence for the law and my respect for the lawyers, judges and teachers of law that I have known. But it would be naive to assume that the courts occupy any more dominant moral role than the churches in the poll-conscious society of today. I suppose that sin (unfortunately thought of as our special commodity) has increased. I am daily assured by editorials and governmental bodies that crime certainly has. The daily diet of man's guilt has grown both in sheer size and in complexity. The latest findings that document your plight are from the President's Crime Commission, headed by Nicholas Katzenbach, former attorney general. I am sure you saw the news stories Sunday; I was in Detroit and enjoyed both sides of the battle. Local judges, stung by the treatment dealt out to some of Detroit's courts, replied in kind.

The mildest of these criticisms was that the nation's courts are "undermined, ill-trained and archaically organized." As special targets, the commission selected: (1) disparity of justice (lack of uniform standards); (2) negotiated pleas (with the startling statement that trial by jury is an exception in the criminal process); and (3) abuses in the lower courts due to untrained justices of the peace, the fee system and the failure to follow through with proper rehabilitation, especially of first offenders.

Aside from the Commission's report, the law seems to be plagued today by the dilemma of the freedom of the courts and the freedom of the press, the eternal see-saw between the rights of the accused individual and the right of society to protection, and the interplay of politics in certain areas of judicial selection.

There was a day when both Church and Court enjoyed a greater dignity in the social stratification. There were clergymen and bishops, advocates and judges. Thomas Cromwell, in the days of Henry VIII, could strike a cord sympathetic to the vulgar ear when he exclaimed:

> What Englishman can behold without Awe
> The Canvas and the Rigging of the Law?

Is this still valid? And God's dominion is incarnated in His churchmen, yet sometimes today it seems that the finest clerical compliment is, "A great guy! You'd hardly know he's a priest! (or minister! or rabbi!)"

I will not attempt to assess how far the men of the law are culpable for this alleged disarray of the Amercian system of laws. But I will humbly admit that on our side we have not as a body measured up to the servant ministry enshrined in the Judaic code and personalized for Christians in the Suffering Servant, Jesus. Instead of a public confession on behalf of the ministry, a litany of our shortcomings, I will cite a handy symbol. A best-seller when first published and still going well is a symptomatic little book called, "How to be a Bishop without being Religious."

If the church is reckoned as a private club with a sign on the door excluding some ten million Americans because they are not white; if the pulpit is silent on poverty, hatred, war and peace and most of today's relevant issues; and if the desacralized clergyman becomes more of a counsellor, a sociologist, a politician or a practitioner of the pleasant platitude — should we be surprised that our people go elsewhere for inspiration?

This dilemma, our present trouble, is serious. Can we help each other?

There is a wide plateau of responsibility on which the Church and the Courts meet, but each has its own equipment, its own instruments, a distinct function — and each institution has its own proper *raison d'etre*, its essential role. Our equipment and instruments are drawn from the storehouse of revelation, the emergence of faith, the discipline of theology. And the Church exists to lead men to their eternal destiny with Christ our Head, in God our Father.

The Courts, on the other hand, draw on the massive accumulation of laws, an "essential morality" (sometimes called the natural law), the rights and duties of both man and his society, the reservoir of man-made laws that aim to safeguard this morality, these rights and duties. These are the instruments of the Courts. And these Courts, the law as a profession, exist to lead men to their temporal destiny, a contemporary person able to cope with his own identity, the slings of outrageous fortune and the hostile maneuvers of other men.

Thank God, the Church and the Courts no longer, at least in this nation, are blurred by a false identity. We have had enough theocracy in human history to allow us to close happily the chapters of Calvin's Geneva, the Puritan colony, and certain Catholic states, of the nineteenth and early twentieth centuries. When religion takes on the robe of magistrate, or civil law takes up the burden of sacred things, only bitterness and then chaos can result. Man's ears have not been tuned to the theme of Oliver Cromwell's conscience: "I and God." The personal conscience grown majestic and righteous grows even more. It becomes untouchable and bitter.

Eugene Carson Blake, distinguished Presbyterian churchman, holds that the sin of pride (the Greek *hubris*) is the source of history's worst evils. Reinhold Niebuhr, another outstanding Protestant scholar, agrees: "Man, who is a creature, is continually tempted to assume the role of God." Thus the dichotomy so popular in the TV Westerns: the good guys (that's us) and the bad guys (that's them). This dichotomy springs from the screen into party politics, world affairs, crime, and even the pulpit. It's always the "other party," the Communists, the Mafia, juvenile delinquents, and in the language of the pulpit, "secularism," or the world's evils.

Neither one man nor one body of men can alone speak for God. And in terms of this address this morning, no one can be both shepherd and judge, minister and advocate. We cannot blur our vocations although we must seek mutual friendship and understandings. We are partners, not competitors. But our training, methodology, sanctions and ultimate functions differ.

In respecting this proper antonomy, I must leave your judgment of the Church to you. But I would like to suggest a few ways in which we, as churchmen, might enrich this partnership:

1. We see the law, civil as well as canonical, human as well as divine, as a causeway, to paraphrase Thomas More. It is not a light to see by nor primarily an instrument of equity. It is a causeway, said More just before his martyrdom, "upon which, so long as he keeps to it, a citizen may walk safely." And the civil law is a necessity of life. Again in More's words:

> This country is planted thick with laws from
>   coast to coast - man's laws, not God's.
> And if you cut them down - d'you really think you
>   could stand upright in the winds that would
>   blow then?

2. If a priest or rabbi is speeding, he may claim no exemption from the traffic law. And I submit that men of law may claim no exemption from the moral law, properly understood. Perhaps more than other professions, yours (like ours) must inquire and live and judge by the law of God in things eternal. For example, in the Presidential Commission's report there are certain points in which we share responsibility for the moral consensus and the moral methods:

(a) We are morally concerned if justice is diminished by the disparity of sentences, by the lack of judges or their necessary training.

(b) We are likewise aware that our open system of law (as opposed to the Star Chamber of earlier England) is seriously impaired by "negotiated pleas" of guilt that lack judicial scrutiny just in the interest of speeding up the legal calendar.

(c) We recognize the need of extensive rehabilitation, especially of first offenders, and regard such care as inconsistent with a political structure weakened by justices of the peace, the fee system, and the political choice of judges.

These are your problems, but they are equally ours. When justice is diminished, or public scrutiny is denied or rehabilitation is ignored, God's voice is not heard by a puzzled, disillusioned humanity. I can cite these offenses in good grace only if you reciprocate. You have equal right to criticize the working of religion, especially when the churches become irrelevant, uncommitted, affluent or absent-minded.

3. We meet in a common bond of responsibility. Yours is civic, ours is pastoral. This conviction of responsibility is losing out today; legal relativism sees no crimes, only abnormalities. Situational morality sees no sins, only conduct beyond the control of the person. In the words of Bishop John Wright of Pittsburgh, "The philosophy of responsibility has been replaced by the philosophy of excuse."

I fear that one reason for this creeping relativism has been the stagnation of its opposite — moral absolutism. If we define law as something always and everywhere the same rigid set of abstractions, it should not surprise us when anthropology, sociology, medicine and psychology shoot holes in it. Was the abandonment of babies wrong when it was the common practice of destitute, starving primitive people? Was usury based on money wrong in the Middle Ages when men knew only an economy of land? Was human sacrifice evil among underdeveloped people who put dumb gods before living creatures? These "exceptions" to the universal moral law do not destroy that law; they are sociological facts and circumstances which only modify or interfere with the law.

In the laws that you and I uphold, it is necessary to avoid both the bleak rigidity of absolutism and the shifting sands of relativism. The trouble with an abstract moral absolutism is that it is constructed from concepts, not realities. We must look at it more critically and restore to it the value of the individual, the sacredness of the person, and the responsibility of free men. We must recognize and allow for the inadequate and the unfortunate; their dignity and their protection are high on the list of society's obligations.

But, just as surely, we must not let this responsibility of free men degenerate into a "wasteland of relativism," as Paul Ramsey, Protestant theologian, terms it. The posters and luncheon club slogans that read, "Who is the real delinquent, this boy or society?" are misleading. They are only a few steps short of Jean Paul Sartre whose existentialism prompted him to say:

> There is nothing in heaven, nothing good or bad,
> no person who can give me an order.

As Blake puts it, "The code of ethics in public life must be absolute because the driving forces of self-interest and altruism are not sufficiently restrained by an absolute, objective right and wrong." But this code must at the same time be relative because God's law suffers by man's misuse of it. He can overcome the temptation to play God only by seeing the actual circumstances as well as the abstract law.

The original Christian use of the natural law allowed for this relativism. This is what one Catholic writer, Dr. Frederick Flynn, has called "essential morality." It is what Dr. Theodore Gill of the San Francisco Theological Seminary, means by "contextual ethics" in which God is the only total context in which moral decisions must be made. And even Bertrand Russell, who professes no theological preoccupations at all, has compromised:

> Without control, there is anarchy;
>   Without initiative there is stagnation.

In the Church, these are days of renewal. Vatican Council II has shown us the vision of the open Church, the relevant Church, the flexible Church. While the Word of God remains immutable, we are exploring a new theology, examining the moral imperatives, revitalizing our liturgy. But creed, code and cult are not the only subjects for renewal. There is a new vitality in its birth-pangs. It has its source in a deeper grasp of Scriptures, its accompaniment in a wider practice of ecumenism. The Catholic Church is in transition, and it is too early now to judge how far, how profoundly, how broadly the change will affect us.

The other great religions, especially Protestant, are experiencing a like transition. No religion could run this century's gamut of war, poverty, collectivism, racism and despair without awakening to the new world. There is evidence of this theological scrutiny on every side. It must not be confused with the spiritual revival that was so publicized and so disappointing in the decade following World War II.

From this new posture, the churches look at the Courts. Are you experiencing a similar renewal? Laymen to the law find snatches of this in their newspapers and books, although the present focus seems to be mostly on the legal side of President Kennedy's assassination and on a flamboyant string of criminal lawyers who never lose a case or an expense account. We must come to you to ask if there is really a renewal, an *aggiornamento* of the realities that have made the American vocation of the civil law an honorable profession?

Theater-goers and movie fans have found in "A Man for all Seasons" a hero whose faith and whose profession make Saint Thomas

More almost unique in the annals of Church and State. In his introduction to this brilliant dramatic study, the author, Robert Bolt, explains that More became for him

> . . . a man with an adamantine sense of his own self. He knew where he began and left off, what area of himself he could yield to the encroachments of his enemies, and what to the encroachment of those he loved.

He served his king, the nation, the civil law brilliantly and "he was able to retire in wonderfully good order, but at length he was asked to retreat from that final area where he located his self." The play silhouettes those instances where he could give in, his silence in the face of the king's divorce, for example. But in its final, gaunt scene, the play finds him

> in a little . . . little area . . . where I must rule myself. It's very little — less to him, the king, than a tennis court.

Here he shows that he has not blurred his king and his God in a theocracy. He recognizes the king's position, and in civil matters he admits its autonomy. But he knows, as he knew right along, that God's Word and God's minister, the pope, have their own autonomy too. He never loses the absolute law in the trees and thickets of relative situations. He goes to his death, saying

> I am the king's true subject, and pray for him.
> I am and all the realm.
> But God's true subject first.

OPEN EDUCATION IN THE OPEN SOCIETY

When Archbishop Hallinan accepted the invitation to address the graduating class at Charlotte, North Carolina, he did not realize, as he said himself, the implications of the situation that existed in that explosive city. He knew where he stood, and he knew also where his audience stood on the racial question when he delivered this address on 28 May, 1967. On this, as on other occasions, he proved himself to be both a true ecumenist and a sincere apologist.

When I accepted your gracious invitation to speak at this baccalaureate, I did not realize that your experience of 1965 and 1966 had become a topic of national interest. Churchmen, educators and civic leaders are keenly interested in this baccalaureate, in the "Charlotte experience." For example, in the current issue of the *Christian Century*, the experiment is set forth and ably debated by Rabbi Israel Gerber, of the Temple Beth El in Charlotte, and by the Protestant editors of the magazine.

The precise question at stake is the use of prayers at such public events as this, so I am only indirectly involved. My contribution is not a prayer, but a sermon, or more accurately an address. But I am profoundly concerned about the basic disagreement between the rabbi and the editors. The rabbi asks:

> Is it right for a majority to take advantage of such a situation to impose its religion on the minority? People of all faiths can join in public prayer if the basis for such prayer is communion with God.

The *Christian Century* disagrees:

> Let all people speak out in the strong, clear language of their own communities. Let each who hears do his own adding. subtracting, issuing of inner-reserve clauses. Let there be charity in those who listen as well as in those who pray.

As a Catholic citizen, I am (at least in the South) a member of a minority, just as the rabbi is. For more than two centuries we have

173

had little option. We have patiently heard God saluted in Protestant accents in school prayers and classwork, at graduations and Fourth of July celebrations, PTA meetings, kick-off dinners, even football games, and possibly in opening contests to select Miss Georgia Peach or Miss Piedmont Beautiful. I can sympathize, therefore, with the rabbi because usually the context of public prayer has had a long-standing Protestant content.

But I do not conclude that the answer is a prayer or a sermon that is nothing but a reduction to common terms. Prayer has its roots in the conscience, not in the consensus. I do not agree that democratic rights on the one hand, and religious etiquette on the other, so bind us that only the uncommitted prayer will do. I do not think that God is authentically worshipped or our human community well served by a common denominator set of prayers. Will Herberg, the American sociologist, documented several years ago how far our nation has already gone this route. There is, he concluded, one national religion. It has three forms: Protestant, Catholic, Jewish. This is hardly God's revelation; it is, more accurately, man's compromise.

I believe strongly that when any churchman speaks to the community or for it, he should speak up in the unquestioned accents of his faith. I want to hear a rabbi talk like a Jew, a minister like a Protestant, a Catholic or Orthodox priest like a Catholic. Clergymen of other forms should speak in accord with their principles.

Pluralism, the American way of life, can go several ways. It can issue in a bland, inoffensive, uncommitted no-religion. Or it can raise a healthy climate where each man speaks his own faith undiluted, and this can easily include the Moslem, Buddhist, and those who profess other ways to God. I have learned much of how to pray from the prophets of Israel and Juda, from Hosea, Micah, Isaiah and Daniel ... from the Methodist John Wesley and the one-time Baptist Roger Williams and the founder of Congregationalism Jonathan Edwards, and from many others.

When I listen to a Protestant clergymen pray, I become more aware of our single redemption in the Lord Jesus. When the Jew prays or speaks, I become more conscious of the Book of Genesis, of Moses, David and Job. And I hope that my Catholic accents will reflect the unity and universality of our Church with the long, Catholic panorama of Augustine, Aquinas, Francis of Assisi, Ignatius Loyola, Philip Neri, Thomas More, John Henry Newman, William Gaston, the Catholic statesman from this state, and the pioneers of the Georgia Catholic Laymen Association. I recognize the differences in our approaches, but I know that Jesus was a Jew by birth and education and the Lord of the universe to all Christians.

Of course, there must be rules of etiquette. In our American manner, pro-Catholic must not become anti-Protestant; pro-Christian must not degenerate into anti-Semitism. Courtesy, civility, kindness, love of each other, these virtues have no denominational barriers. Each faith must have its turn at gatherings such as this. We may feel that the atheists and those currently serving as pall-bearers for the funeral of God are no more disturbed by a religious prayer than they would be by an announcement that there are more seats down front. But in courtesy, charity and legality, it would be much better to excuse from attending at all.

We do not want the union of church and state. We do not need to violate the conscience of adult or child by forcing them into a "majority-religion" format of worship. But equally we do not accept a "no-God" nor an "anti-God" in our secular city's public polity. Nor will we find an adequate solution in a prayer of the lowest common denominator. It is my firm belief that we need not resort to any of these ersatz remedies.

If in charity and courtesy we agree to let each churchman pray and speak and act in his own religious idiom, then his conscience and our own will be held sacred. Then and only then will our communities draw upon the spiritual values and the God-awareness that have built the conscience of our nation.

I do not apologize to today's graduates for these comments on a current situation. More than earlier generations, like our own, they have already begun to probe such issues as these. This June's graduates, both high school and college, have had their own Head-start program for maturity. A diploma is no longer a badge of past achievement nor a credit card of future promise. It is simply a tag of identification, your new ID card, entitling you to continue your thinking, your love, your action, your decisions. And I am sure that, along with poverty, Vietnam, racism, automation, you are as much concerned with which way our religiously plural society goes as are your pastors and parents.

We have seen the spirit of rebellion grow: the militant students taking sides; the young Negroes fighting for their civil and political rights; the college bodies demanding the truth about Vietnam; the spirit of academic freedom growing. And in none of these headline-catching, sometimes productive, sometimes silly, sometimes frightening episodes have I ever found reason to lose my confidence in this new generation, the graduates of tonight — you. We have lived with war and poverty, dishonesty and injustice long enough. And I express my heart-felt hope to you tonight that the three remaining years of the 1960's will hear your questions, share your doubts, and thus shall we force the break-through of the status quo, the destruction of the packaged morality of our times, the reconstruction of our American society on political, social and economic applications of the moral law.

What is the Open Society? It is the assembly where the majority are citizens of the whole world as well as their nation and their region. The Open Society is characterized by a restless curiosity, a quest for truth, an escape from escapism. It is marked by a large majority of people to whom, in Robert Frost's words, "life is a pursuit of a pursuit forever." It is shaped by a compassion not just for abstract humanity, but for those close to us. And this compassion must go out to the anonymous — the deprived, the depressed, the depersonalized. The Open Society has a contempt for the superficial — the TV commercial, the spectator sport, the packaged culture. It is the willingness to dig and sweat for depth. Its atmosphere is charged with new ideas and insights, a will to use the true-or-false test on social experiments. This is what Walter Lippmann's *Good Society* was about. It is the spur to the modern term, "The Great Society." It is able men and women refusing to be anonymous men in David Reisman's *Lonely Crowd* or to be the dehumanized figures of George Orwell's terrifying prediction about 1984.

How does the Open Education, at secondary and college level, prepare for and serve and preserve the Open Society? Education exists, of course, to preserve the knowledge and culture of earlier times; it is to teach this to new generations, not in the boxes of formal courses, each carefully marked with the passing grade and all wrapped up with a big bow from a diploma. The Open Education teaches in order to help students to apply this knowledge to contemporary demands, issues and cultures. It must not just conform to the prevailing mind-set of today's society, but it is to form men and women who are impatient with today's serenity, a false serenity in the midst of growing poverty and senseless war and a voracious appetite for excess, serenity in the context of sin, respectable sin, serenity in a church which has often tailored itself into a private club with private membership and dues, and a No Admission sign for millions of our fellow Christians who happen to be black instead of white.

I suggest, first, to go past the now to the beyond. We can to a great degree control the present. We cannot control the future. But the hopes and ideas that come to you so passionately today can measure what manner of man or woman you will be. You will not be seventeen or eighteen very long, but your thirties and forties will stretch out. For the person with a purpose they will fly by, but for those who drift, they can become almost endless. A good marriage comes from an honest and sophisticated plan of dating and courtship. A productive job and career, with at least some openings of creative effort, can only come with the blood and sweat and tears of the lab, the classroom, the final exam and the above-passing grade. These are not new revelations; they are eternal truths. In the *Open Society* these are only the *sine qua non.*

Second, this graduating class must be a generation of realists. A dream world is a dangerous one in which to sow your visions. Not all hallucinations come from marijuana or out of a pot; many young people maintain their own do-it-yourself LSD kit. It is not produced from burnt bananas, but it can produce its own psychedelic world: day dreams, frustrations, laziness and diluted romance. It is a tiny compact existence, self-deceptive and self-defeating. The realist, whether he is twenty or forty or sixty, scorns it. Rest and recreation, relaxation, each has its role in life. But the turnip and the turtle can rest and recreate and relax, too. Only men and women can break out of Hamlet's dilemma.

Finally, our vision can be improved by standing on the shoulders of the past. This is not an easy posture to maintain but it surely improves the vision. The impatience of youth is usually directed at the messed-up society their parents left them. At most moments of human history this has been a fairly accurate diagnosis. You didn't invent nuclear warfare. You didn't buy up slums and rent them at exorbitant rates; you didn't start to segregate the Negro; you didn't prostitute your talents in politics by bribes and corruption. Our generation and those before us did these things. But, to their credit, they did one thing that was noble; parents and teachers that they were, they produced you. No matter how humble you may be, no matter how low you estimate yourself, you began life anew, and you owe this to the generation that now holds the reins. For good or evil, you have our experience, our mistakes and our achievements to examine and to use, to renew or discard. If I may be permitted one ministerial quote it is this. So live that the next generation will gain by your experience.

Because you have much to say that is worthwhile, we are listening. Because your capacity for curiosity and restlessness seems greater, we envy you. Because you have room for mercy and compassion, we

can learn from you, and because you are our own — all of us, children
of the same God — we offer you what you need most, our trust. Today
you are society's potential. Tomorrow, you are its reality.

We have faith in you. Under God, in whom other than you can
we place it?

FAITH AND THE HUMAN CONDITION

This is a pastoral letter issued jointly by Archbishop Hallinan and Bishop Joseph L. Bernardin in commemoration of the Year of Faith called for by Pope Paul VI. It first appeared in the 29 June, 1967, issue of the Georgia Bulletin.

"Do you believe in the Son of Man? . . . Lord, I believe!" — *John 9:35, 38.*

During Sunday Mass, the people of God stand for their profession of faith. Priest and laity assembled, they speak out with confidence and humility: "I believe in God . . ."

Toward the end, they tell why their faith is firm: "He spoke through the prophets . . ."

When they have been dismissed, they go their way — to cars, homes, recreation and work. Now, on Monday, Tuesday, week after week, do their hearts, enkindled at Mass, continue to burn within them? During the Creed, both the ordinary man and the intellectual understood what they professed at least obscurely. But many fail to follow through with their prayer, thought and meditation. Our instinct to believe is not sharpened. Our faith is openly professed, but quietly betrayed.

Our Lord knew this. Like the seed planted in the field, our faith is liable to misfortunes. Sometimes, the Word is snatched away by the usual forces of evil (in the Gospel, it is the birds). Trials and persecutions stifle it (it has no roots). Again, it may be diminished by worries or the pressures for wealth (it is choked by thorns).

What is the "rich soil" that generously produces a fine crop, the fourth possibility noted by Christ? Such soil is the open mind and will, heart and body and emotions, the social views of the man who hears the Word, understands and keeps it. This is the Christian man or woman of faith. In the Creed and in daily life, they answer Christ, "I believe!"

It is no secret that the Catholic world today is tense with anxiety. Modern man (and we are that man) reaches out in conquest, proud of his own self-awareness. Out of this has come a collective turmoil. We are impatient that man who can do so much can solve so little.

In a sense, the bottom has fallen out of our world. In more papal language, Pope Paul VI on the anniversary of Peter and Paul, the apostles of faith, has made this comment:

> Where God has no place, there is no longer a final explanation for reality, no inspiration for thought, no compelling moral sense that our human order needs.

A new generation of Catholic thinkers was unleashed by Vatican Council II's "Open Church." Study has opened up the riches of Scriptures; liturgy has opened new doors to God. Ecumenism has built a new bridge to other religions. The Church's social teaching has cut new paths through the inner city, suburbia, the minorities and emerging nations, and especially through the areas of God's poor wherever they are.

The Holy Spirit, moving over the assembled bishops, has re-awakened the whole body of Christians to a fresh, adult way of life. Faith — its meaning, application and loss — is being re-examined. This should not surprise us. The present pope is encouraging new "energies of Catholic thought in the search for fresh and adequate expression." But his chief role is pastor and father, and he has not abandoned John XXIII's formula for renewal:

> The substance of the ancient doctrine of the deposit of faith is one thing, and the way it is presented is another.

But what of Layman X, Father Y, Bishop Z? Faith, contained in the Church, is personalized in each of us. Am I waking to a fuller awareness of the faith, enlivened, purified and strengthened? Unless, on this anniversary of the apostles of faith, we can answer "Yes," then the Council and its aftermath remain only events of history.

A LIFE NOT A LIST

The Church, closely following the Bible, identifies faith as the acceptance of a person, Jesus Christ, the Son of God. When you read St. Paul's letters to the Romans, Corinthians and Galatians, you notice that the old catechism simply will not do. Faith is no single act, or series of steps or list of things to believe. Paul, speaking to unbelievers, describes the living faith. James, speaking to Christians, takes a more practical view and insists that behavior must harmonize with this living faith. There is no contradiction: faith to both apostles is not a one-time thing, static and fixed. It is an experience.

It is the apostle John, closest of all to Christ, who describes faith as a lived experience:

> We proclaim what was from the beginning, what we have heard, what we have seen with our own eyes, what we have embraced with our own hands.
>
> I refer to the Word who is and who imparts life. To you, we proclaim that we have seen and heard, that you may share our treasure with us . . . union with the Father and His Son, Jesus Christ.

Contemporary man is more concerned with the fact that things exist than why they exist. He reads more newspapers than books of philosophies. To such an existentialist mood, the ancient but fresh Christian faith speaks with far more meaning than it did a generation ago. Man is not asked just to accept a list of truths which surpass human knowledge. He is summoned to an encounter with Christ who speaks to us all that God wants to say to men. We are not just pupils of faith. We are participants and witnesses of it.

A recent *Pastoral Catechectics* (Hofinger and Stone) comments: "God comes to believers through the biblical, liturgical witness and doctrinal signs, unveiling His personality under the impulse of intense love." De Chardin addresses God in his hymn to the universe: "It is not just your gifts that I discern; it is you yourself that I encounter."

The theologian, Karl Rahner, links the Church to Christ: "This reality (the people of God) means a presence, as it were, an incarnation" of Christ's truth, will and grace.

Christianity has more than a message; it has a mission. It communicates to us not just an idea, but reality itself. Faith is a lived response. Robert Louis Stevenson, a man of deep religious sensitivity, put it in a way most men can grasp:

> In the harsh face of life, faith can read a bracing gospel.

THE BEGINNING OF FAITH

Every experience unveils something new. When the Council of Trent called faith "the origin, foundation and root" of our salvation, it meant that God was unveiling for us all the truths He wanted us to know.

St. Paul's classic definition of faith stressed the unveiling:

> Faith is the substance of things to be hoped for; the evidence of things that are not seen.

But faith does more. God speaks to us. Ours is not the fate of remaining silent observers of the silent God. "He has spoken to us through His Son." And we respond to this forthright language. The dialogue is obscure, of course. God uses our faulty languages: Hebrew, Aramaic, Hellenic Greek. We listen to the translated readings at Mass. We meditate on the texts in private.

Our reason plays its part, although the call to faith is God's gift. The French theologian, Jean Moroux, assures us that the Church "has always refused to admit a break between faith and reason." God would hardly have given this man the superb tool of the intellect if he had not expected man to use it in the noblest task of all. Despite those who rest their religion on a pillow of emotion, men of letters bear a long witness to reason's role. Robert Frost, our New England poet, asks:

> Grant me intention, purpose and design—
> That's near enough for me to the Divine.

Other writers like G. K. Chesterton insist on more than that. In his essays and short stories, the jolly Englishman demonstrated both the work of reason and the free gift of faith.

When the baby is brought to the parish church for baptism, the first question put to him is, "What do you ask of the Church of God?" The godparents answer, "Faith." In one word, his intention. In the words and rite of baptism, its fulfillment. The tiny creature of God becomes a child of God, a brother of Christ. Belief is on-going. It is our daily response carrying that simple answer. Faith, through the sacraments of penance, anointing and Eucharist received as death approaches.

In practically every document of Vatican Council II, faith is noted. Parents are its "first preachers." Educators give it "clarity and vigor." Priests strike its spark and then nourish it. Bishops confirm their people in it. In the liturgy, men grasp by deed what they hold by faith.

We have been blessed in this gift of faith, and we must not hold it lightly. Our reason played its part. So did preaching. So did the whole impact of Catholic life — God's goodness, our readiness, the example of those around us, the heritage of our parents. Faith started us on our rugged pilgrimage to God whom we will one day see face to face. What shall each of us do about it now?

MAN THE PILGRIM

A time of tensions is a time of choice. We do not always grasp this. Many Catholics fight the renewal because it is their nature to fight change. Others see it as a time to tear down the old, destroy old ways and experiment with new uncharted paths. The truth is, renewal is a time of choice. Karl Rahner states that today's Christian has discovered the sharply painful nature of choice:

> Each individual has to achieve [his faith] afresh for himself; it is no longer a heritage from our fathers.

This painful struggle may be at the root of what this generation calls an identity crisis. It is difficult to tell who we are unless we are more sure of what we are — flawed children of God, flawed by Adam's sin, restored by Christ, illumined by faith, enlivened by grace. Because faith will not be static, its alternating current in us can drive us wild. Christian men and women must ask:

(a) How is faith strengthened?

(b) How is it weakened and lost?

(c) How can it be restored?

(a) INCREASE OUR FAITH (Luke 17:5)

Father John Powell has observed that although the virtues sound sweet, "their practice is costly." Difficulties abound everywhere, but as John Henry Newman pointed out in his *Apologia,* there is a radical difference between a doubt and a difficulty:

> Ten thousand difficulties do not make one doubt .... I have never been able to see a connection between apprehending, however keenly, and multiplying them to any extent and, on the other hand, doubting the doctrines to which they are attached.

First, then, we must meet our difficulties head on. They are no more than symptoms of a malady that is subject to cure. But faith lives best in the whole man, not in a bland and superficial state of mind. Newman, again:

> The heart is commonly reached, not through reason, but through the imagination, direct impressions, the testimony of facts and events, by history and description.

Faith must permeate the whole man, each of us giving to its enrichment the best that he is. The ordinary layman strengthens his faith by repeated prayer, gratitude, hard work and perseverance. The Christian intellectual adds to these his own reflection, his reading, his skill of intellect. Surely the believer who leaves his Bible shut and his liturgy unlived is not strengthening his faith. Newman's prayer for faith works for us all:

> Oh Lord, here I am — I will be whatever you will ask me — I will bear whatever you put upon me ... Never will you bring me into any trial which you will not bring me through.

(b) YOU OF LITTLE FAITH (Matthew 8:26)

Faith can be weakened, and it can be lost. Our present society does little to help. Materialism, relativism and secularism are poor soil if we expect a good harvest from our faith.

But it is more likely that the torpor starts within us. If a man fails to relate his faith to the everyday facts of life, the bond intended by God becomes weakened. If he is harsh and critical to other persons and institutions, without love and compassion for them, his vision of the Church grows bitter. There is evidence of this in the well-publicized critiques of the Church by men whose faith has diminished, or even disappeared.

Our vigilance must be constant. We must meet difficulties with wisdom. Even doubts can have two effects: although they can enervate and weaken faith, they can also try and test it. Catholics must not rest comfortably on their belief. They are called to suffer many a struggle of doubt. Under pain of decline, the habit of faith must keep stretching toward a perpetual renewal and growth. It is not an insurance policy or a guarantee of a serene mind. Its exercise, amid difficulties and even with the resolution of doubts, is a necessary part of God's discipline.

The young people of today are both pioneers of an uncertain future and relics of a mixed-up past. Are they more apt to lose their faith? Our colleges and universities, neighborhood groups, the protests and demands seem to underline the crisis of belief. The Fathers of Vatican Council II honestly faced up to this young impatience and rebellion: "Aware of their own influence in the life of society, they want to take their role in it at once." As we think of it, this strong desire to assert oneself and to protest authority is not exclusively for the young. Women, minorities, the deprived and the disadvantaged are all asserting a new independence. Church, state, schools may not find this comfortable. But we must remember that these are tests of authority, a discipline; not of belief, a faith.

We must not forget either that history is on the side of the young. So is their zeal and innovation and hard work. So is their optimism about the future and pessimism about the past. To the extent, and only that far, that the adults of society share these young virtues have we earned the luxury of criticizing them.

Our Christian hope in these youths and in special minorities is a more attractive virtue than gloom. And it is far more effective.

Faith is not lost in one sharp act of disengagement. It dies slowly and painfully. Whether the cause is within or without, man can wake to a dreary life without faith, a series of fragmented days centered not upon God, but upon self.

The non-believer is an alienated person. He is also among the world's most lonely men.

(c) I HAVE KEPT THE FAITH (Paul to Timothy, II, 4:7)

There is much in today's Church that reminds us of the trials of Corinth in St. Paul's time. The Christians there let their faith be diminished by jealousy, shallowness and overpersonalization of their preachers. Paul dealt with them sharply. But near the end of his first letter to them, the apostle opened his heart:

> Be awake to all dangers. Stay firm in the faith. Be brave and be strong. Let everything you do be done in love.

For the man whose faith has lapsed, this is sound advice. When he is unduly drawn by fame or pleasure or popularity, when he resents the humility that must go with faith, when he is distracted or preoccupied with the personal — let him read Paul's advice and do whatever he does in love. For the Christian, Paul never separates faith and charity. In the same Corinthian letter, he gives the chart and dimension of authentic love, "the greatest of the virtues," the sure and steady bridge to God.

The doubting man, even the unbeliever, can still walk this bridge of love. The humanist and the socialist does not have the faith, but he still loves his fellowman. The poor man too, all who are in need, can join him on this crossing. "Those who are poor according to the world, God has chosen to be rich in faith." Charity is a generous avenue, and crossing it, every man can link the burden of his good works to the gift of belief. As Paul adds, "In Christ Jesus, faith works through charity."

God calls whom He will. But His love is for all, even the redeeming love of the Son of God, and His will is that all men be saved.

Religions of men, whether they acclaim mankind or some "unknown god," will not do. But they can provide the soil in which the Word of faith can sprout, take root, and bear the harvest of a full faith.

ONE LORD, ONE FAITH, ONE BAPTISM

Vatican Council II has made the Catholic world more aware of its mission to those within it, to other Christians, and to those of other faiths or of no faith. Never as much as today is the Church a city set upon a mountain. The world is watching.

What of Catholics so complacent that they do not even walk the road of good works, much less the higher plane of faith? What of Catholic thinkers more concerned with self prestige than the humble spirit of Christ, more anxious for the flattery of their peers than for the hard work of truth, more prone to novelty and revolt than to meekness and humility of heart?

What of our own index of faith? Have fear and prejudice and hatred and impurity corroded our spiritual life?

The human condition is our own, fashioned by us, lived out in the context of our home, our work, our leisure. God has spoken to us through his prophets. Faith is our personal encounter with him, an on-going experience, a lived response.

Blessed is the man whose human condition has been permeated by this faith. Blessed is the society in which it can flourish.

THE CHURCH—THE OPEN CIRCLE

As many speakers frequently in demand before various audiences quite generally do, Archbishop Hallinan developed this theme on a number of occasions before groups throughout the country. This version he used at the installation of the Most Reverend Gerard L. Frey as the Bishop of Savannah on 10 August, 1967.

There is going on in the Church today a radical, far-flung, inner reformation. To *reform* means to *reshape* — to consider the past and present not simply as dreams or visions but as the working materials of the future. Out of the ideas, the dialogue and the interaction that make up our daily fare, out of the guidelines of Vatican Council II and the theological studies and sociological surveys which have followed it, a new Catholicism is taking shape.

Christ is the Head, our brother; we are the members, sons like Him of our Father. We guard the same deposit He gave us, but we hope with Augustine, Aquinas and Newman that we will deepen our understanding of it. The God-given code of right and wrong is still our way of life, and it is conditioned not by popular vote or polls, but by a fresher, more relevant grasp of God's will. We still pray and praise God in our worship, but we have made the remarkable discovery that God understands English, French and Bantu as well as Latin.

What is the shape of things to come? A great deal more freedom, much flexibility. And lest these two conditions might destroy the skeleton and flesh of our faith, we need a growing fidelity to Christ and those He chooses to carry out His will — laymen, religious, priests and bishops. They, as in the parable of the sower, hear the word of God, understand it, keep it and bear its rich harvest.

For centuries the Church has been pictured as a pyramid, the pope at the peak, and the laity at the bottom; the bishops, priests, deacons and religious in between. It was symmetrical, pleasing to look at, easy to understand. But it was closed and tight, a little too smug, a little too secure. It failed to catch the high spirits and daring of fire cast upon the earth, a light burning on a mountain, a fishing boat setting out from

187

shore, a net cast into the sea. The shape of the pyramid satisfied the eye, but not the mind and certainly not the heart of man.

Every page of the record of Vatican Council II points to a totally different shape. The lay-clerical distinction is qualified by the striking concept "priesthood of the faithful"; the levels of priest, bishop, pope are now conditioned by a sharing of service and authority that is now called "collegiality." We might find many figures of speech to describe the new shape of the Church, to replace the pyramid. Perhaps the phrase open circle defines it best.

Remember the engravings in the old catechism. There was a hint of the open circle on the very first page. God the Father, arms extended, gazing at the new creation — plants, animals and the happy man and wife before him.

In the Last Supper of da Vinci, the open circle is indicated by the central figure, the high priest, Christ, turning to His apostles on either side, speaking with them in every day dialogue, feeding them with the sacrament of His Body and Blood, climaxing the eucharistic sacrifice. There is nothing closed or tight or pyramidal in this scene. In fact, it has been observed that for centuries priests turned their backs on their people at Mass in sharp and ironic contrast to our high priest, Christ, who stood in their midst, sharing His presence, words and even Himself with them. I recall no artist who ever painted a Last Supper that had Our Lord facing the wall.

The open circle received its final sanction the day after the Last Supper. The God-man hung from the cross facing in a minority His enemies, in the majority those who loved Him. He sees them all, the faithful, the separated brothers, Christians and Jews and pagans. The arms are extended wide in a full embrace of mankind. Saints and sinners, His mother and the thieves — all are swept up in those weary arms. His blood mixed with our sweat and sins and tears. This was no pyramid; this was the open circle of redemption: "God our Savior wishes *all men* to be saved and to come to a knowledge of the truth." (1 Tim. 2:4)

This new form of the Church is not a novelty nor an invention. It is a correction. It is a rediscovery of the gospels — what God wants His Church to be. In other times, other shapes may have been effective. But in a world grown used to self-reliance, dialogue, involvement and the democratic way of life, the pyramid just will not do. The open circle is scripturally authentic and historically appropriate.

A bishop can be located at the top of a pyramid, but an open circle calls for a different position. The Vatican Fathers gave a full picture of this new role for the bishop: "He gathers God's people together through the Gospel and the Eucharist ... he teaches them the faith and the realities of freedom, of family, of education, civil society, the arts and sciences, the just distribution of goods, peace and war, and especially the poverty of those whom Christ loved the most. In the liturgy of the Mass in the cathedral, the bishop takes his encircling role, in a single prayer, at one altar with the full, active participation of all God's holy people, surrounded by his college of priests and other ministers."

In this open circle, the Council itself defines the position of the bishop not at the top, but "in the midst of his people, as one who serves." Around him are his faithful, "living and working in a communion of love." He welcomes and loves his priests, listening to them and trusting them. And his arms, like Christ's, stretch out to all the brothers baptized and part of the Church, as well as the non-baptized everywhere — because like Christ he loves them.

The view is better from the center than the top. The bishop does not take, as the military does, the high ground. He walks and lives among his people. The pyramid is gone; the Church is now the open circle, and the bishop is in its midst as one who serves his people.

A TIME TO CREATE—A TIME TO RECOVER

Observers of the liturgical movement in the United States have frequently noted that the liturgical week which convened in Kansas City, Missouri, 21-24 August, 1967, was a highwater mark in liturgical development. For the Archbishop it represented, as this address makes clear, an occasion to continue his efforts — in spite of failing health — to advance the liturgical goals so clearly set forth by the Council's Pastoral Constitution on the Liturgy.

We have in this country a liturgical underworld. Since its citizens defy statistics, it is impossible to estimate how far-flung and effective it is. Whether the majority comprise earnest, imaginative priests and laymen, or a generation of novelty seekers is equally obscure. When its spirit is a true zeal, it rises out of the "providential dispositions of God in our times," as Vatican Council II said. When it is born of impatience with rules and frustration with delay, the purity of the motives is more suspect.

Is this underworld of the unauthorized experiment a phenomenon only of our times? Is it an heir to the Frankish adaptations of the Roman Rite when the empire was coming apart? Or of the Jesuit missioner, Matteo Ricci, whose fresh experiments almost made Christ and His Church come alive in China, until Benedict XIV ended the experiments in 1742.

A pioneer trail can even be traced back to the reforms brought from central Europe in our own century by Virgil Michel, Gerard Ellard, Matthias and Martin Hellriegel. Was their lonely experimentation, while bishops frowned and Rome cautioned, the American forerunner of the underworld that now stretches across a hundred colleges, seminaries and parishes?

There is a time to create, Cardinal Lercaro wrote recently, and a time to "fully uncover and live by all the riches of our liturgical heritage." He was speaking of translations but his words are applicable to the entire reform. The difficult choice is ours today. The task of discovery of the Mass, its scriptural and patristic core, is complex and long. The creative task is more challenging and vibrant. It is suited to the young, to contemporary needs, to the people's voice. It is not fitted to the old-time sacramentaries, the exhausting work of scholars, the dust of the past.

The Cardinal, who is president of the Consilium, the Church's primary instrument of the liturgy, is writing of the problems of reform. His own dynamic will to create and to recover are coupled with a profound love of divine worship, but he knows well that liturgy has a social, pastoral dimension. Is it of rubrics or pastoral needs he is speaking when he states, "It is not opportune to 'jump the gun.' "? The question at issue is simply this: How best will the community of God's people be pastorally served?

"Liturgy is for men, and not men for the liturgy," was the key of the second Vatican Council's reform. It was the call of Cardinal Montini on the fourth day of the Council, October 22, 1962. During the debates of 1962-63, the conflicting words of the traditionalists and the progressives were often heard, but Montini's phrase was still ringing at the end of the second session. All but four council fathers voted the new historic direction for the liturgy. Then it hit the Catholic world with a mighty impact. It proved dramatic for those who wanted a scriptural, pastoral shape suited to modern man. And it has almost proved traumatic for those whose faith was locked and secured in the old rigidity.

Unlike collegiality and ecumenism, the new liturgy touches every Catholic. The effects have been strikingly diverse. Letters to most bishops blasted the changes, and hurled such unkempt slogans as, "Throw the ironing-board altar out!" but gradually the Consilium in Rome settled down, and diocesan and parish commissions began to reach the people. This new climate was especially noted in those parishes which had begun moving with Pius XII's *Mediator Dei* in 1947, and now linked learning by instruction to learning by doing.

The road of the Consilium has been rocky. During a meeting of the Vatican Council's commission, one very high Roman prelate, deeply offended at the idea of local bishops making liturgical decisions, cried out, "Impossible! Every change must be approved by the Congregation of Rites." The old cardinal-chairman, hardly a liberal himself, demurred, "You forget, Ecellènza, that the Vatican Council is above even the Congregation of Rites."

But the intransigents held on, and their brand of heavy centralization is still a vigorous weed stifling the growing tree of a vital liturgy.

Meanwhile, back at the parish, four years have brought many changes in Catholic worship. Too often they are one-dimensional (ver-

nacular, gestures, novelties like the Offertory procession) and lack the
depth of understanding and involvement that the Constitution requires.
One of today's myths is that resisters are the Curia and the bishops,
while the reformers are the young priests, religious and laity. There are
eager experimenters in every sector. And from the new generation,
bishops often receive letters of protest about the kiss of peace, the presence of the lector, and the use of guitars that would curl the hair of
the most reactionary prelate.

This is not the place to defend the American bishops. But the snide
comment, "The bishops were brave in Rome, but timid back home,"
can leave an unpleasant error for history to devour. This group of men
helped to prepare, and spoke out forcefully for the liturgy schema. They
voted in November, 1963, and April, 1964, to use all the vernacular
possible, and continued to press for more English and further reforms.
The hierarchy helped to launch and finance the gigantic task of preparing a fine international text for the ten English-speaking nations. They
put a Music Advisory Board to work. The bishops were the first large
hierarchy to obtain the vernacular canon, and then approved the new
text by a 95% majority. This is hardly the picture of a group of bishops
"blighted with conservatism, slavishly submissive to the Roman Curia,"
as one critic recently termed them.

In 1963, the liturgical constitution ordered a revision of the entire
rite. Minor refinements of gestures were effective June 29 this year, but
a more far-reaching revision is due this year for the whole eucharistic
rite. The prayers at the foot of the altar will be cut out, probably the
Kyrie and Gloria will be rearranged, the Offertory prayer shortened.
Most significant will be the inclusion of more than one form of the
Canon. These changes will go far to produce the "clean liturgy" called
for by the council fathers when they sought

> a noble simplicity . . . short, clear and unencumbered by useless rep-
> etition . . . within the people's power of comprehension . . . normally
> not requiring much explanation . . . with an intimate connection be-
> tween words and rites.

Gratitude is due the teams of theologians and liturgists, pastors and
missioners who are preparing the revision. But this is experimental only
in a very broad sense. It is a process of recovery and of testing. Its
scholarly preparation, absolutely necessary, is the task of men concerned
with the past and its rich heritage. But such revision does not guarantee
a contemporary shape. The living tree must have its trunk and roots. But
it is the growing arms that give it strength, the flowering leaves and
buds that give it beauty.

These revised forms come to us for a term of testing. The new funeral rite is being used today; the new form of the Mass will be tested soon. But again, testing is not creative. It satisfies the past, but it may not reach out to the present. There is still too much of the formal, the official, the prescribed in this state of the revision. Is it true that the "time to create" is not here?

A modicum of "spontaneous experimentation" is beginning to appear. Its course: preparation by local experts, local conference approval, form determined by the Holy See, and a period of testing. In the United States, a very necessary modification has been made — a committee on liturgical experimentation to examine the proposal and to advise the bishops. Under the direction of Bishop Victor Reed and Father Charles Riepe, a well-qualified committee has been formed. It includes theologians and liturgists like Fathers Bernard Cooke, Godfrey Diekmann, Aidan Kavanagh, and Gerard Sloyan with such "practitioners" as Fathers Paul Byron, Rollins Lambert and Theodore Stone, and the lay advisers Robert Rambusch, Mary Perkins Ryan and Donald Quinn.

Only progress can be expected with experimentation in such hands. The first proposal, a Mass form for small groups (home Masses, university, etc.) is now in the final stage of formation. Others will come.

Why then are the liturgists of the country rising? Is not this two-way avenue of experimentation due to become a very busy street? There are delays and frustrations. But the underworld's travail goes deeper. The cry sounds ominously like, "Liturgists of the world, unite! You have nothing to lose but your rubrics!" Enter the "Dutch Canon," self-communion, new twists with rite and word. Enter, on a lower key, the new pop art forms described in the New York *Times* of May 15, 1967: an altar surrounded by 76 oil cans to symbolize "Christian involvement in the world"; a maze made out of seven-foot walls of paper boxes labelled "Get with the action!" and "I must be what I am." Enter on a piteously low note, the Mass that features a bottle of drugstore wine and a loaf of grocery bread.

What are these things saying to us? Whether vibrant and relevant, or drained of all meaning, creativity and reverence, they express an unrest with our churchy tradition. We pastors need not feel alone in this. It is no secret that unrest, and not only that of the young, has eroded family life, the university world, business and labor, the old certainties of political life and the sure principles of international polity.

General unrest must have a root. And if the old liturgical forms have lost their meaning for modern man, the root probably is in their rigidity, their unintelligibility, their formalism. Today's dissatisfaction —

or worse, its apathy — is the penalty we pay. Godfrey Diekmann argued persuasively in 1966 that the most significant note of the new liturgy is "its profound respect for the mysterious, inviolable dignity of the human person." It pours out in personal participation in the community, the restoration of roles for celebrant, deacon, lector, choir and congregation, the willing engagement of free persons. "It seems not improbable that the highlighting of responsible personhood will historically be deemed the council's most far-reaching overall achievement."

A more spontaneous liturgical experimentation will not produce a panacea for this unrest, but it will reach out, in the full spirit of the constitution, to creative minds and open hearts. It will amplify the voice of praise and sanctification beyond the sanctuary to the daily concerns of the inner city, the outer city and suburbia. It will not silence the sounds of undisciplined rites, but it can give an authentic voice to them. The cry of anonymous man, of unsatisfied youth, merits an audience at God's altar as surely as that of the child, the repentant, or the suffering victim. It is the liturgists' role to see that they all get there.

Leaders of the liturgy — bishops as "principal dispensers of the mysteries of God" and priests as their fellow-workers — must see how Vatican Council II pushed out the dimensions of their role.

They must listen to the voices, no matter how untrained and un-disciplined, of this unrest. Underneath the twanging of the guitars are sounds of hope and haste, sometimes bitterness, and even despair. In their attachment to vintage Gregorian, the old hymns, or even the new chants, the leaders must still catch the rhythms of the new beat. It can speak with the same authenticity as Bach did when he began to write church music that shocked the traditionalists.

It is not enough for the leaders of the liturgy to listen. They must live with, talk with and suffer with those who are caught up in today's grossness. When a young man rejoices, the liturgist must collaborate with him in the composition of a new hymn or a fresh prayer.

And because he is a leader for the Lord, he must lead. The structuring of Christian life is his, and so are correction and reproof. But a shepherd must lead, a father must take the initiative. Bishop and pastor must stand in the midst of their people, not in a shady corner or a protective cover. He serves by love and compassion, but he must daily serve by seeking out the way.

Bishops, either personally or collegially, today have almost all the means they need to strengthen the liturgical life of their dioceses. They can teach, urge and exemplify. They can prod those who are indifferent to the changes, a more important task than curbing those whose enthusiasms outdistance their experience and skill.

In this reaching out to those who lack and unwittingly desire the experience of a living liturgy, bishop and pastor must, of course, be as conscious of the universal need of an orderly, structured worship as of the spontaneous desires of their own local church. Given man's flair for the novel, an authentic liturgy needs order, norms and competent authority. Few would opt for an anarchy of the altar. But given any institution's built-in centripetal force, the leaders of the liturgy must find the time to experiment, to change, to adapt — in a word, to create. The last thing the renewal needs is a liturgical Pentagon.

Another visitor to Atlanta, and another Council friend, Archbishop Robert Dosseh, Lome, Togo, West Africa, visits Archbishop Hallinan.

Marking the beginning of the first Archdiocesan Synod on November 20-23, 1966, Archbishop joined Monsignor P. J. O'Connor, Fr. Noel Burtenshaw, Fr. John McDonough, Fr. Jerry Hardy, and Fr. John Stapleton in concelebrating Mass at the Cathedral of Christ the King.

In August, 1967, in ceremonies attended by his two brothers, Gerald L. Frey, former monsignor in the New Orleans diocese, was installed as Bishop of Savannah, Georgia. Archbishop Hallinan delivered the sermon. Left to right: Fr. Andrew Frey, Bishop Frey, and Fr. Jerome Frey, with Archbishop Hallinan at the right.

At an ecumenical dialogue held in Atlanta, December, 1966, Archbishop Hallinan (center) introduces Archbishop Egidio Vagnozzi, then Apostolic Delegate to the United States, to Rev. Daniel Brand, a Presbyterian minister.

Archbishop Hallinan (center) was the major speaker at the Southern Catholic Leaders Conference on "Social Change and Christian Response," in August, 1965, in Atlanta. The conference, attended by five bishops, several hundred priests, nuns and laymen, discussed the impact of the 1964 Civil Rights Act on the South. With Archbishop Hallinan at a dinner during the conference are Dom James Fox, O.C.S.O., abbot of the Trappist Abbey, Gethsemane, Kentucky, and Dr. Benjamin E. Mays, president of Morehouse College in Atlanta and a noted Negro Baptist educator.

Archbishop Paul J. Hallinan, first Archbishop of Atlanta, died March 27, 1968.

A LIVING LITURGY

A new phenomenon appeared in the United States after the Second Vatican Council. Liturgists began to meet in regional groups to implement the decrees of the Council. Undaunted by opposition in higher and lower ranks, Archbishop Hallinan continued to press forward the need of continuing implementation and experimentation in matters liturgical. In October, 1967, he delivered this keynote address to the Catholic Congress on Worhip of the Southeastern United States in Greenville, South Carolina.

Keynote speakers come in a wild assortment of styles, shapes and sizes. About all we have in common is a table of contents, a theme. First, we look at the condition of the world and announce that it is in bad shape. Second, who is to blame? We give you a choice: communists, secularists, the undertakers at the death of God, and the Supreme Court. Second choices are the power structure, those who live in suburbia, General de Gaulle, the younger generation and the Roman Curia. Thirdly, what can we do about it? Get involved, be detached; get committed, stay loose.

Bishop Unterkoefler has already welcomed us, and Father Riepe is about to speak to us. I know that you are hoping that I will "keynote" fast. Besides, I agree the world is in a pretty confused shape, that somebody is to blame, and that something must be done. I want only to share two of my liturgical ideas with you.

1. We are the beneficiaries and the agents of a *Living Liturgy*. Every paragraph of the Constitution on Sacred Liturgy breathes this new concept that God's worship grows and adapts, prunes off what is outdated and adds what is needed. The Council Fathers called loud and clear for a war against rigidity. They cast a vote (with only four negatives) for flexibility. When they wrote that the laity's role was to be full, conscious and active, they meant that it was no longer to be half-hearted, non-intelligible and passive.

I do not think enough priests and laymen, whether old or new breed, grasp this. They ask us almost plaintively, "Are the changes over?

196

Have we stopped at last?" It is not easy to explain to them that the liturgy will never again be fixed and passive. As long as our world changes, and man's moods shift, so long will the forms of Mass and the sacraments be changed. The Church is not a dead rock. She is a living vine. A liturgy that is not contemporary is no liturgy at all. It is only a dead set of ceremonials fit for a museum. You and I must not let the Church retreat into that stifling situation again.

We must not let the new practices freeze into molds. I do not want to shock devoted liturgists, but two of our finest new symbols, the offertory procession and the unleavened whole-wheat bread, could become stylized. We smile at the recollection of the outmoded vesting, unvesting and revesting of a bishop at the throne before a pontifical Mass. Someday the procession and the special bread may be only a memory of these early post-conciliar days. Right now they have a point, but they are not of the liturgical substance. They are strictly on the perimeter.

2. No man, parish or diocese lives only to itself. When bishops speak out on war and peace, they are part of the American Catholic consensus. When Father Groppi marches and fights for the rights of Negroes in Milwaukee, he is helping Catholics in Atlanta, Charlotte, Charleston, Savannah, Jacksonville and Miami see the harsh truth about our cities, the riots, the frustration and the violence.

This unity of action gave the Church a new direction in such fields as the collegiality of the bishops, the new layman-priest cooperation and the ecumenical efforts. Collegiality brings bishops together; at times with their brother-bishop, Pope Paul VI, sometimes with the other bishops of their own nation. Another step away from isolation toward teamwork is the increased role of the laity. Here, of course, we have only begun. After centuries in which the laity prayed, obeyed and paid, they are called now to rise not just with new rights but with new duties, to be informed in truth and formed in grace toward a full acceptance of their new responsibility. And thirdly, the wonder of our times, the Catholic process of ecumenism is opening doors to knowing and respecting those of other faiths, working, praying and worshipping with them. In these three great conciliar areas, we are working together.

Why is it that this teamwork has broken down in the case of the liturgy? Nearly every week our Catholic papers carry bitter stories of priests denouncing bishops for doing nothing. Every pastor knows with anguish the divisions in his parish — those who stubbornly resist change of any kind, and those who want to push aside law, order, tradition and even the reverence due to God's worship. Meanwhile, bishops have their troubles with the old guard at the top who act as though to abandon a dead language is to abandon the faith, and who assume that Our Lord pronounced the holy words at the Last Supper not in his own native Aramaic, but in faultless, Ciceronian Latin.

If we ever needed liturgical teamwork, mutual trust, pooled energies and skills, it is right now. Out of it could emerge a true unity, not imposed from above or forced from below, but a unity in which every part of the Church could give its best to the Eucharist, the Word and the sacraments. There must come about a mutual trust in which bishops declare a moratorium on their angry repressions and condemnations and priests stop thinking of their bishops as the authoritarian baron-bishops of the ninth and tenth centuries. As we work together, forgetting our prejudices and curbing our self-will, we can serve our people not from the top of a pyramid of power, but in your midst where we can hear you and heed you.

As a bishop in a southern See, speaking to a representative audience of southern Catholics, I ask you to share our deep confidence in our priests. New breed and old breed, they move in today's society as the finest clergy the South has ever known. We in turn trust our laity and our religious, sure that the day will come soon when the stubborn resistant lion and the eager, restless lamb will lie down together. If there is one sure thing in American Catholicism today, it is the breathing, urging movement of the Holy Spirit over these southern states. For a century we have been the Church's orphans, the butt of the Ku Klux Klan, dioceses with a memorable history of the past and little evidence of any real future.

Now there is a season of new birth. And you are a part of this second spring. Not for us the huge dioceses, the preposterous faceless parishes, the curates who may never become pastors and the Sunday Masses where success is measured by getting in and out of a parking lot without smashing fenders. Ours is a simpler life, thank God. The religious sister doubles her value the moment she crosses the Mason-Dixon line going south; the lonely missionary still plods his dusty trails, and all of us go out begging money for our survival.

Now in the wake of Vatican Council II, the Holy Spirit is stirring the South once more. We meet head-on a new set of problems: racial injustice and unrest, the despair and crimes of the cities, the depopulation of fields and farms, the weakness of public officials. We are meeting them out of our own southern background and ideals. It is not that of New York, Detroit or Watts or Haight-Asbury in California. It springs out of red clay and scrub-pines, and its voice is not only that of the Tom Watsons, Bill Tilmans and Huey Longs. It is the echo of the poet. Sydney Lanier, Booker T. Washington, Judge William Gaston of North Carolina, and Flannery O'Connor of Milledgeville.

Does our liturgy reflect these good things out of the southern culture, the love of the Bible, the close linking of worship and life, our warmth to friends and our hospitality to strangers? Much as the Catholic Church, after a late start, has done in ecumenism, integration, and areas of need, I do not think our liturgy is keeping pace. We need more good lay lectors, more good hymn singing, more powerful preaching, more Masses in the homes.

The Catholic South can do this if it keeps an open eye to the ongoing flexibility of the liturgy and an open hand for all — laymen, religious, priests, bishops, working together. Your Catholicism is not enshrined in prestige, but it knows how to love and to share. You are few in numbers, but you are great in faith. Wherever two or three are gathered together in His sacred name, you know Who is in our midst.

SERVANT CHURCH—SERVANT PEOPLE

During the time of the first worldwide Synod of Bishops in Rome, Archbishop Hallinan addressed another pastoral letter to the people of the archdiocese. Again he was joined with his auxiliary bishop, Joseph L. Bernardin, in signing the statement. It appeared in the 12 October, 1967, issue of the Georgia Bulletin.

One of Christ's last gifts to us was peace. It was a special kind of peace which was to be the hallmark of those who believed in Him and loved Him: "Peace I bequeath to you, my own peace I give you, a peace the world cannot give, this is my gift to you."

Today, however, this peace lacks the universal dimension Christ intended it to have. People everywhere are restless and at odds with each other. This restlessness has become so much a part of the contemporary scene that many wonder whether the Easter gift of Christ can ever be a reality again. Our Christian faith answers this question with an emphatic "yes." But the same faith requires that we seek and then remove the causes which make that peace so elusive today. It would surely be too simple to ascribe all of society's difficulties to one cause. Our problems are too complex for that. Still, there is one cause which is unquestionably more basic than most. That cause is poverty.

Poverty — that condition wherein man lacks basic necessities and basic dignities — is directly linked with much of the social unrest and conflict that exist today simply because it strikes at the heart of the human community, man as man. Peace, as Pope Paul has reminded us in his encyclical, *The Development of Peoples*, will be achieved only when the basic human needs of all people are satisfied. This, of course, will be accomplished only if all people are permitted to enter into the mainstream of modern economic and technological development. "To wage war on misery and to struggle against injustice," the Holy Father stated,

> is to promote, along with improved conditions, the human and spiritual progress of all men, and therefore the common good of

humanity. Peace cannot be limited to a mere absence of war, the result of an ever precarious balance of forces. No, peace is something that is built up day after day, in the pursuit of an order intended by God, which implies a more perfect form of justice among men.

It is vital that in considering the global dimensions of poverty we not overlook the problem which exists here at home. There are millions of poor people in the United States, and northern Georgia is no exception. The poor live in every section of our archdiocese. Perhaps poverty is more apparent in the city of Atlanta where the contrast between the "haves" and the "have nots" is sharper and more dramatic. The new, handsome skyscrapers which are a symbol of the city's progress often form a backdrop which only highlights the ugliness of the slum areas.

In considering poverty, a distinction must be made between the Christian spirit of poverty and material poverty. Christian poverty was praised by our Lord in His Sermon on the Mount: "How happy are the poor in spirit; theirs is the Kingdom of Heaven." It is a virtue which one freely choses. The person who possesses the spirit of Christian poverty is always aware that everything in this world is a gift of God to man for his enjoyment, use and perfection. He understands, therefore, that all men have a right to those things which are needed for their normal, human development. In acquiring material things for himself and his family, the man who is poor in spirit will not overlook the rights of others; he will seek to satisfy his personal needs with a certain maturity and sense of purpose; there will be a detachment which will make it possible for him to take a more genuine and profound delight in the things of the world and at the same time turn to God with more confidence and trust and to his fellow-man with greater generosity and interest.

Enforced poverty, on the other hand, is an entirely different matter. It is quite clear that people must have the things needed to live a life consistent with their human dignity and it is our duty to help them acquire them. A material poverty which denies opportunities and thus stifles development is degrading to the human personality. It destroys initiative and enthusiasm, qualities which are so important for human progress. It is this evil which today afflicts so many people, including millions in our own country.

While the Christian spirit of poverty and an imposed material poverty are different, it should be evident that the two are intimately related to each other. The evil of material poverty will continue as long as men generally are not animated by the spirit of poverty. For it is the Christian spirit of poverty which prompts men to consider the needs of others as well as their own; it is this spirit which is needed to create a climate where all men will be given the opportunities so essential for their full, human development. Without this spirit, attempts to alleviate material poverty must fail simply because they will have fallen short of the mark in their consideration of why these conditions must be corrected.

Resolving the problem of poverty involves much more than alleviating some of its affects. As Pope Paul indicated in *The Development of Peoples*, it is not just a matter of eliminating hunger or other evils stemming from poverty, although this is surely necessary as an immediate, temporary measure. "It is a question," as he said, "rather, of building a world where every man, no matter what his race, religion or nationality, can live a fully human life, freed from servitude imposed on him by other men or by natural forces over which he has not sufficient control, a world where freedom is not an empty word and where the poor man Lazarus can sit down at the same table with the rich man."

In this task of building a better world where everyone can live a fully human life, no one is exempt; no one can claim that it is not his concern. It is a task which demands great generosity, much sacrifice and unceasing effort on the part of all.

It is important to remember, too, that what is true of individuals is also true of nations. In the "Pastoral Constitution on the Church in the Modern World," the fathers of Vatican Council II stated clearly that advanced nations have a very serious obligation to help developing nations. In his encyclical, Pope Paul has not minced any words in spelling out the practical implications of this obligation:

> Every nation must produce more and better quality goods to give to all its inhabitants a truly human standard of living, and also to contribute to the common development of the human race. Given the increasing needs of the under-developed countries, it should be considered quite normal for an advanced country to devote a part of its production to meet their needs, and to train teachers, engineers, technicians and scholars prepared to put their knowledge and their skill at the disposal of less fortunate peoples.

WE ARE ALL SERVANTS

While the duty of relieving poverty rests on all individuals and groups, the Church has a special role to play. She must be a servant church, always identifying herself with those who are poor, as Christ did. When the Church removes herself from the poor, she loses her effectiveness; she loses her ability to serve as the bridge which joins men to one another as brothers and to God as sons.

In stating this, however, it is not implied that the Church must not also be vitally concerned about the welfare of those who are not poor. The Church must surely serve the influential and the affluent. Their needs as members of God's people are no less important, no less real, no less our concern. But in serving them she must constantly lead them into the various areas of human need; she must always draw from them and their resources in fulfilling those needs. It is precisely in her ability to bring the rich and the poor together that the Church finds her strength. It is in this mutual collaboration in which men accept each other as equals before God that they find Christ who is their salvation. It is by putting the parable about the Good Samaritan and the Sermon on the Mount into practice day-by-day, in the ordinary circumstances of life, that the Church finds her life and vitality.

It is not the role of the Church to displace or replace what government and other secular institutions can and must do to eradicate the evil of poverty. She can only supplement it. However, beyond whatever programs the Church may sponsor as her part in the war on poverty, there is another contribution which she can make. It is the Church's responsibility to help her members acquire a truly Christian sensitivity to the needs of the poor. It is this sensitivity which makes us realize that in discharging our Christian obligation of service in the world, we must offer the far more precious gift of self that is entailed in face-to-face compassion — the sharing of suffering — with those who need us, not just our money or our institutions. As a prominent churchman said recently,

> Unless (we) somehow sit for a while where the poor are sitting, the Church and the Christian cannot really minister to the poor, the disinherited, the powerless, the outcasts, the captives. It may not be the only place where we will sit, and we may not sit there forever, but in some genuine and unfeigned way Christians and the Church must cast their lot with the captives. Only then can we hope to lead them out of their captivity, not by remote control and not by paying another to go in our stead, but by our own hands.

THE ARCHDIOCESE IS COMMITTED

It was within this context that our lay congress and synod last year committed the archdiocese to an important role in alleviating human suffering. The synod made it clear that here in northern Georgia "the Church must be the very act of Christ within this particular southern area where, adapting to the press and flow of modern society, she feeds the hungry, heals the sick, clothes the naked, and preaches the Good News to the poor. Her role is to be the servant Church, the praying Church, offering the Eucharistic sacrifice as well as the personal sacrifices of her members in their work of service." Then, becoming more specific, the synod declared: "To the poor, the Church must be a healing force to remedy the causes of their poverty as well as the effects of it. The Church must strive to identify herself with the poor man, not as a part-time visitor to his section of town, but as a permanent, active neighbor. . . ."

The people of the archdiocese have always given evidence of their concern for the poor. In addition to what they have done as individuals in their parishes and communities, they have supported both by their money and their service Catholic Social Services, the Village of Saint Joseph and the Saint Vincent de Paul Society. Through their generosity to national collections, e. g., the Bishops' Catholic Relief Service, the collection for Latin America, etc., they have taken part in the Church's efforts to help the poor in other countries.

Today all of our institutional programs are being reevaluated to make sure that they are truly serving the needs as they exist today. In this task of evaluating and planning, all segments of the Church are involved — bishops, priests, religious and laymen.

The department of Catholic Social Services seeks to restore families and individuals to a normal life, wherever possible, through a program of social services directed toward strengthening the positive values in family life. It carries out this objective through direct services, e. g., counselling, and through cooperation with existing social agencies and community facilities. Beyond this, the department coordinates all of the Church's welfare efforts with the programs of other churches and the community.

The Village of Saint Joseph, which recently moved into its new home in Atlanta, is for dependent children. Instead of giving custodial care, the Village is now oriented toward resolving the emotional and psychological problems of both the children and their parents. Expert therapy is available for this purpose.

The Saint Vincent de Paul Society, through its parish units, has traditionally given financial assistance to the members of the parish who are in need of help. While this program is as necessary today as it ever was and will continue to be, the work of the Society is taking on a new dimension. Its members are now crossing parish lines and going into the community at large to seek and to help the poor wherever they are.

Together with other agencies, both public and private, the Society is developing educational programs for children, e. g., Headstart, tutorial programs, and for adults, e. g., classes in basic subjects for school dropouts, homemaking, etc.

The work of the Vincentians in the inner city is now aided and supplemented by five Franciscan Sisters who moved to Atlanta in mid-August. These Sisters will live among the people whom they serve. In addition to assisting with the work of Saint Vincent de Paul, they will develop other programs to meet the needs of the community in which they live.

CHALLENGES FOR THE FUTURE

Our efforts so far, however, have only scratched the surface. They do not begin to satisfy our obligations as one of the major Christian churches in our area. What, then, must we do?

(1) We strongly urge all of our people to give some of their time to the many poverty programs now underway under church and civic auspices. Financial generosity, as important as it is, cannot substitute entirely for personal involvement. We must overcome our "checkbook charity" mentality; we must give of ourselves as well as of our goods. While we especially recommend the Saint Vincent de Paul Society and the work of the Franciscan Sisters, it is our hope that our people will also play an active role in ecumenical and government-sponsored programs.

(2) Every parish must examine its budget (just as the archdiocese must do) to see where savings can be effected in order to make more money available to the poor. We cannot afford frills as long as there are people in our midst who do not have the essentials. Moreover, wherever possible, parishes should permit their facilities to be used for programs which benefit the poor, such as Headstart, tutorial programs for school children, adult education, etc.

(3) We urge our Catholic people to use their influence to correct the inequities which are often the cause of poverty. We must do everything we can to help secure good education, adequate housing and equal job opportunities for all of our citizens, white and Negro alike.

(4) As a more immediate goal, we ask everyone to contribute generously to a special collection to be taken up in all the Atlanta churches on October 22 for the work of the Saint Vincent de Paul Society in the inner city. The proceeds from this collection will make it possible for the Society to finance, in conjunction with other agencies, a number of educational programs which are urgently needed.

SERVANT CHURCH

From apostolic times, when the lower classes made up the first harvest of Christian love, down through the times of Saint Francis of Assisi and Frederick Ozanam and the Vincentians, the Catholic Church has written a long record of living with the poor. Indeed, her most fruitful and even her happiest decades have identified her as the "Church of the Poor," not the Church of wealth and power.

We cannot forget this history because what we do now should reflect our past, in order that we plan and carry out our future. Now the crisis of need is greater and much more urgent.

If this pastoral message is to be realized before it is too late, the Church — you and we — have much work to do in the weeks and months ahead. Our synod of 1966 highlighted the coming decade of decisions.

Let us together move ahead. Are we not convinced that vast and pitiful needs lie all around us, that we must deepen our compassion as we jolt our complacency? Are we not determined to use the many channels that reach into these dark areas of degradation, that we must share our time and energy and money and skills and prayers so that the victims of enforced poverty will be led back to human dignity, the promised American style of noble living, and to the Christian way of life which is Christ?

COMMUNITY AND LITURGY: THE INTERACTIONS

This address was given at the University of Dayton on 23 October, 1967. The Archbishop delivered many other addresses concerning the liturgy, but this was chosen because it represents a continuation of the thinking between worship and social action that the founder of the liturgical movement in the United States, Dom Virgil Michel, O.S.B., insisted upon from the beginning. The Archbishop was a devoted disciple of both Virgil Michel and Monsignor John A. Ryan.

It is a post-conciliar surprise that of all sixteen documents, that on the liturgy seems today to be the chief battleground. The average observer of the Catholic scene finds a Church which has accepted ecumenism, collegiality and even religious liberty with serenity and not a little pride. But the liturgy schema, moved up by Pope John from eighth to first place in the agenda, immediately raised father against father. The spearheads of the battle were the vernacular and the centralization of liturgical authority. But in the final vote of November, 1963, the schema became the Constitution on the Sacred Liturgy, and only four bishops voted against it

Four years have now passed, greeted with increasing joy by some, designated as four years of survival by others. The resistance of the hard-core traditionalists has noticeably melted; those who wanted the open and flexible liturgy of the Constitution now exult in the mother tongue, the altar-turned-around, and the Prayer of the Faithful and, not noticing that these are all externals, cry on for more.

The battle now has shifted because the old resisters have either changed, or they have grown sullen and silent. This is a real casualty because the liturgy is the public act of all God's people. Perhaps we did not instruct and motivate them. Our own impatience to get at the changes before the Church's contemporary vitality was doomed as "too little, and too late," could have left many good Catholic people confused and embarrassed. In any case, we must, as we push ahead, pause long enough to be understanding of and patient with them lest we lose our compassion. Was Our Lord teaching us, in the parable of the Good Samaritan, that there lie by the roadway others who are bruised and hurt, perhaps even dying? After all, the priest and the levite were concerned with their duties. They were the liturgists. It was the Samaritan stranger who stopped, nursed, bathed and provided for the bleeding victim.

But the shift of battle put laymen, religious, priests and bishops in sharp conflict over experimentation. The seeds of this open and creative process are already in the Constitution, in Chapter I, No. 37-40. The guidelines are simple but clear: this "radical adaptation of the liturgy is needed. ... The episcopal conferences must prudently consider which elements from the traditions and genius of individual peoples might appropriately be admitted." The Apostolic See will grant to these bodies of bishops power to permit and direct the necessary preliminary experiments.

But this idyllic picture is not being realized. Nearly every week, our Catholic papers carry bitter stories of priests denouncing their bishops for doing nothing and bishops denouncing priests for doing anything. Every pastor knows with anguish the divisions in his parish, not only over experiments but even authorized changes, and on the other side those who would push aside law, order, tradition, and even the reverence due to the praise of God. Meanwhile, bishops have their troubles with the old guard at the top who sometimes act as though the liturgy had never changed, and if it were to do so today it would mean the abandonment of the faith.

There is needed urgently a mutual trust in which bishops declare a moratorium upon their angry edicts of repression and condemnation, and priests and laymen stop thinking of their bishops as the authoritarian baron-bishops of the ninth and tenth centuries.

It would be foolish to underrate the bitterness of this conflict over experimentation, adaptation and an open, flexible liturgy structured for the men and the needs of our time. With conflict can come crisis. That it has not reached that stage yet has been due to the vision, the courage and the good will of hundreds of the faithful, priests and bishops who love the Church as much as they love the worship of God and the sanctification of men.

But a more pertinent cause for the new shift of the battle lines *in re liturgica* is the rather sudden emergence of a question more intense than change, more far-flung than experimentation. The question, put bluntly, is this:

> Is it in fact true that the source of the Christian's active, fruitful, redeeming presence in the world is the liturgy?

As soon as we note the word "source" we recall the words of Vatican Council II: "The liturgy of the Church is the fountain from which all her power flows." This phrase, now classic, ties in with others — "a sacred action surpassing all others . . . no other action of the Church can match its claim to efficacy."

In his book, *Honest to God*, Bishop John Robinson strips liturgy of its eucharistic substance as well as its role of proclamation. He defines the function of the liturgy ". . . to focus, sharpen and deepen our response to the world and to other people." Parenthetically, may we ask, "Where did God go?"

But it was Daniel Callahan, one of Catholic America's most perceptive minds, who dramatized the question. By doing so just before the opening of the 1967 Liturgical Week in Kansas City and with pungent, almost angry words, headed "Putting Liturgy in its Place," in the most widely read *National Catholic Reporter*, he almost took the focus away from the liturgical sector of experimentation, retiring innovators and non-innovators alike to their underground altars and their chanceries.

He has raised questions that had to be raised: Has the liturgy inspired the faithful to become "of one heart in love?" Has the liturgy, no matter how sound and inventive, produced automatic miracles of Christian community and service to the world? Should we put Christ's presence in the world in a secondary, subordinate place in the light of the liturgy's insistence that Christ in the Eucharist is the primary source of grace?

I am grateful for these questions. They force liturgists by study, pastors by experience, and bishops as chief priests in the diocese to reexamine the Vatican Council's Constitution. Have we paid too much attention to the externals? Have we talked of diverse canons and the need of new forms to a point where our guidance has failed to put the eucharistic covenant into the hearts of men and "set them afire"?

Have we expected miracles, and made too much of the conciliar phrase that "zeal for the liturgy is rightly held to be a sign of the providential dispositions of God in our time"? A sign, not a cure-all. We have no right to act as if the key to heaven were a liturgical credit card.

In preaching the liturgy as the chief ingredient of the desperately needed renewal, have we forgotten the two great basic documents of Vatican II, The Church and The Church Today? The liturgy is the complex of actions and words, the ritual which gives expression to man's need for praising God and helping to redeem his own community. But the Constitution on the Church stresses the People of God, and The Church Today opens with the unforgettable words, "The joys and the hopes, the griefs and the anxieties of the men of this age, especially those afflicted, those too are the joys and hopes, griefs and anxieties of the followers of Christ."

The liturgy document is no competitor of these basic principles. It is not an either/or situation. Each of the three constitutions is in harmony with the other. Indeed each interacts, even interfeeds on and internourishes the other. The Church is Christian community; The Church in the World is human society; The Liturgy prays that the faithful of the Church community may grasp by deed what they hold by creed, that it may be a like witness to the world in which man lives.

In fact, the foreword to the liturgy document, in stating the case for renewing and fostering the liturgy, puts it in this context: The Council seeks to intensify the daily growth of Catholics in Christian living, to change Church observances to the requirements of our time. Those who are striving to know the liturgy better and love it more vibrantly have spent four years trying to make this cult-community effective, to make more evident the nexus between Christ in the Eucharist and Christ in the Poor.

Callahan merits Catholic thanks for shifting the battlefield from the externals, like experiments and formats, to the heart of the matter — man's love for his fellow-men and through them for his God.

But Dr. Callahan is also a journalist and uses a journalist's tools with more talent than he uses those of liturgy (cf. Margaret Mead's delineation of the human necessity of ritual), or theology (cf. Bernard Cooke "We cannot expect Christian unity to take place apart from the influence of the Eucharist. The Eucharist unifies the Christian community."), or history. In fact, the imprecision of Callahan's history in this essay is surprising because his writings have thus far been woven of the authentic threads of the past.

So we must excuse his bad habit of buttressing his main point, the loss of community in the overshadowing of cult, with a rather tired tirade against "brick-and-mortar Catholicism," i.e., building churches, and a diversionary foray into Freud's reduction of ritual to repetition to neurosis. He did not need these side issues to establish his emphasis on community and service.

The Benedictine, Aidan Kavanagh, finds Callahan's piece wanting in its over-simplification of interrelated issues, and its theological and historical naivete. Father Robert Hovda, a long-time pioneer, asserts that it is the liturgy's very lack of primacy that is to blame. We have, for centuries, simply centered ourselves in almost anything but a Eucharistic deed and assembly. Genuine liturgy, says Father Hovda, has not been tried.

Perhaps Lucille Hasley's question is the best critique of Callahan's technique. "How in the world do you gather statistics as to whether or not the Mass 'carries over' into the world?"

I grant the Callahan critics their points and I could add a few more places where I think even Daniel nodded. But I submit that his main point — that *homo liturgicus* must be *homo servans, homo patiens, homo frater*, — is so urgent that like the good journalist that he is, he puts that in the lead of his story, flings pertinent paragraph after irrelevant paragraph, and then writes a bold and flashing headline, "Putting Liturgy in its Place."

I have read many accounts of the sinking of the Titanic, but I have never seen one in which the catastrophe was buried in a recital of the weather conditions, the ship's rules, the percentage of millionaires on the guest list, or the Raising and Care of Ice-bergs.

The name of the game is "cult or community," or which came first, the chicken or the egg? It must be noted that we are not discussing the old rock that stubbed even the philosophical toe of Jacques Maritain: public liturgy is private devotions, prayers, meditation or the silence of reverential reflection. Vatican Council II dealt gently with that dilemma and decided that it was not a dilemma at all "since the liturgy by its very nature far surpasses any of them." Each has its place in man's life, but Christ is present in the liturgy of the Mass in His priest, in His Word, in the assembly and especially under the Eucharistic species.

The cult-community relationship (whether dichotomy, identity or dilemma) must also be narrowed because of the limits of our time. Godfrey Diekmann, the pioneer Benedictine liturgist, asks the question, "After our people pray and sing together, will they be better Catholics, better Christians?" And he answers it by an orderly review of four levels of community: mankind, the Universal Church, the diocese and the parish. Let us omit the first two, the world-wide dimensions of our community, not only because these are unwieldly areas and theologically sophisticated, but for the homely reason that the community of God's People with the bishop in the midst of them, and the priest as his co-worker in the episcopal order, is close at hand and full of personalities, bonds and irritation. This is where our energy can best be expanded. To paraphrase Saint John, it is easier to love the pope whom I cannot see every Sunday and the bishop whom we know only in a miter or a pastoral letter. It is an old human saying that I can love mankind with great charity, but it is my boss or neighbor or mother-in-law I find difficult to take.

So we shall concentrate in this final part on the smaller community: the diocese (and the state or metropolitan area) and the parish (and the town or suburb or inner-city or outer-city). We can note certain trends and signs: (1) Man was meant for community. Geography, race and money may separate him. So does sin. But there is a power in him that draws him to others — that bond of man and wife, of parents and child, our need for each other and our ability to love and cherish each other. In a less complicated culture than our own, his community was much more evident: family, tribe, nation. As Gerald Sloyan puts it, "Liturgy was easy for him because he already had community. He *was* society, and as society he prayed (or cursed or pleaded)."

(2) In our times, community has been fragmented. Following the Industrial Revolution of the nineteenth century, farms and fields began to be forsaken and cities became swollen in size and lonely in their anonymity: The village disappeared. Home life was dehumanized by television and packaged meals. Children got lost in summer camps, pre-school and pre-kindergarten classes, and in houses where the parents were indefatigably employed in the pursuit of leisure. In every city and in every parish, the elements of community grew thin (warmth, familiarity, concern, teamwork and mutual sacrifice). These days when Catholics go to church on Sunday, they come from no given community. Hardly any speak to each other going in. Social, economic and racial lines divide them. The closest attempt to contact is the crunching of fenders in the parking lot.

(3) In this mass culture in which dehumanization follows closely upon depersonalization, the sense of community is losing out. This has been partly caused by our apathy toward others, especially the needy, the deprived, the underdog, the disadvantaged, the unemployed, the desperate — as Callahan maintains. But it has also been caused by our own mislearning of the meaning of liturgy, as the professional liturgists replied to Callahan. The worship of God is not a set of words, actions, gestures and other rubrics. It is man's corporate praise of God and men's corporate act of redemption and sanctification. Anyone who has read the words and deeds of Christ in the gospel knows this. His impatience with empty rubrics and His many parables of mercy lead relentlessly to that set of accusations that will test our redemption and sanctification before Him as our Judge. You gave me nothing to eat, to drink . . . . Saint Paul

and Saint John are equally explicit in their stress on charity, service and compassion for others, the consciousness of a just social order — in a word, community.

(4) Vatican Council II did not compartmentalize the liturgy and community. In the Constitution on the Sacred Liturgy, their bond is urged: "Efforts must be made to encourage a sense of community within the parish." In the Decree on Priests, the pastor is reminded that his office extends to the formation of a genuine Christian community: "This cannot be built up unless it has its basis and center in the celebration of the most Holy Eucharist." Then, the Constitution on the Church Today traces the steps whereby *God* made men into a single people, *Jesus Christ* pleaded that the sons of God should treat one another as brothers, that all should be one, and *the Church* became His Body, "a new brotherly community composed of all who receive Him in faith and in love."

Not content with generalities, the Council Fathers examine the fields of economics, politics and the international community of nations. In each of these, the Christian imperatives of justice, charity and peace are clearly spelled out for every man to read. The Church lives not in a tower, nor on an island, nor in a cathedral. She lives on Main Street, Wall Street, Broadway, in suburbia, the inner city and the United Nations.

The subject of this talk is not Liturgy *versus* Community but rather their *interaction*. To make effective a true Christian assembly, they must constantly interact and surely with more awareness and agility than we are using today. Men of other Christian professions may employ a different method. Those not Christian may not grasp our Catholic problems at all.

But Catholics have to solve the issue of oversized dioceses and preposterous faceless parishes, of curates who may never become pastors. We have to repersonalize ourselves to escape the anonymity of the masses. The Church cannot remain, in our big cities, the ecclesial equivalent of the lonely crowd. Our bishops must know all their priests and guide them in a firm bond of fraternal love. Priests must work incessantly to see their people not as baptismal statistics or fund-raising possibilities or even as frequent communicants or regular retreatants, but as brothers in Christ. Their vocations and duties differ, but their baptism, their faith, their Lord is one with our own. With this kind of human inspiration, our laity will be more apt to witness the Church to the world, to spend themselves in the common good of the community, to sacrifice and suffer that they will see Christ in their needy brothers, and these in turn will see Christ in them.

It was at the Last Supper, when Christ gave us the Eucharist, that He also said, "By this shall all men know that you are my disciples, that you love one another."

Twice Pope Paul has spoken urgently of the bond between worship and community. As Archbishop of Milan, he said:

> We cannot be content with having the church full of people, with having an amorphous crowd of individuals . . . . We need to inform to all the sense of communal action, which is knowing about the communal sense. As Saint Augustine described it, "The Church is a sort of personification of justice. She prays in common, works in common, suffers in common." (Pastoral Letter, 1958)

And in 1963, as pope, he spoke on the *aggiornamento*:

> Tell the people to come to church and not to stay away. Tell them to come together always . . . do not let yourselves be separated from the Church by not being united into one, for you are members of Christ.

The building of community within the Church and the cooperation of it and the world is our tremendous task today. We are finding it in the liturgy; the Prayer of the Faithful, the kiss of peace, the readings and responses, the hyms are but the beginning. Perhaps the Mass in the homes and the liturgy for small groups are the most hopeful signs of a deeper grasp of community within the Church. The parish of choice, not of boundaries, can be another important step against the oversized parish and the anonymous parishioners.

When Catholics enter into ecumenical efforts with Prostestants and Orthodox, or services of prayers with Jews, the community grows. And our late arrival in the secular city is compensated somewhat by our present-day absorption in poverty (Headstart, Vista and low-cost housing plans), racism (Project Equality and inter-racial councils), the morality of war and crime, economic inequalities, and our growing awarness of world problems and involvement in them (from Peace Corps to United Nations).

Are a people opening up to the riches of the liturgy also extending themselves to their fellowman? The timing would indicate that they are. The question, are people praying, singing, worshipping especially in the Eucharistic action "better Catholics, better Christians?" is being slowly answered too. The progress is slow, but then it is only four years since the renewal initiated by Vatican Council II began. The comprehension is slow; so is the willingness of our people to be concerned, to dare to be different.

But as the goal of community is more clearly seen, so are the power-weapons Christ has put to our use — the Eucharist, love, obedience, patience and humility, and our function as servant.

Permit me to give the second last word to an English philosophy professor, Father Peter de Rosa of Saint Edmund's College. Writing on our precise subject, "The Sense of Community and Liturgical Prayer," he says:

> The flight from community in prayer is paralleled by the flight from the community in love .... What we have to learn is that we must try to discover God in our neighbor here and now. This alone makes sense of loving our neighbor, and not when he is safely separated from us by several city streets or at least a decently thick wall.
> Instead of saying, "I'll go away and pray for him," we should learn to say, "I'll stay here and pray *with* him and *in* him and *for* him."

And as my last word, I must observe how close this prayer-in-community is to the prayer-in-the-Eucharist. In the great doxology, we pray that all honor and glory is given to God, Almighty Father, in the unity of the Holy Spirit, "*through* Him and *with* Him and *in* Him."

Is Father de Rosa's phrase just a coincidence, or could it be an invitation to interaction?

THE WORD IN THE WORLD

On 9 January, 1968, Archbishop Hallinan was invited to address an anniversary symposium at West Virginia University. The general theme of the meet was, "Through Changing Knowledge to Enduring Wisdom." In his opening remarks he explained the title he had chosen and from there went on to explain the necessity of wisdom for a truly educated man.

More than a century ago, when William Wordsworth, poet and sage, saw the world as "too much with us; late and soon, getting and spending," his painful conclusion would not fit the twentieth century: "We lay waste our powers." Imagine his disquietude today as the world and its machinery permeate our breakfast cereal, our paychecks, the news media and our machines of war.

If the world is overmuch with us, what of the word — ideas, aspirations, memories and proposals? We have the assurance of Marshall McLuhan that words, whether spoken, written or printed, are being phased out by the media which have become the extension of man. When you grasp the implication of the chapter in his book, *Understanding Media,* "The Medium is the Message," you are reminded of what the Duke of Gloucester said to the historian, Edward Gibbon, when he had published *The Decline and Fall of the Roman Empire*:

> Another damn fat book, eh, Mr. Gibbon?
> Scribble, scribble, scribble, eh, Mr. Gibbon?

Are we spawning a generation of Gloucesters? Where have words gone? Television commercials no longer sell with words. They stimulate by rhythm, repetition, and a singsong, reminiscent of the lesser talents of Mother Goose. Much popular music is only sound, signifying nothing, certainly not words that have meaning. And even political campaigns, once the haven of words, are now mechanical; from opinion polls, through the staged hysteria of the convention and the blatant trumpeting of the candidate's image, clear through to the electronic telecasters which announce the votes before they are even cast.

216

The historic interchange of word and world has shifted. We are being stifled by the world of things. And we are intellectually starved because the food of words is receding. It is hardly, in 1968, a fair contest. The world even with all its tensions and grief is simply more alluring, more satisfying than the poem, the essay, the speech, the editorial, the lecture or the biblical homily.

I have taken the liberty of particularizing the theme of this anniversary meeting, "Thru Changing Knowledge to Enduring Wisdom," in my title, "The Word in the World." The wealth of facts is a vast flux, formed out of the constant changing data derived by science and technology. The world in the title stands for the source, depository and application of those changing pieces of knowledge. On the other hand the word, as stripped of its literary style and philosophic backlog, is that wisdom which endures. The Jewish Word is God's way through the world. On Mount Sinai the people responded to this word, given through Moses, by affirming, "We will do it, we will hear it!" The Moslems, and the great Asiatic and African religions in different ways hear a word from their Gods.

The classic Christian affirmation of the Word is found in Catholic, Orthodox and Protestant scriptures. In the epistle to the Hebrews, we find:

> God, who at various times and in different manners, spoke to the fathers by the prophets, but in our times he has spoken to us by His Son. (1:1-2)

This must be coupled with the primal revelation of the world:

> For since the creation of the world, His invisible attributes are clearly seen — His everlasting power and divinity have been there for the mind to see in the things He has made. (Romans 1:20)

Nature first, then the prophets, and finally Jesus, the Word of God, are the means of God's revelation.

In the Christian Scriptures, word and world meet. But as H. Richard Niebuhr has clearly shown in *Christ and Culture,* there are many ways of meeting. If we substitute "culture" for the "world" (its resources, development and achievement), Niebuhr sees diverse relations with Christ the Word. Tertullian and Tolstoy lead those who range Christ *against* culture; the Gnostics and Abelard, and later Albrecht Ritschl and Schleiermacher find Christ the great enlightener — Christ is not *against* culture but *of* it. Thomas Aquinas proposed a synthesis with Christ *above* culture. Luther, more of a dualist, sees Christ and culture *in paradox.* Relying strongly on St. John's gospel, Augustine interpreted Christ as the *Transformer* of culture.

In a world more than ever marked by our preoccupation with things, almost bloated by the products of the sciences and technologies, what shall we say of the enduring *word* and the changing *world;* of living and creative wisdom and the accumulation of shifting knowledge; of Christ the Word, as Christians know Him, and culture, the progress made by mankind? Will any of the old ways suffice? Can man live fruitfully in the conflict posed by Tertullian on the one hand or the materialists on the other? Is Christ *of* culture or *above* it; is the relationship one of *paradox* or of *transformation?*

Honest and skilled men are incessantly asking this question today. Scholars and preachers and pastors of the word are coming to grips with *secularity,* the world-view that centers on this here-and-now world, the end-product of the process of secularization. (It differs radically from the ideology known as *secularism;* the process is open and concerned with deliverance from static world-views, especially religious; secularism is closed, and dangerously liable to the imposition of its ideology by the state or some other institution.)

Heidegger and Bultman tilled the theological soil for this new concept of secularity. Vahanian, Altizer and the other death-of-God theologians have nourished it to a bold degree. The popular Harvey Cox has brought together the secular elements in his book, *The Secular City.*

Cox starts with Dietrich Bonhoeffer's questions from his prison cell, "How do we speak of God in a secular fashion?" Cox answers that we must tackle *the sociological problem* (chiefly of language); the *political issue* ("How does the Church find out what this politician-God is up to, and move in to work along with Him."); and the *theological issue* (Amos Wilder has said, "If we are to have any transcendence today, even Christian, it must be in and through the secular. Grace is to be found in the world and not overhead.").

As we go back to Genesis and Wisdom, to Paul and the Fourth gospel, we become more immersed in our guidelines. Primitive man knew that the Creator saw all He had made and indeed it was good. Then He took man and settled him in the garden to cultivate and take care of it. Here indeed was secularity without loss of divine origin and concern. God created all nature, but He did not definitively develop it. Man was due for that role — to develop creation's potentialities. In the Fourth Gospel, the role of man, world and God is clarified:

> For God sent His Son into the world, not to condemn the world, but so that through Him the world might be saved.

And Paul adds:

Paul, Apollos, Cephas, the world, life and death, the present and the future are all your servant. But you belong to Christ and Christ belongs to God.

It is in the light of this Christian secularity that chapters 14, 15, 16 and 17 of the Last Gospel illuminate any false dualism or unhealthy dichotomy of the word and the world. In the first epistle of John we are warned, "Do not love the world or the things in the world." James adds, "Friendship with the world means enmity with God." Certainly historic conditions have stressed the evil of the world around them. It had (and still has) a dangerous and enticing power in the face of our service of God.

But the extended treatment of this duality in the four Joannine chapters help us to use effectively Saint Paul's two-edged sword, "Alive and active, cutting more finely, judging secret emotions and thoughts." The world cannot receive the word; it cannot give that peace which comes from Christ alone; it will be proved wrong about sin, joyful and troubled at the wrong times. Deprived of the presence of Christ and the witness to His Word, of His prayer, of belief in Him, the world remains in a religionless state, foreshortened and despairing. No wonder that the dominant forces of power, pleasure, gain, security will hate Christ, the Word, and those who believe in Him. The ultimate stroke will be the two-edged sword, "Be brave: I have conquered the world."

And in the manner of this victory: "I kept those You had given me true to Your name. I passed Your Word on to them, and the world hated them because they were not of the world. I am not asking You to remove them from the world, but to protect them from the world."

In the full light of this biblical issue it is not hard to see why at certain times, the Church held the world by its fingertips, not wishing to embrace a genuine secularity. Tertullian and many other Fathers took with deadly seriousness the dangers of a world which hates Christ and His disciples, whose leader is Satan, and whose goods are corruptible. When Cyprian and the desert monks understood that "Man, greater than the world, should not be borne towards it, but towards God," they were narrowing the rule of Christ, "What does it profit a man if he gains the whole world, but suffers the loss of his own soul?"

We have seen that the greater minds, Augustine and Aquinas, saw it differently. To Augustine, especially in *The City of God*, Christ (the Word) transformed the world and its culture, while Thomas Aquinas built his synthesis in which Christ was above culture.

As the world speeded up, multiplied its tempo, piled up the products of technology, scientism with its measure and matter became more and more dominant. Secularism became its world expression. More open Christian thinkers like Aquinas no longer were heard. But heritage was decadence, not creativity. The flight from the world, was nothing but a return to the romantic. Even its proponents found it wanting because it impaired the unity and universality of Christianity.

This vital theme, word and world, suffered the hardening of theological arteries, both Catholic and Protestant. There were moderates like Niebuhr, Tillich, Maritain, Chenu. But the present scene is dominated by Bonhoeffer, Hamilton and Van Buren. Compromise was strong on both sides, but at least the probing was honest. Then a French paleontologist, a Jesuit, Teihard de Chardin, entered the theological picture:

> The originality of my belief is that it has its roots in two spheres of life which are usually looked upon as mutually antagonistic. By education and intellectual formation, I belong to "the children of heaven." But by temperament and professional studies, I am "a child of the earth".... I have set up no inner dividing wall. I have let two apparently contradictory influences react in perfect freedom, in the depths of my being. Now at the end of this process, after thirty years devoted to the pursuit of inner unity, I have the impression that a synthesis has taken place between the two streams that make their demands on me.

In every scientific work he touched, in every theological process he proposed, he asked the implied question, "Ultimately to be a Christian, must we renounce being human?"

Again, "To divinize is not to destroy, but to create anew."

This was the self-effacing, tortured man of whom the scientist, Aldous Huxley, wrote:

> Through his combination of wide scientific knowledge with deep religious feeling and a rigorous sense of values, he has forced theologians to view their ideas in the new perspective of evolution, and scientists to see the spiritual implications of their knowledge.

This is the Christian thinker of whom the young Emory theologian, Thomas Altizer, has said, "Teilhard de Chardin has reached the most radically Christocentric theological conception of the divine life and energy, and it is also consoling to know that it is in the Roman Catholic world that theology today is most revolutionary and alive."

In Teilhard there is no false dualism but a creative emergence. There is no irreducible dichotomy but rather a healthy interchange of word and world. There is in him much of Pascal and Bergson, the poetry of nature of Paul Claudel and Charles Péguy. There is the same respect for development to which John Henry Newman gave his life.

No wonder that he was the spirit infusing so much of Vatican Council II. The Constitution on the Church in the Modern World begins:

> The joys and the hopes, the griefs and the anxieties of the men of this age ... these too are the joys and hopes, the griefs and anxieties of the followers of Christ. This community realizes that it is truly and intimately linked with mankind and its history.

Is this not the echo of the French Jesuit?

Catholic theology today has a strong Teilhardian thread. The obscurity of his scientific and theological work to the average reader broke forth in Vatican Council II when eminent thinkers gave voice to his world-view. Edward Schillebeeckx, the Dutch Dominican, has based much of his teaching on the theme, "Our salvation comes about within the one reality that is ours, within the scope of our own life in this world." The ethical commitment imposed on Western man by underdeveloped countries, the plans for a society upon earth built on a dynamic blueprint, and the new science service calling for a closer unity — all these conditions have forced Christians to reject faith as a mere superstructure. In the beginning, the Bible desacralizes and unmystifies the world, God handing it over to itself into the hands of men for God's glory.

The Dominican, noting that there is a Christian reaction against religious practices alien to the world, wants a process that is vibrant and thoroughly Christian. "There is obviously going on throughout mankind a process of bringing things into the Church, and in the Church there is a process of secularization that conveys sanctity," he concludes.

Johann Metz, professor of theology at the University of Münster, in like manner, flaws the Christian who sees the worldliness of the world as fundamentally contrary to a Christian view of the world. Yet the "Spirit of Christianity" has permanently infused "into the flesh of the world history."

God, in fact, is the God of history, not just a random fact within history. "He is not a competitor, but the guarantee of the world ... the creatureliness of the world always stands against the background of the history of salvation." And if we cannot disassociate them, how can the world be in opposition? The enduring wisdom of the word and the changing knowledge of the world can be in tension, but not in conflict.

In an essay entitled "The Christian and the World," Metz writes:

> Precisely as God, he does not appear within the horizons of the world, but he lets the world be worldly .... to Christianize the world means to secularize it. Grace builds on nature.

A third Catholic thinker concerned with Christian secularity is the Louvain professor, Gerard Philips. He makes a sharp distinction when he says: "The Christian's separation from the world is spiritual, not sociological." It is caused by sin. Mankind, however, the totality of men living in the world, saints and rascals both.

The world, repeats Philips, consists of all earthly values and those tasks that men must accomplish in the temporal order. God created all but he did not develop it. That is man's work, and through its achievement he reaches the eschatological kingdom. He states:

> The Church lives in the world and with the world . . . . It will have to be involved in the world; not the world of sin, but the one created by God, disfigured by sin, redeemed by God. It does not set itself up between the world and sin, but attaches the world to God.

These thoughts lie at the basis of any sound Christian theology of the world. Philips concludes, "The Church is at the service of God. Because of this, and not in spite of its religious mission, it is at the service of men."

This secularity at the service of the Word has been growing. At its base is a spirit of mind which lets things emerge on their own terms.

A reduction of the holy to the wordly, or the sacred to the secular will not work. Neither the Reformation, the Enlightenment nor the Romantic movement will solve our problem. Only a Christian secularity is realistic enough to accept the world as it is — its culture and its changing knowledge — and then permeate it by the Word, Christ and his enduring wisdom.

Otherwise the giant of the world, fat and sloppy, will rest on the glory of the past accomplishments. If we permit that, the world will cease to be creative and emergent. Instead it will be sluggish. The clarion call of Vatican Council II will not be heard; the document on the Church in the Modern World will go unheeded.

The choice is ours. Either we accept our world and make it a matrix of our life, enfleshed by the Word of God, or we dismiss it and lose the world to its own devices.

In the words of the world diplomat, Dag Hamarskjold, "In our era, the road to holiness necessarily passes through the world of action."

And the word of truth traverses the world of daily concern.

POSSIBLE EXPERIMENTS IN THE LITURGY

The leadership of Archbishop Hallinan in matters litur-
gical, both in the United States and during the Second
Vatican Council, has been a cause for rejoicing and
admiration to any keen observer of the Church in the
1960's. Invited to address a meeting of bishops and
major superiors of religious in New Orleans in March,
1968 — the same month he was called by death — the
Archbishop wrote this address. Ill health, however, pre-
vented him from delivering it personally and his repre-
sentative was the Reverend Henry C. Gracz, pastor of
St. Joseph's Church, Athens, Georgia.

We find the theme of peace underlying the entire mesage of salvation which we share as followers of Christ. Yet, at this time, candid
honesty forces us to admit that peace is quite elusive during this era of
liturgical change. I am sure you realize I am not speaking about the
external peace found by someone who attends a hastily mumbled Latin
Mass. The elusive peace I am speaking about comes when one knows
that he has accomplished the work of the Lord, and that he has done it
well.

We certainly have come far since the days when Pope Alexander
VII in 1661 stated:

> We have learned with great sorrow that in the kingdom of France,
> certain sons of perdition, itching with novelties detrimental to souls
> and despising the laws and practices of the Church, have lately
> come to such madness as to dare to translate the Roman missal into
> French and to hand it over to persons of every rank and sex. Thus
> they have attempted by their rash actions to degrade the most
> sacred rites, to lower the majesty which the Latin language gives
> to them, and to expose the divine mysteries to the common gaze.

We know that we have at least begun the work of the Lord, and I
think we can rest assured that most persons do not identify us with sons
of perdition. (Notice that I said *most*.) It surely has been the work of
the Lord, for who can imagine so much being done in so short a time?

223

I remember Father Jungmann having said during the planning sessions of the Council that he would be a happy man if half of the requested items were approved. Just imagine! We thought in 1963 that someday we may hear the actual Scripture lessons of the Mass proclaimed in our own language!

But remember that serious liturgists have *never* said that language alone was the answer to our problems in the Church. We must take note of the more serious problems that we face if we are to see even the need for experiments in the liturgy. Recently, articles have filled our periodicals and journals stating, analyzing and elaborating on the widespread crisis of faith among American Catholics, particularly as regards the structure of the Church. We ourselves have seen priests and laymen, educated and informed, leave our Church; but even more tragic is the departure of the uninformed and the young whose search for relevance cannot be satisfied within the Church.

Again I want to make it clear that I am not saying liturgical reforms more extensive than language will answer these needs, but it would be scandalous if the irrelevancy of the liturgy proved to be an additional reason for their departure from the Church. As members of the American Church, we cannot allow ourselves to be deceived by a distorted view of tradition, for two of the discernible characteristics of American Catholicism are its brevity (we are less than 200 years old) and its immigrant origin. This is the hour, this is the day when we must find our identity as a people whose worship flows from their very life — a life that has been both enriched and emasculated by the dissolution of our ethnic ghettos, by the mobility of our population, by the inauguration of a computerized technology, by the environment that is saturated with gadgets and an overpowering media, and lastly, by an affluence that can be used for the service of mankind or that can isolate us from the cries of our brothers in the world.

Within the present framework of our Church, there is no oportunity as great as the repetitive assembling of men to engage in that work which we call liturgy. We — members of a nation whose identity has been forged from the anvil of the unknown, and who politically have sought a league of nations, a new deal, a new frontier, and a great society — cannot be afraid of experimentation within the confines of the ecclesiastical. This experimentation is rooted in the concept of radical adaptation, an adaptation that has taken place in our liturgy as it went from the upper room and the paschal meal, the *Eucharistia* of the *Didache*, the Leonine, Gelasian and Gregorian sacramentaries, the Romano-Frankish Mass of the tenth century to the missal of Pius V. Jungman's words are telling:

... after fifteen hundred years of unbroken development in the rite
of the Roman Mass, after the rushing and the streaming from every
height and out of every valley, the missal of Pius V was indeed a
powerful dam holding back the waters or permitting them to flow
through only in firm, well-built canals. At one blow all arbitrary
meandering to one side or another was cut off, all floods prevented,
and a safe, regular and useful flow was assured. But the price paid
was this, that the beautiful river valley now lay barren and the
forces of further evolution were often channeled into the narrow
bed of a very inadequate devotional life instead of gathering strength
for new forms of liturgical expression.

We are now emerging from a period of fixity and rigidity which was
unnatural in the Church's life. The Constitution on the Sacred Liturgy,
as are so many other documents of the Council, is not a completed blueprint to construct the edifice of a new liturgy. The constitution is a
declaration of principle with practical norms and a style of its own. If
we evaluate it solely in juridical terms, it will share the same fate as the
decrees of the Council of Trent, "which the theologians considered for
several centuries as the complete epitomy of the whole tradition of the
Church." We must understand that this declaration of principle must be
applied and adapted, tested and evaluated with a healthy respect for
anthropology as well as theology.

It would be narow for us not to consider the ecumenical dimension
in the future. It may not be an achieved fact for some years to come, but
we can certainly look forward to a uniform text for Catholics and other
Christians, not only in the ordinary of the Mass but also in a newly
translated Lord's Prayer. We have only talked about the Eucharist, but
we can be sure that forms and rites will be appearing for the remaining
sacraments as well. This brings us to the problem of the experimenter
or adapter.

You already know that I feel a grassroots approach is absolutely
essential if our liturgy is to be truly expressive and creative of a people
dedicated to God. At this time, you know that our request to authorize
centers for liturgical experimentation in dioceses has been refused by
Rome; but we cannot call a halt to our efforts to seek experimentation
from the bottom up, to complement those experiments which we received
from the scholars and theorists. We have assurance that our requests will
receive prompt attention, but now these requests must come; from men
who are pastors, working among the people, from individuals whom we
release for training in the necessary scholarship, not only theological
and liturgical, but also adequately prepared in the sociological and an-
thropological studies of our era. These men need to integrate the disci-

plines. They can give us a solid basis for a sociology and psychology of community. While these men are working and preparing, they must have our solid encouragement, not merely our permission. And our encouragement will extend not only to these men, but to all the people of God with whom we must communicate the spirit of renewal. Periodically we hear that men are wearied of liturgical discussion. This weariness is all the more reason for our increasing an effective catechesis of our developing liturgy. For we are professional men and professional liturgists, yet this professionalism is not the conviction of us all, as it should be. We can hold our rather solemn banquets with every detail socially correct and yet haphazardly celebrate that banquet which is of life-giving importance. Can you imagine any one of the apostles rapidly racing through the breaking of the bread in which they came to know the presence of the Lord because of a heavy schedule or an approaching appointment? We have an already existing flexibility today which is not used because men say, "It's not the law; it doesn't matter; it's not necessary."

Our concern cannot be exclusively aimed at those who are excessive, but must also be strongly directed to those who err by defect. To lapse into a new system of rubrics as rigid as the old is premature and death-dealing to the spirit of the liturgy. Our prayer must be that we worship and that we lead in worship with renewed hearts, that we worship our Father in spirit and in truth through Christ our Lord. This is our life.

Topical Index